AFTER THE BLAST

AFTER
THE BLAST

THE ECOLOGICAL RECOVERY
OF MOUNT ST. HELENS

ERIC WAGNER

A Ruth Kirk Book

UNIVERSITY OF WASHINGTON PRESS
Seattle

After the Blast was published with the assistance of a grant from the Ruth Kirk Book Fund, which supports publications that inform the general public on the history, natural history, archaeology, and Native cultures of the Pacific Northwest.

This book was also supported by the Northwest Writers Fund, which promotes the work of some of the region's most talented nonfiction writers and was established through generous gifts from Linda and Peter Capell, Janet and John Creighton, Michael J. Repass, and other donors.

Design by Katrina Noble
Composed in Scala, typeface designed by Martin Majoor

24 23 22 21 20   5 4 3 2 1

Printed and bound in the United States of America

UNIVERSITY OF WASHINGTON PRESS
uwapress.uw.edu

LIBRARY OF CONGRESS CATALOGING-IN-PUBLICATION DATA ON FILE

ISBN 978-0-295-74693-7 (hardback), ISBN 978-0-295-74694-4 (ebook)

INTERIOR PHOTOGRAPHS: Page 10: Eruption of Mount St. Helens, 11:00 a.m., May 18, 1980, National Archives 95-GP-4017-529645. Page 36: Ash-blanketed clear-cut, northeast face of Mount St. Helens in the background, National Archives 95-GP-4017-529585. Page 110: Downed trees after the eruption, June 10, 1980, National Archives 95-GP-4017-529708. Page 160: Mount St. Helens from the northeast, October 2017, photograph by the author. MAP: Pease Press Cartography, www.peasepress.com

The paper used in this publication is acid free and meets the minimum requirements of American National Standard for Information Sciences— Permanence of Paper for Printed Library Materials, ANSI Z39.48–1984.∞

For Mom and Dad

On my volcano grows the Grass
A meditative spot —
An acre for a Bird to choose
Would be the general thought —

How red the Fire rocks below
How insecure the sod
Did I disclose
Would populate with awe my solitude

—EMILY DICKINSON

CONTENTS

AFTER THE BLAST

PROLOGUE

AFTER

THE STORY OF the eruption of Mount St. Helens as most of us know it begins with two prepositions, *at* and *on*, usually in that order and in quick succession: *at* 8:32 a.m., *on* Sunday, May 18, 1980, a powerful earthquake shook the mountain. The summit rippled, churned, and then collapsed as more than two billion tons of rock, snow, and glacial ice fell away in the largest landslide recorded in human history. The landslide took with it all the weight and pressure that had until then kept a bulging chamber of magma contained under the mountain's northern flank. With that release, superheated water and gas both in and surrounding the chamber flashed to steam and burst out in searing clouds. The clouds raced over the land, obliterating the trees closest to the mountain and flattening others as they flew on, until their force finally dissipated. Mudflows followed as the mountain's glaciers and snowfields melted. Called lahars, these flows swept down drainages and river valleys, swallowing boulders, trees, logging equipment, cars, trucks, trains, bridges, and houses. From the heart of the mountain, meanwhile, a column of ash from the exposed vent rose fifteen miles into the sky.

The main eruption lasted nine hours and caused the deaths of fifty-seven people. When it was over, Mount St. Helens was 1,314 feet shorter. Where the summit had been gaped a crater a mile wide and two thousand feet deep. In a 180-degree arc to the north, 234 square miles of forest were buried, knocked flat, or left standing but scorched. The landslide traveled more than fourteen miles down the valley of the North Fork

Toutle River. The lahars went farther still, destroying hundreds of miles of roads and railways, knocking out twenty-seven bridges, damaging more than two hundred homes, and clogging commercial ship traffic seventy-five miles away on the Columbia River. As it was blown east, the towering plume of ash blocked out the sun for miles. Several inches of ash fell in the city of Yakima an hour later, and streetlights flickered on. Two hours after that, the plume reached Spokane, more than two hundred miles away. The plume eventually climbed to the stratosphere and floated across the US, dusting seventeen states. In fifteen days it had circled the Earth.

Back in the blast area, the sense of desolation was greater than mere statistics could convey. Mount St. Helens had always been the most beautiful of the Cascade peaks, its summit the most symmetrical. Gone now was that perfect white cone, the dark forests that had cloaked it, the deep, clear lake that had reflected it. In their place was a hollow volcano in a wrecked landscape of black and gray. When President Jimmy Carter toured the area by helicopter four days later, he could only marvel at the waste. "The moon looks like a golf course compared to what's up there," he said to a scrum of media when he returned. Local reporters were less glib. "Death is everywhere," wrote one in the Portland *Oregonian*. "The living are not welcome."

———

A couple of weeks later, on a bright morning in June, another helicopter lifted off from Vancouver, Washington, albeit to considerably less fanfare. Riding in it were Jerry Franklin, Jim Sedell, and Fred Swanson. Franklin and Sedell were ecologists with the US Forest Service, and Swanson was a geologist also with the agency. The helicopter rose and turned northeast above the city and its suburbs. From there it crossed into Cowlitz County and flew over the Lewis River, which was still running gray-brown and high. Here the pilot turned to angle more to the north. Tracts of forest appeared, with stands of tall old trees next to short young ones, and brown patches of fresh clear-cuts between them: the checkerboard grid characteristic of the Pacific Northwest. Roads noodled in and among the squares like veins, but no one was looking at them. Their thoughts were drawn east, to Mount St. Helens.

The misshapen hulk of the mountain lay in the distance, still shrouded in cloud. Franklin, Sedell, and Swanson gazed at it. The *whup-whup* of the helicopter's rotors was so loud that it was impossible to hear anyone speak, but it did not matter, because no one had anything to say. The eruption had overwhelmed their professional vocabulary. They were flying toward something for which they did not yet have the language.

Franklin and Sedell were certain that nothing could have survived. It was impossible, and in this way almost perversely exciting. In overwriting the landscape, Mount St. Helens had presented ecologists with what was in effect a huge natural experiment. It was as if the volcano itself had posed a question: What happens when every single living thing for hundreds of square miles, big and small, plant and animal, is burned away or buried, and nothing is left but rock and ash?

Franklin and Sedell had discussed the question at length in the weeks leading up to their flight, both between themselves and with their colleagues in Oregon, Washington, and beyond. Their working hypothesis was that although it might take decades or even centuries, plants and animals were sure to return at some point. Here then was an unprecedented opportunity to document how living things crept back in from the outside world, to test on the grandest of scales some of the oldest and most durable theories in ecology and evolution about how life responds to a massive disturbance, how it recovers from one, or how it does not.

The helicopter neared the mountain and flew past the still-steaming crater. The pilot scanned the ground for a safe place to land, eventually settling close to Ryan Lake, about twelve miles distant. Franklin, Sedell, and Swanson prepared to disembark. The safety officer, who was 6'4", weighed over three hundred pounds, and had introduced himself as Tiny, reminded them that they did not have long to stay and were not to walk far. They might have to get out of there in a hurry.

So it was that Franklin opened the helicopter's side door and hopped out. His boots sent up little puffs of ash when they hit the ground. He glanced down, but instead of the gray he expected, he saw a bit of green poking up next to him. He knelt. It was a plant shoot, maybe two or three inches tall. *I'll be damned*, Franklin thought. It was *Chamaenerion angustifolium*, a plant much more widely known by its common name, fireweed.

———

Fireweed is a perennial plant in the evening primrose family. It ranges across much of the temperate Northern Hemisphere, from sea level to subalpine meadows to altitudes as high as fifteen thousand feet in the Himalayas. Individual plants can grow up to nine feet tall, but most are closer to three feet. Their leaves are long, narrow, and pointed, like spearheads. Their small flowers grow in dense clusters, and the petals may be pink, red, or purple, or sometimes all those colors at once, depending on the play of sunlight and wind.

Fireweed can spread through the soil by means of a system of roots that lie a few inches beneath the surface. If the stalk above the ground has been damaged, the plant can regrow from as little as an inch or two of remnant root. The stalk itself grows quickly, up to one inch per day. Mature plants can also produce tens of thousands of seeds. Each seed is topped with a cottony tuft of fine white hairs to help the wind carry it away, sometimes for miles. Fireweed thus can travel across long distances. Botanists describe the species as aggressive; to some gardeners, it is a pest.

Pest or not, fireweed gets its American common name from its habit of being one of the quickest plants to sprout in newly burned forests, clear-cuts, and any place that has been suddenly and drastically denuded. It thrives in habitats with bare soil and a lot of light. In England, the species is called rosebay willowherb, but it is also known informally as bombweed, since it was often the first flower to appear in blast craters after German air raids during World War II. "London, paradoxically, is the gayest where she has been most blitzed," wrote one journalist in 1944. "The wounds made this summer by flying bombs are, of course, still raw and bare, but cellars and courts shattered into rubble by the German raids of 1940–41 have been taken over by an army of weeds which have turned them into wild gardens."

Now Franklin considered this fireweed sprout so close to Mount St. Helens. It could not have come from a seed; fireweed would not set seed for a couple of months yet, near the end of summer. It had to have come from a piece of root that had somehow survived under all the ash and debris. He imagined the new shoot emerging from the root fragment, pushing up through the ash once the ground had cooled. He imagined the probing spread of the slender tendrils below, the slow and tenacious unfurling of bud and leaf above, the eruption of the flowers, the establishment of the plant.

Franklin stood and took in the landscape again. He realized that this fireweed was one of tens, hundreds, maybe even thousands of little green shoots emerging from the ash. He saw the beginnings of thistles and pearly everlasting, a flowering plant. More than plants, he noticed evidence of other forms of life. Beetles were scuttling over the downed trees. Ants trooped along the ground, leaving trails of dimpled footprints. Dark mounds of dirt showed where a pocket gopher must have pushed up from its subterranean tunnels. Roving herds of ungulates—elk, probably, judging by the size of the hooves—had already planted prints in the ash as they picked their way through the tangle of trees.

Franklin clambered over the trunks—how hard it was to get around!—and stumbled toward a stream that was working its way through the ash to the old surface. The water was almost clear, and a film of algae was starting to spread in it. He was astonished, elated. "Right off," he said later, "all of us smart ecologists realized we didn't have the correct working hypothesis."

———

What follows is an account of the hypotheses about the regeneration of life at Mount St. Helens that would spring from that first incorrect one. The fireweed that Franklin saw not only changed the ways that he and other ecologists approached the eruption and the landscape it created, but also led to new ways of thinking about how life responds to seeming total devastation. Some of these ideas grappled with such things as disturbance, resilience, succession—topics in the gauzier realms of ecological theory. Others had more explicitly practical applications, for even as it had destroyed the land around it, Mount St. Helens would help usher in new, wiser ways of managing forests and streams.

Although the effects of the eruption were widespread, from the lahars that clogged the Columbia River to the plume that left deep drifts of ash hundreds of miles away, most of this story is set in or near what is now the Mount St. Helens National Volcanic Monument. Covering 110,000 acres, the monument encompasses most of the land immediately north of the mountain, in what is popularly thought of as the blast zone or the blast area. From here, Mount St. Helens presents its open face to the hundreds of thousands of people who come to see it every year, whether they are walking out a mile or so from the Johnston Ridge Observatory to the northwest or going on longer treks along Windy Ridge in the northeast.

"We can take pride," Forest Service chief Max Peterson said at the monument's dedication ceremony in 1983, "in having preserved the unique episode of natural history for future generations." This was to be the monument's significance, as a place for the landscape to reshape itself on its own; or, as the legislation put it, a place that would allow "geologic forces and ecological succession to continue substantially unimpeded." Scientists would watch these processes in action and so learn how plant and animal communities act when left alone. But Mount St. Helens has many facets, and as the years passed, managers and ecologists found themselves having to ask just how unimpeded they could afford to let the processes be. When threats to public safety arose, how would this idealistic purpose fare?

The story of the eruption of Mount St. Helens and its aftermath is also one of the human endeavor of science encountering a staggering unknown. None of the biologists who would work in the blast area had begun their careers focused on volcanoes or volcano ecology, but the eruption compelled them to bind themselves to a place and study it at an extraordinary level of detail, and in a variety of ways. Some arrived early and stayed for a few years before moving on, even as the eruption shaped their thinking for the rest of their careers. Some arrived at the blast area later, drawn both to its uniqueness and to the opportunities created by those who had come before them. A few devoted their lives to the mountain in ways they could never have anticipated. One researcher who spent nearly four decades here told me, "Mount St. Helens can give you a lot, but she takes a lot from you, too." Then he said he would have it no other way.

PART ONE

MORE THAN THE BOOM

I

PAPER 1250

THE SUMMIT OF Mount Margaret is a craggy pile of rock about six miles north of Mount St. Helens. As one pile among several along this ridge, it does not seem any loftier or more distinguished than its neighbors, but it is the only pile to have a small bronze disk bolted and cemented to it. Inscribed on the disk's face is the legend "U.S.C. & G.S," which stands for the US Coast and Geodetic Survey. Beginning in the mid-1800s, the survey sent people all around the country to affix markers to points of natural and national interest, and in 1906, a surveyor with the initials J.S.H. affixed one here. His original site description is spare ("appears as a rocky summit"), but forty years later another surveyor, W.R.H., noted that the marker was on a "rocky pinnacle that overlooks a small canyon to the north." W.R.H. also left directions for future surveyors:

> To reach the station from the lodge at Spirit Lake, go west for
> 0.2 mile to a sign on the right Coldwater L.O.H. [lookout hut], Mt.
> Margaret Trail. Turn right and follow a well defined trail for 3 miles
> to a Forest Service shelter and at trail forks, take the right fork and
> continue on this trail for 3 miles to the summit of Mt. Margaret and
> the station as described. Approximately six hours travel by horse.

All of W.R.H.'s landmarks—the lodge, the sign, the shelter—are gone now, destroyed thirty-four years after he wrote of them during the eruption of a nearby mountain he did not think it necessary to mention. New trails have replaced the old across this portion of the monument, now called the Mount Margaret Backcountry. The present path to the summit of Mount Margaret is an unmarked spur from the wider Boundary Trail. You climb about a tenth of a mile until you come to the base of the rocks. Scramble up thirty feet or so and there you are, 5,862 feet in the air.

On an afternoon in the middle of the summer, the sky is cloudless and the view splendid. West Coast snowpeaks ring the horizon: the sharp profile of Mount Hood rises sixty miles to the southeast, with Mount Jefferson dimly visible behind it, more than one hundred miles away. Beveled Mount Adams is thirty miles east, and Mount Rainier, grand and round, is fifty miles to the north. Mount St. Helens stands to the south, dominant because of its proximity, but in fact the lowest of the bunch. Spirit Lake sits before it, with thousands and thousands of bleached logs forming a tremendous mat on its surface.

In the space between Mount Margaret and Mount St. Helens, varying shades of green show life's steady but uneven progress in reclaiming lost territory. To the southeast, at Windy Ridge, the green is dark and rich, but closer to the volcano it becomes faint, like a scrim that might blow away in a strong wind. Immediately north and west of the prominence, the ground is as gray as naked rock. The patch of gray flows out to the west, down into the valley of the North Fork Toutle River. The river winds across this wide gray plain until it disappears behind some more hills, where it continues to carve new channels for itself every year, unable as yet to make up its mind where it wants to go or how it wants to get there.

As always, though, Mount St. Helens is what draws the eye. Its crater gapes toward Mount Margaret. Gazing into it is like staring down the barrel of an enormous cannon, against all of whose strength and fury this modest summit and its bronze disk stood fast. They are none the worse for wear, other than being a little scratched up. Around Mount Margaret, the most obvious signs of the 1980 eruption are all the fallen trees: a forest knocked flat in seconds. Almost to a tree they lie along a roughly north-south axis, like iron filings aligned to a magnet's pull. That so many could be so swatted down eight miles from the crater speaks to the eruption's awesome power. That the bleached and decaying trunks are now increasingly covered with grasses and shrubs speaks to the quieter power of something else.

———

Fifteen or so miles northeast of Mount Margaret and a couple of thousand feet lower in elevation, down near the Cispus River, is the Tower Rock U-Fish RV Park and Campground. The park's namesake, a basalt pillar more than 1,200 feet tall, projects out from the neighboring hills. The park itself, set among a peaceful mix of forest and meadows, offers tent sites and RV hookups, and, in the middle of one of the meadows, a large artificial pond stocked with rainbow trout. An enterprising osprey will sometimes perch above the pond and hurl itself in. Humans are welcome to try their hand for six bucks per fish.

Tower Rock bills itself as a sleepy little hideaway, but when I pull in on a warm evening in late July, cars and pickup trucks fill the parking lot to overflowing. People mill about, chatting in small groups or setting up tents around the edge of a wide meadow. A big white pavilion has been erected, with plastic tables and chairs set under it. Next to all of this is a large catering truck, its generator bucking and roaring. To its side someone has taped a huge poster of Mount St. Helens and its surroundings, showing an enlarged satellite picture taken from directly above the crater. The caterers rush about, already harried to exhaustion. I see their leader crouched behind a Port-a-Potty, chewing on a cigarette and speaking slowly but intensely into a satellite phone: "We are going to run out of food very fast. Send more now." He exhales a cloud of smoke. "Thanks."

All of these people have come to Tower Rock for an event called the Pulse. About every five years since 1980, scientists who have worked at Mount St. Helens have convened to gather benchmark data from sites and plots established more than three decades ago, share their findings, and toss around ideas for new studies, syntheses, or collaborations. Well over one hundred people are at this gathering. They come from various fields: ecology, geology, hydrology, sociology. (A few artists and writers are also here.) They are at all stages of their careers, from twentysomething technicians on the seasonal field crews to graduate students, postdoctoral researchers, young faculty, older scientists, retired scientists, and, more and more often these days, the spirits of the deceased: at the opening ceremony, after everyone has gone around and introduced themselves, we listen to memorials for three people who have died since the last Pulse.

Recent Pulses have lasted about a week. The first full day of this one is devoted to a bus ride through much of the blast area. The tour is long, with hours of driving and stopping and debussing, then standing and listening as one scientist after another tells the story behind their studies. They talk about the ways the eruption has contributed to soil formation, its effects on water quality in nearby streams, how trees fared near and far, the fate of flowering plants, the travails of fungi, spiders, beetles, other invertebrates, birds, fish, amphibians, small mammals, and larger mammals. Undergirding this range of topics is a persistent theme: the eruption of Mount St. Helens has enabled ecologists to ask things that they had no other way to ask. "Most people," one ecologist had said during the afternoon, "looked at the devastated area and just saw death and destruction." She smiled. "But for us, the mountain was loaded with more questions than we ever could have dreamed."

After we return to Tower Rock, I walk back to my little green tent to relax for a few minutes until dinner. Next to my tent is a big red one that belongs to Fred Swanson, the geologist who flew over the mountain after the eruption and is at the moment sitting in a circle with some of the artists and writers. Swanson is in his seventies now, tall, thin, and long-limbed, like a great egret. His short gray hair fringes a shining dome of head before it joins with his thick but well-tended beard. Folded into a camp chair, his body is a study in right angles.

"People engage with Mount St. Helens through what we call science," Swanson is saying, "but this volcano encompasses a lot more than just science." Interdisciplinarity is a favorite topic of his, and Mount St. Helens, he says, is one of the best places in the world to see it on display.

He is one of only two or three geologists among all these ecologists, but he wants to draw attention to the layering of new ecology atop a new-old geology in this volcanic terrain. Although he spent a few years after the eruption studying this geo-eco connection, as he calls it, he still frets that it does not always get its due. Everyone is here to talk about what has been happening above ground, but the ground itself provided the stage for all the biological events that followed the eruption. It is therefore essential to understand the many ways that volcanic disturbance processes have shaped these spaces. Before you look at all the life, he says, you have to look at the land. It is impossible to know one without the other.

"So what was the land like?" I ask. I have become generally familiar with the terms used to describe the area after the 1980 eruption: *barren, lifeless, a wasteland, a moonscape*, and so on. I have taken these to mean a widespread and almost uniform sterility.

No, Swanson says, that was hardly the case. For all the fire and fury, the effects of the eruption were quite varied across the landscape, differing in subtle but profound ways.

I confess that I have never thought of an erupting volcano as a subtle thing. Swanson grins. "You'll want to look at Twelve-Fifty," he says. "Just a second." He gets up from his chair and disappears into his tent, returning a few moments later with a big book, which he hands to me. I am unprepared for its weight, and it slips through my hands and drops into my lap.

"Oof," I say.

"There you go," Swanson says. "That'll start to give you an idea of what we were dealing with."

Twelve-Fifty is practitioners' shorthand for the US Geological Survey Professional Paper 1250. Titled *The 1980 Eruptions of Mount St. Helens, Washington*, it is a collection of sixty-two individual papers that occupy nearly 850 pages. Published in May 1981, it represents geologists' first efforts to make sense of the events, and in this it has the hybrid character of being both a definitive account and a rough draft that anticipates the significant work yet to come.

I open Swanson's copy, which is clearly well loved, and leaf through the bureaucratic front matter. In the foreword, Dallas Peck, then the director of the USGS, writes that "exceptional opportunities were presented for scientific observation of infrequently occurring volcanic processes." (I am starting to appreciate just how pervasive this sort of intellectual salivation was at Mount St. Helens.) Opposite it is a touching dedication to David Johnston, the young geologist who died during the eruption when he was swept from the ridge that now bears his name.

The main text begins with a brief history of Mount St. Helens by Donal Mullineaux and Dwight "Rocky" Crandell. Their names had come up earlier during the day's tour in connection with a paper they had published in the journal *Science* titled "Mount St. Helens Volcano: Recent and Future Behavior." After summarizing all of its volcanic activities, the two had ended with their educated guess that "an eruption is likely within the next hundred years, possibly before the end of this century." This they had written in 1975. "Mount St. Helens has done so many different things in the past that hardly anything would be a surprise," Crandell later said in an interview. "The only thing it hasn't done is blow itself apart."

Writing after the mountain had blown itself apart, Mullineaux and Crandell focused on placing the 1980 event in broader geological contexts. Mount St. Helens sits in the Cascade Range, itself a short segment of the Ring of Fire, an arc of volcanic activity stretching nearly twenty-five thousand miles around the edge of the Pacific Ocean, from New Zealand up through southeastern Asia, north to Russia and across the Aleutians, and down the western coasts of North, Central, and South America. Of the hundreds of active volcanoes scattered along it, eighteen are in the Cascade Range, which stretches more than eight hundred miles from the Silverthorne Caldera in southern British Columbia to Lassen Peak in California. Among these volcanoes, Mount St. Helens is the youngest, at only forty thousand years old. Its conspicuous prominence is younger still, most of it less than four thousand years old. The mountain owed its former roundness and graceful symmetry to its youth. Unlike Mount

Adams and Mount Rainier, both of which are much older, its summit had not been eroded and dissected by the movement of glaciers.

What glaciers could not do in four millennia, an eruption can accomplish in a few minutes. The most active of the Cascade volcanoes, Mount St. Helens has erupted several times in the past five hundred years; the event in 1980 followed a quiet period that had lasted 123 years. The mountain is in a state of almost perpetual adjustment. It builds itself up and then knocks itself down and starts again. Reading Crandell and Mullineaux, it does not seem improper to think in these anthropomorphizing terms. The two write of the birth of Mount St. Helens, and they refer to its conduct "throughout its lifetime." Their implication is clear. This is living stone.

———

The rest of 1250 is devoted to the time just before and after May 18. A section called "Volcanic Deposits" comprises more than half the book. Here geologists parse the main eruption into a series of processes according to the nature of their leavings; or, as Swanson said in one of his delightful euphemisms, by what each process had "contributed to the landscape."

What contributions and processes they were! The eruption let geologists see a volcano behave in ways that they could previously only have imagined or carefully reconstructed from geological evidence. First had come the debris avalanche. In 1250, it goes from being simply "the largest landslide ever observed in human history," as I often hear it denoted, to something much more nuanced and devastating. After the initial earthquake, the summit and north face fell not as a single slab but in three large blocks, one right after the other, and each rockfall had its own implications. The first block plunged into Spirit Lake, turning its mirror-still waters into a giant oscillating wave called a seiche. The seiche may have sloshed more than 850 feet up the slopes of the hillsides, dragging almost every tree back down into the lake basin. Moments later, the second block crashed northward, overtopping a ridge more than one thousand feet high before it came to rest four miles away. The third block, by far the largest, rumbled fourteen miles in ten minutes down the valley of the North Fork Toutle River. Once it settled, twenty-three square miles of the valley were buried under hot, steaming piles of sand and rock up to 650 feet deep. Unlike the first two blocks, which came from the mountain's skin, the third originated closer to its core. Twelve days later, the material still simmered in spots, at temperatures between 158 and 212 degrees Fahrenheit.

After the avalanche came the directed blast: the explosion of all the gas and superheated water from the deep magma chamber the summit had covered until just moments before. In addition to the gas and steam, the blast clouds were filled with heat-shattered shards of rock. Rather than blowing upward, as volcanoes were generally thought to do, Mount St. Helens blew laterally, out and away. The clouds rushed over the landscape at up to six hundred miles per hour, outpacing and overtaking the more sluggish debris avalanche within a few seconds. At first those blast clouds were so powerful that they were unrestrained by topography, but as they traveled from the volcano and lost momentum, they followed the land's contours, swirling and eddying around hillsides and ravines. The directed blast left comparatively little in the way of volcanic deposit: a bit more than three feet of gravel close to the crater, a few inches of silt-sized rock fragments at its farthest reach seventeen miles away. Its destructive power came from its force. The avalanche buried or plowed over every tree in its path; the blast clouds shattered the trees closest to the vent into fragments or ripped them from the ground and hurled them through the air. Farther away, it toppled trees over like cut grass. The energy released with the blast was greater than that of an atomic bomb. Even as that energy started to lessen after three or four minutes, the cloud was still so hot—over 500°F in places—that when it had spent itself, it marked its extent with a fringe of standing dead trees, their foliage charred or scorched off.

Within a minute of the lateral blast, a column of ash, pumice, and steam began to billow from the new crater. This was the beginning of the Plinian phase of the eruption, the towering plume named for Pliny the Younger, the Roman magistrate who wrote of watching Mount Vesuvius destroy Pompeii in 79 CE. The column climbed fifteen miles into the sky in less than fifteen minutes, carrying more than five hundred million tons of ash and pumice and rock. The plume that resulted was more than forty-five miles in diameter at its widest and shaped like a giant anvil. Around the mountain, lightning flashed from the clouds of electrically charged particles, igniting the trees that still stood on its southern flanks. When prevailing winds started to blow the plume northeast, ash and pumice—or tephra, as geologists call anything solid a volcano spits out, from the finest ash to boulders that burst like bombs on impact—fell back to earth in a wide swath. Compared to the avalanche and blast cloud, the tephra was almost a gentle particulate rain. Less than eight inches deep, these deposits at their warmest were just 122°F and cooled quickly.

Three and a half hours after the Plinian column began came the pyroclastic flows. *Pyroclastic* means, roughly, "rock fragments born of fire," and the flows were mostly hot pieces of rock, some fine and silty, some larger and more gravelly. The flows boiled up and frothed over the crater rim, wave after wave of porous, gaseous rock tumbling down the mountain's sides at eighty miles per hour. While this was happening, the Plinian column occasionally collapsed under its own weight and added to the flows. These deposits, called the pumiceous pyroclastic flow, formed a plain more than three thousand acres in area and up to 120 feet deep. The pumice was extraordinarily hot—in some spots over 1,500°F, the heat so intense that the ground shimmered for days afterwards.

Nine hours after it began, the Plinian column dispersed, and the cataclysmic eruption was over. Smaller pyroclastic flows occurred every now and then until the following October; magma was extruded onto the crater for the next several years, building a series of domes, until the eruption as a whole was officially declared finished in 1986. By then, the technical jargon for Mount St. Helens's revised geographies had become a more casual argot. The one billion board feet of timber blown down by the lateral blast became the Blowdown Zone. The pyroclastic flows led to the gray Pumice Plain in front of the mountain, a six-square-mile area that reached to the southern shore of Spirit Lake. On the lake's surface drifted a huge mat made up of tens of thousands of logs. The surface of the lake itself was 180 feet higher than it had been before the eruption, and its area had increased from 1,300 to about 2,200 acres. Rubble from the debris avalanche and pyroclastic flows blocked the lake's natural outlet to the North Fork; downslope, new lakes formed from impounded creeks and streams. Bordering the lake's southern shore were large, lumpy hummocks left from the second block of the debris avalanche, with more than one hundred ponds filling in among their topographic depressions. The third block, the one that buried the upper Toutle River valley, remained simply the debris avalanche.

Sitting back in my chair with the book in my lap, I try a quick mental exercise to compare these four processes, the volume of material they produced, and the area that it covered. The debris avalanche left the most material, but all that material covered only the third-largest area. The lateral blast was the most powerful process, and it affected the second-largest area, but it contributed the smallest amount of material. The pyroclastic flows had the hottest material by far, but the flows affected the smallest area, also by far. The tephra, conversely, covered many thousands of square miles, but was the thinnest and coolest deposit.

Hundreds of feet of rubble or a thin layer of ash, scorching temperatures or tepid ones, effects localized or crossing state lines—my thoughts are soon a tangle. What is clear is that the diversity of these processes and their effects shaped the ways life returned. This, I gather, is what Swanson meant by subtleties.

I heft 1250, feel its weight again. In the twenty minutes or so it has taken me to page casually through it, both the debris avalanche and the lateral blast would have run their course, and the ash column would have climbed to its full height. A crazy thought. Amazing, too, that geologists figured out so much in just a few months, while ecologists are still feeling their way more than three decades later. During the bus tour I had mentioned this difference to a geologist who had been one of the first to visit the blast area after the eruption. He chuckled. "We had a handle on the mountain pretty much within a few weeks," he said. "Then we watched everything disappear under all that damn life!" As if all the organisms that now lived here had somehow conspired to conceal a part of Mount St. Helens's essential nature. As if they had not instead revealed it.

———

I close 1250 and set it on the grass. Across from me, Swanson is still regaling the artists and writers with stories from the early days. Even though he is a geologist, he is not one of the dozens to have a chapter in 1250. He spent his career with the Forest Service rather than the USGS, and 1250 is a USGS publication, but he knew the geologists well and joined them on some of their early forays to the blast area. "What a head trip those were!" he says. On his own first flight just ten days after the eruption, the mountain was still spitting and mud balls splattered against the helicopter windscreen. Once the USGS team landed, Swanson had dug down into the ash a few inches, creating a little pit. When he got on his knees, he saw lacy strands strung throughout the pit; on its walls, particles of tephra dangled at the ends of the strands where his trowel had severed them. He later learned the strands were mycelia from a type of fungus that flourishes in the ground after forest fires but apparently is not finicky about its heat source. "The ground was still warm from the eruption, and they were already spreading all over the place!" he says. "The initial biological response, and in just days."

With Jerry Franklin, Jim Sedell, and a few others, Swanson has become one of the intellectual pillars of the Mount St. Helens posteruptive landscape. He worked around the mountain for several years, focusing on what he calls "secondary disturbance processes" occurring in the volcanic deposits over time: the channels and gullies that winter rains dug through the ash, which created openings for vegetation; the landslides large and small that ripped down the slopes of the steeper hillsides, at times carrying downed trees with them. But his interests are much more expansive, and now, long after ending his field research, he remains a staunch advocate for the mountain's value. At the Pulse, he argues against a view that the 1980 eruption was essentially a one-off event and so of limited ecological interest. "You can't think that way," he says. It is too restrictive a view, trapped within puny human time horizons. The mountain has an actual situatedness in much larger thought structures. It is part of many dialogues and webs of knowledge, and these knowledges keep being unveiled, or unveiling themselves, to anyone willing to pay attention. "There are many ways of seeing the mountain," he says.

I sit in my chair, listening happily. I have met scientists, and I have met people who speak of mountains with deep spiritual reverence, but Swanson is the first person I have met who combines these traits. He sometimes refers to Mount St. Helens as his Zen mistress, saying that as a teacher she has presented us with a Zen riddle: challenge after challenge, change after change. Owing to Swanson's beard, which can amplify his direct and dark-eyed gaze, Jerry Franklin once likened Swanson to a religious fanatic. This strikes me as far too severe. Swanson is certainly a believer of a sort, but he is no zealot, having instead a gentleness that couples with his capacious interests. His ideas start mildly, build in pitch and moment and pace, branch in curious ways. He gestures broadly when he talks, moving his hands in full circles to emphasize certain points.

"This is the interpretive form of my argument," he says.

"The mountain is more than the boom," he says.

———

When Mount St. Helens went boom in 1980, Swanson was one of the scientists at a US Forest Service research station down in central Oregon called the H. J. Andrews Experimental Forest. He had arrived there by way of Delaware, where he grew up, and Penn State, where he studied geology and ran cross-country. (Even now it is easy to envision him loping across a grassy course, although he says he mostly bikes these days to spare his Achilles tendons.) After he graduated, he packed his car and drove west. In college he had read the poetry of Kenneth Rexroth and Robinson Jeffers and admired Edward Weston's landscape photography. Their ideas of the American West appealed to him: the ambivalence they felt in the seeming serenity of the natural world, the frictions they found there.

After spending some time in southern Oregon and the San Francisco Bay Area, Swanson settled in Eugene and began his PhD in geology at the University of Oregon. For his dissertation, he studied gravel and pebbles in the Elk River, in the southwestern part of the state. When he was not looking at sand and cobble in the river, he was often hiking up or around Mount Hood and the Three Sisters, the nearest Cascade volcanoes. His beard was even longer and thicker then, so much so that he could put it in a kind of ponytail. He was, he says, "quite the mountain man."

He finished his PhD in 1972 and went to work at the Andrews, as the experimental forest is widely known. As a postdoctoral scientist, his first job was to map the geology that underlay the forest, which covers approximately sixteen thousand acres. Much of the woods are old-growth conifer, under which grew a lush, wet understory. "You couldn't see much because of the damn vegetation," Swanson says. His research soon pivoted from pure geology—the nature of the rocks alone—to the study of landforms and land-forming processes, and how they interacted with and influenced the growth of the forest. He became a geomorphologist: one who studies how the Earth moves and grows and changes, be it fast or slow, and how vegetation can slow those changes or speed them up.

On the West Coast, he saw, the land could move and grow and change quite a lot. Conditions facilitated frequent and at times extensive rearrangements. Rain and snow were plentiful, especially west of the Cascades. Much of the rock was liable to crumble and collapse, and often did down the steeper slopes. At the Andrews, Swanson developed a professional interest in the disturbance processes that arose from these instabilities, most specifically a phenomenon called an earthflow. This is a slow-motion landslide, which might creep somewhere between one inch and several feet a year . It can persist for decades, or centuries, or perhaps even longer. This sort of landslide can be so subtle that it might be imperceptible to a person standing right on top of it, save for quiet signs: the paved road that buckles a little each year, or the mature tree splitting in two as the shifting ground on which it stands slowly pulls it apart. Such incrementalisms may not feature in the earthquakes, volcanoes, and other spectacular exhibitions that bring professional glory, but they are just as much a part of the larger exchanges between land and life.

In the forest community, Swanson immersed himself in these exchanges. He was introduced to a holistic practice of science he had never encountered anywhere else. Researchers at the Andrews were encouraged to work together, even (or expressly) if they came from different disciplines. Groups ranged widely, setting up stations to monitor the rhythms of the forest and its watershed. Swanson, who eventually became a research leader, learned what it meant to look at a place for a long time, to try to study its every twitch and tremor. He saw the forest as habitat provider, lab, nexus, classroom, sanctuary. Nowhere had done more to shape his thinking. "The Andrews is a special place," he tells me at one point. "You should come see it sometime. It would help you get a better understanding of what we tried to do at Mount St. Helens."

2

A PORTAL TO OTHER WAYS
OF KNOWING

THE ANDREWS FOREST is a couple of hours southeast of Corvallis, Oregon, where Fred Swanson lives. (Julia Jones, his partner, is a geography professor at Oregon State University, and Swanson has an appointment there as well.) The drive takes us through the fertile, flat Willamette Valley. Fields blur by, many with large white placards that tell their contents: fescue, rye, sweet corn, hazelnuts. Bracketing the fields to the west is the Coast Range, old and dark and gloomy with rain; to the east are Mount Jefferson and Three Fingered Jack, two of the Cascades' southern peaks.

After thirty-odd miles Swanson leaves the interstate for the McKenzie Highway, which curves along the McKenzie River. Fir boughs hang heavy over the road, blocking what little sunlight the clouds let through, until we arrive at the entrance to the Andrews about an hour later. Drizzle veils down. Even in May the air is cool, verging on cold.

Swanson pulls into a parking lot outside the headquarters, the squat brown buildings forming a sodden outpost in the dark forest. (In the old days, the headquarters was a collection of junker trailers known half-affectionately as the Ghetto in the Meadow.) "This is probably the most closely studied patch of trees on the planet," Swanson says as we head into the main building. Our arrival has coincided with that of a passel of students who will spend the next few weeks here. We run into Jones while she leads them on a tour; to provision them, Swanson has brought bags of kale from their garden, which he wants to drop off. While he does, I wait in a conference room, study the walls. Hanging from one is an enormous poster, a time map of the Andrews that begins with its founding in 1948 as the Blue River Experimental Forest. (Its name was changed in 1953 to commemorate Horace Justin Andrews, a forester who died in a car accident.)

The poster shows rows of colored bars marked with tiny names and varying in length and thickness. When Swanson returns he orients me to the scheme. At the top are slim green bars that span the tenures of the various research leaders. Swanson's bar is the second of the stack, running from 1972 to the present day; a couple of bars under his is Jerry Franklin's, which goes from 1957 to 1989, when he left to take a position at the University of Washington. Below that grouping are the National Forest leaders at the federal level—the Andrews sits within the Willamette National Forest—and below them are thicker bands for the main research themes, each over its year of inception: vegetation in 1950, hydrology/small watersheds in 1952, information management in 1955, and so on.

At the bottom is a second timeline, or rather a recapitulation of the scroll of years from the top, with little amber pyramids indicating significant incidents in the forest's history. There is a pyramid for the first clear-cut (1950), a pyramid for the year when all the soils were mapped (1962), one for the Christmas flood (1964). The only pyramid that does not pertain to the forest's own history is at 1980, beneath which is written, "Mount St. Helens erupts."

———

Mount St. Helens did not touch the Andrews in any physical sense. The eruption was not even visible this far south except on TV, although some people in southern Oregon later reported hearing a series of odd *whoomps* early in the morning. But even if the mountain had no direct impact on this forest, its scientists have done much to shape the ways people perceived the blast and its effects, and few have done more than Jerry Franklin.

Franklin grew up in Camas, Washington, a small logging town just across the Columbia River from Portland. He was the son of a sawmill worker, and so ingrained was forestry in his being that his middle name is "Forest." He started as a research forester at the Andrews right after he graduated from Oregon State and did research there for a year before going off to earn a PhD in botany from Washington State University. He returned to the Andrews in 1966 to stay, becoming the chief plant ecologist in 1975.

From the beginning, it was clear to his colleagues that Franklin had a knack for seeing big, thinking big, scheming big. Swanson jokingly told me once, in an attempt to describe the scale of Franklin's ambitions, that "he wanted a numbered tag on every tree in the Pacific Northwest." Jim Sedell, who was Franklin's colleague in the Forest Service for years, described him as the Andrews's "effervescent arm waver and synthesizer."

This role became more pronounced in the late 1960s and 1970s, with the onset of a project called the International Biological Programme, or IBP. The IBP proposed to do basic scientific work on a range of natural systems, including grasslands, tundra, and old-growth forests. Scientists envisioned large, interdisciplinary groups studying whole ecosystems, or biomes, teasing out as much information as possible on the mechanisms of those landscapes and how they contributed to the state of the planet.

In 1969, the National Science Foundation, which administered the IBP in the United States, selected the Andrews as one of a few representatives of the coniferous forest biome. Scientists from Oregon State and the Andrews received funds to study the finer workings of stands of trees there that were either managed younger forests or remnant old growth. They were to look specifically at the relationship between the trees and the streams that threaded through them. With this charge, the Andrews went from being the workplace of a few Forest Service scientists to a much more freewheeling laboratory for government biologists and academics. The research topics grew as well, shifting from the pragmatic, applied-research questions of how best to grow trees as a crop to much more descriptive ecological work. Teams set out to learn how nutrients cycled between terrestrial and aquatic habitats, how energy flowed across the oft-blurred boundaries between the two, and how the forest ecosystem organized itself, from the fungi in the soil to the creatures in the canopy far above. They established permanent plots to track how the forest responded to logging and other human acts, and to big, more natural disturbances, such as windstorms, floods, and insect infestations.

"The kind of studies that can be accomplished by large integrated research differs from that which can be done by individuals or small groups," wrote one biologist in 1974 for one of the IBP's periodic bulletins. This was especially true in an ecosystem densely woven of many thin but interrelated threads. Before the deeper work at the Andrews, foresters had thought of old-growth stands as sterile and useless. What was the harm in cutting down all those big trees to rid the land of them and free up space so that more young trees could quickly grow? Adopting a more integrated view, Franklin and Swanson and their colleagues began to upset those prejudices within just a few years, helping to reveal the tremendous number of organisms that quietly and discreetly made their home in the old growth. They were thus disposed to look at places people thought bereft of life and show otherwise.

When Mount St. Helens began to stir with a series of small quakes on March 20, 1980—the official start of the eruption—Franklin watched from the Andrews with more than a casual interest. He knew he was seeing something big, and he started to think big. No one could be sure what would happen at Mount St. Helens, but the eruption was sure to be interesting, and he wanted personnel from the Andrews to help lead the study of it. "It was an extraordinary opportunity to shift our focus to a different place, a different environment, where we could explore developing ideas," he says. "We were a cadre out in front in terms of looking at natural ecosystems and processes." It was only fitting, then, for the Andrews teams to turn their gazes north to that newly restive mountain.

Swanson is driving up an old logging road that follows Lookout Creek, which bisects the Andrews almost exactly. The road winds and splits, and soon I have no idea where we are, a disorientation that seems characteristic of being among these big trees; but Swanson, thankfully, knows where he is going. He pulls over at a nondescript spot where stubborn patches of snow cling to the ground. The Andrews ranges from 1,300 to over 5,000 feet in elevation; these higher hills have only lately melted out.

We strike out into the forest. The trail is spongy, the understory overgrown. Dripping shrubs soon hide the road behind us. It is curious to be here, to juxtapose this old green with the new gray-green of Mount St. Helens, where almost everything is less than forty years old; but as Swanson walks, he talks of the processes at work in both places: disturbance, succession, resilience, forces of earth and nature working in opposition or in concert. For him, to move from one habitat to the other is to attune to a dialectic with a great teacher, or teachers. "Both the Andrews and Mount St. Helens are seedbeds for communities, for discoveries," he says. "It speaks to the influence of powerful landscapes, and their humbling effect, too. These are high-karma places."

We are in this part of the woods to see one of the Andrews's more famous experiments—the sort of thing Swanson says could only be done here, given its charter. The experiment began in 1985. Best practices in forestry at the time dictated that as much woody debris as possible be removed from a site once it was logged, so that new seedlings would have room to grow. But a biologist named Mark Harmon thought to ask what seemed a simple question: What happens to a tree after it falls to the ground? This simple question branched into many less simple ones. How long does it take a log to release the nutrients and carbon it holds? How does the carbon then find its way into the soil on which the log rests? What colonizes the log, makes it a home, springs to life upon it or from it? Previously, no one had ever had the years or wherewithal to study this process from start to finish. At the Andrews, it was possible.

Harmon arranged for five hundred trees from four conifer species to be cut down and bucked into logs, each about twenty feet long. These he spread around six sites. He then monitored each log's density, its moisture and nutrient content, the gases it released, and the organisms that moved into it. He set a run time for his experiment of two hundred years, assuming that others would see fit to continue the work. Swanson shows me one of the logs now. It lies with four or five others, carefully, if haphazardly arranged. Numbered metal tags festoon it, along with bits of plastic and a white bucket that is itself covered with a film of green slime. "This one is a Pacific silver fir," Swanson says of the log. He presses the bark with his finger. "With some species it can get kind of hard to tell after a while, but silver firs go fast."

After more than thirty years, the log's bark is crumbly and soft under a heavy quilt of moss and fungi. I can push my finger into it almost up past my middle knuckle. It feels akin to touching a famous painting: the same sense of awe that turns to titillation, with a hint of desecration. I also get the sense no one has been here in quite a while. Swanson tells me people only visit the logs every year or so now, to cut round slabs called cookies from them. Like most ecologists these days, they are adept at modeling processes from intermittent streams of data gathered through periodic sampling. "That seems to be the way things are going," he says. Still, the logs will remain until the earth absorbs them, covering with forest litter both the trunks and the tools used to study them.

Swanson recites a few of the project's main findings: how the logs slowly bequeath the nitrogen they contain back to the forest, how the different species of trees decompose at different rates. Critters also swarmed all over the logs almost from the moment they hit the ground. Even a medium-sized log might have as many as twelve thousand beetle galleries after just one year, the little tunnels and chambers spreading out across the wood like glyphs. "Just think if Mark had done this for a few months or a year and said he'd learned everything," Swanson says. This is the value of embedding oneself deeply in a place, in a question. Swanson stands over the log, considers it. "Work like this is an honoring of death," he says. "It is a way of showing the amount of life that can continue after death." Hearing this, I think of how he thinks of Mount St. Helens.

———

The IBP program ended in the late 1970s, but the seeds of method and philosophy it sowed continued to flourish at the Andrews under another NSF initiative called the Long-Term Ecological Research program, or LTER, established in 1980. The Andrews applied and was selected to be one of the first six participating sites around the US. Ever since then, its scientists have enjoyed extensive support for monitoring projects that span decades and address issues such as climate change and its effects on vegetation; the relationship between forests, water quality, and salmon populations; and patterns in biodiversity.

On the time map in the conference room, the establishment of the LTER shares the little 1980 pyramid with the eruption of Mount St. Helens. I think back now to that map and what it represents, comparing it with Mount St. Helens and its community of scientists, a hundred or so of whom had been at the Pulse. While I had not dared to try counting all the names on the poster, in addition to Swanson and Franklin I had recognized several from the extensive bibliography on Mount St. Helens.

"Has anyone ever done something like this for Mount St. Helens?" I had asked Swanson back in the conference room. Simply as a display of institutional memory, the time map was a remarkable piece, exhibiting the administrative labor needed over and above the labor of research. In that visual record was the Andrews's evolution and the challenges implicit in its project and projects that would seek to emulate it: How do lines of inquiry persist as the world of questions around them changes? How does one ensure continuity in a community of thought as people and their ideas come and go? This was science as social enterprise.

Swanson had shaken his head. "We want to do something this—" he started, before catching himself. "We *should*," he corrected, and smiled ruefully. "But it's all in the heads of three or four people, and none of us has really taken the time to sit down together and map it out yet."

———

After a spell we wander away from the logs to the base of an immense fir that presides over this scientific diorama. Swanson smiles. "It'll be a long time before you see a tree like this in the blast area," he says. He brushes the trunk with his fingertips. The tree's immensity begs a close, tactile inspection. Its bark is tough and thick but flaky, like a pastry. It testifies to great age almost as much as the tree's size does. Swanson leans back and gazes toward its crown, which he can just make out through the overstory. "What is the Andrews?" he muses. "I have a friend who says, 'It is a portal to other ways of knowing.'"

With that he falls silent. I wait for him to go on before I realize he is not going to say anything more. We stand still and listen to the forest. One minute stretches into two, to three, to five, and then Swanson ambles off. I watch him leave in his bright yellow rain slicker and wonder if he is testing me in some way. I feel a flare of discomfort: I am unprepared, exposed. Then I realize maybe I am not being tested so much as welcomed. Swanson is welcoming me to this old forest, this wood he knows so well. In his quiet wake is a question: What is this place saying?

Among the trees I hear faint sounds: fat drops of water striking the earth, the breeze, branches sweeping the air, small birds chittering. But the quiet overwhelms. It is too total, too *loud*. Out comes my notebook, and I start scribbling a list of every noise. There is a chestnut-backed chickadee in the understory, a Hammond's flycatcher calling overhead, the resonant *whumps* of a sooty grouse from deeper in the trees, the nasal monotone of a red-breasted nuthatch, the sweet warble of a Swainson's thrush that sounds a thousand miles away. I broaden my attention some and hear a mosquito's irksome whine, a plane high in the sky, two scolding chipmunks, all over a light patter of rain.

Is the feeling this forest evinces something like the scientific urge, perhaps akin to what Swanson and Franklin and everyone else felt, first here and then at Mount St. Helens all those years ago? Confronted with a phenomenon bigger than the human mind can conceive, there is a rush to document and catalog and so attempt to bring a measure of order to it, which done the correct way might be called discovery. But I doubt Swanson is trying to elicit such an overwrought analysis from me, so I put my notebook away, uncenter my mind from myself, unhumanize my views a little. Through the silence come these other voices. After a few moments, I think I have an answer for Swanson, responding to his question with one of my own: How is being here at the base of all these trees so different from standing on top of a mountain?

PART TWO

NATURAL EXPERIMENTS

3

BIOLOGICAL LEGACIES

JERRY FRANKLIN IS holding court on the shore of Meta Lake. A crowd of biologists sits before him, picking through boxed lunches. (All the downed trees act as convenient benches or tables.) Most have projects in the area, or have had, so they are familiar with this landscape, both in its broad strokes and in its particulars. Still they listen. Franklin knows how to tell a story.

"You have to try to imagine it," Franklin says. "Everything was gray. Nothing had been left standing." He flares his hands for effect. "It was like flying over the *moon*." Under a wide-brimmed hat, his eyes seem to twinkle. He is in his late seventies now, and agile in mind if less so in body than he used to be, back when he would hike twenty-odd miles in a day just to look at something interesting.

He gestures beyond us, and people turn to see what he is pointing at. We are about seven miles northeast of Mount St. Helens, in the eastern part of the lateral blast area, or the Blowdown Zone. The mountain is hidden from here, but within the monument boundaries you always have a sense of where it is. My mind drifts to that quiet morning so many years ago, to what it must have been like for, say, an elk. To sense in my chest the rumbling ground, to feel the warning rustle of wind over my pelt. Physicists later determined the eruption was silent at this distance—something about the nature of sound propagation meant that the *boom* projected up and out and away rather than simply across—and so the first thing I would have heard was all the trees crashing toward me in a wave. I would raise my head as the sky went dark, and the air would get hot and pungent with the smell of flayed evergreens, and then rocks would hurtle down and the leading edge of the blast cloud would sweep over me, and that would be that. Over in seconds.

People around me are laughing, I realize. Franklin has said something funny. I turn back and give him my full attention. "Right off," he is saying, grinning, "all of us smart ecologists realized we didn't have the correct working hypothesis."

I have heard this line before, and so have many others in the audience, but I cannot help chuckling along with everyone else. Franklin has been telling of spotting that first fireweed and the incorrect working hypothesis for many years now, and his delivery is still as fresh as it is polished—a tricky balance. Such a skillful sheen is common to a lot of the stories biologists now tell about Mount St. Helens, as their science becomes oral tradition.

Still, listening to this story again in a young conifer forest, which but for a few features from the eruption might be any young conifer forest in the Cascade Range, is almost enough to make me forget how intimidating this landscape must have been at first, when no one knew what had happened, whether it would happen again, or how soon. But that is the nature of this narrative: those early fears and difficulties are glossed over or elided until the subsequent findings can come to seem almost like a foregone conclusion, as if it was all simple and straightforward, when really it was anything but. For as I have heard Franklin say, also more than once, "Things seem in retrospect much clearer than in prospect."

———

In the weeks following May 18, the prospect of studying the ecology of Mount St. Helens, exhilarating though it may have been, was daunting. Dozens if not hundreds of biologists from the Pacific Northwest and beyond were keen to get in. Accommodating them all threatened to be a real headache, with all the questions of jurisdiction, access, funding, and logistics. To forestall this, several biologists came to Corvallis a couple of weeks after the eruption to meet with Franklin and Swanson and other staff from the Forest Service's Pacific Northwest Research Station, along with a representative from the National Science Foundation. It was a chance for them all to get to know one another, talk about what they wanted to try to do, and figure out who had what money and how much.

Already everyone was antsy. Each second spent in a conference room was time not spent in the field, and the mountain was not waiting for them to finalize their arrangements. But they had a lot to discuss. Mount St. Helens would be a dangerous place to work, and although geologists said a second major eruption was unlikely, it was still belching and fizzing and popping. Lava oozed steadily from its crater as the new dome grew, swelling until it resembled the shell of a snapping turtle. Smaller eruptions took place on May 25, June 12, and July 22; and *smaller* was a relative term, with columns of ash that rose a mere eleven miles into the sky rather than fifteen, pyroclastic flows that poured out in slightly less voluminous blistering waves, and the occasional lahar that sent hot mud down the southern drainages.

To keep everyone safe, access to the heart of what scientists were calling "the devastated area" north of the mountain was restricted. Any researchers who wanted to work in it—and that was more or less all of them—would have to get permission from a host of federal, state, and local authorities. Of course, having permission to go into the restricted zone did not necessarily mean they could get there. Most of the old highways and logging roads were impassable. Researchers would need helicopters, which were expensive. They would be allowed to fly only when visibility was good around Mount St. Helens, and the helicopter would be required to stay at the landing site, with no drop-offs, no ferrying of different groups to different sites. The authorities were clear: everyone was to stay within a fifteen-minute walk (or run) of their ride. Added to the safety concerns was a concern about the effects of human presence on the landscape. It was unique, fragile. No one wanted to get in anyone else's way or to ruin the mountain with needless duplication of projects.

Planning for fieldwork thus became a complex social exercise. The group spent hours in meetings in Corvallis, Portland, and Seattle, back east in Washington, DC, and later in more informal conversations, trying to anticipate and negotiate as many tangles as they could while putting systems in place to resolve the ones they could not. To keep operations running until more money was available, the NSF representative pledged to award a series of small emergency grants, a few thousand dollars apiece, that would need little more than a good idea and a cover letter to get approved. The agency also allowed researchers to divert money from existing grants to study the eruption, given the exceptional circumstances. Congress eventually provided about six hundred thousand dollars in a supplemental appropriation, one-third of which went to Forest Service scientists, one-third to outside scientists, and the rest to logistical support. As for the research projects, Franklin said he would coordinate the work of the terrestrial ecologists; Jim Sedell would handle the aquatic ecologists; and Swanson would work with the scientists interested in geomorphology, while also acting as a link between the ecology group and the USGS geologists, who were already out in force.

By July, once local authorities had deemed Mount St. Helens calm enough to study, the Forest Service offered to fund helicopter flights for eight or ten biologists at a time. Teams were able to tour the blast area, land and walk around as Franklin and Swanson and only a few others had done, and compare their early hypothetical expectations with conditions on the ground. Afterwards, those interested in similar topics—disturbance and succession, the ecology of lakes new and old, the effects of ashfall on vegetation farther from the mountain—met in groups to discuss how they wanted to do their studies and how they could share data. "We were a bunch of fuzzy-headed scientists, but we had NSF funding," Swanson says. "We could do wild science instead of domestic science."

What would the wild science of Mount St. Helens look like? Of actual experiment or manipulation there would be little. The eruption itself was the experiment, and the various volcanic processes and disturbance zones were the experimental treatments. All anyone really had to do was mark out a patch of land in the devastated area and keep track of what happened in it. Doing so was itself a kind of radical modesty. "A final problem," Swanson would note the following November, "is the establishment of long-term plots to monitor changes and recovery in the ecosystem. This is not the kind of hypothesis-testing research that sells at the NSF, and the Forest Service has not eagerly underwritten this mundane activity, yet long-term plots provide the basic foundation for more profound 'quick-answer' science." He was, in his mild way, laying down a marker. If people wanted to understand what had really happened at Mount St. Helens, they would have to be patient and let the landscape speak for itself.

The following September, research began in earnest. Franklin repurposed a team-building exercise he had developed at the Andrews Forest—what he called a *pulse*—and brought it to Mount St. Helens. He and Jim Sedell leased several vans, chartered three Jet Ranger helicopters, and rented space at a campground near the Cispus River. On September 7, dozens of biologists and their field crews arrived. This, the first Mount St. Helens Pulse, lasted two weeks. It was, Franklin thought, a chance for all the scientists to go out and suffer together. In the mornings, the three helicopters *whup-whup*-ed away from camp with their bellies full of scientists, who spent the day working in the blast area, setting up their long-term plots. In the evening, back in the camp's big meeting hall, they gathered to eat and drink and talk about all they had seen and done, "stretching our minds and our experiences and our hypotheses," as Franklin would later say.

One hundred twenty-five scientists participated in that first Pulse; every day, at least forty people were out working on projects. They traveled as far and wide as was feasible. Some focused on the piles of rubble that the debris avalanche had left in the valley of the North Fork Toutle River. Some flew up to Spirit Lake to sample its waters, which were black and stinky and covered with thousands of floating logs, like an enormous millpond. Some looked longingly at the flat white Pumice Plain, although there seemed to be little to see. Swanson flew to the steeper hillsides around Bean Creek and Smith Creek to monitor the rates at which the ash and other deposits were eroding. As for Franklin, he wanted to be among the toppled trees flung across the Blowdown Zone.

Before the eruption, the forests around Mount St. Helens had the region's typical mix of conifers. Douglas fir and western hemlock made up the stands at elevations under four thousand feet; higher up, Pacific silver fir, noble fir, and mountain hemlock dominated. But the composition of the forests was also partly determined by human intervention: they sat on a patchwork of federal and private lands. (Before it collapsed, the summit of Mount St. Helens itself had famously been owned by the railroad company Burlington Northern.) Some had been virgin forest, with trees more than six hundred years old; some were second-growth stands that had been harvested decades ago; and some had been recently clear-cut so that only stumps remained.

Franklin wanted to study the long-term effects of the blast in former forests (clear-cuts), blowdown forest (at both low and high elevations), and, at the edge of the blast area, the rim of scorched forest with trees left standing but dead. He planned to lay out transect lines in each type of forest, at varying distances from Mount St. Helens. (From the air, he had noted that the strength and effects of the blast decreased with distance.) Each of his transects would be 100 meters long and have five evenly spaced 250-square-meter circular plots (about 300 square yards). In total, at thirteen different sites between four and twelve miles from the mountain, he would place thirteen transects in clear-cuts, thirteen in blowdown forest without snow at lower elevations, six in blowdown forest that still had snow at higher elevations, and three in scorched forest. He placed pairs of blowdown and clear-cut transects close together wherever possible, and matched those pairs with scorched-forest transects in a few places; this would make comparing the sites easier.

On paper, in the well-swept and air-conditioned confines of a conference room, this study design looked simple enough. In the field it was not. The days were long, and Franklin and his crews worked in the heat of an unrelenting sun. Moving around and through the tangle of fallen logs and branches, to say nothing of keeping the transect lines straight, was a struggle. (They had decided to lay their lines perpendicular to the general direction in which trees had fallen.) The constant wind kicked up clouds of ash, which dusted their faces, got in their eyes and their ears, and even stuck in their throats if they were not careful. When Franklin worked his jaws, he could taste the grit on his teeth. Volcanic ash is in essence finely ground glass; Franklin wondered what it was doing to his enamel. But once he had laid his lines at all the sites, he was ready at last to measure what was in them, translating the visual chaos of the landscape into data so that he could see which of his hypotheses Mount St. Helens might upend next.

———

Franklin and other plant ecologists working throughout the blast area were coming to their research with an eye on one of ecology's oldest questions: how do plant communities assemble and change? That question had grown out of the straightforward but central observation that certain types of plants—mosses, grasses, flowers, trees—seemed to do better than others at different stages and under different growing conditions, and in ways that were predictable over time.

Plant ecologists now call this process, in its broad outline, *succession*. It emerged as a notion in the mid-sixteenth century, when natural historians wrote of Irish farmers clearing bogs so that they could grow crops and discovering tree stumps buried in the peat—the remnants of past forests. In the mid-eighteenth century, the Swedish botanist and taxonomist Carl Linnaeus wrote in his *Systema Naturae* of how the plants and trees growing in a place could change over time. Henry David Thoreau spoke of this phenomenon in an 1860 lecture, "The Succession of Forest Trees, and Wild Apples." But it was not until the late 1800s that a young scientist named Henry Chandler Cowles began to characterize the patterns that would come to define it ecologically.

Cowles (pronounced "coals") had trained in geology and plant taxonomy at Oberlin College in Ohio. After he finished his undergraduate degree in 1893, he taught natural science at a small college in Nebraska for a year, and in 1895 he decided to go to the University of Chicago to get a PhD in geology. He was doing research on Pleistocene paleobotany until one summer day in 1896, when he boarded the Michigan Central Railroad in Hyde Park. The line ran along the Michigan-Indiana border until just outside the city of Gary, Indiana, when it turned to follow Lake Michigan. From there the train meandered among the great sand dunes that border the lakeshore.

When Cowles first beheld the dunes, he stared out at them, amazed. The largest were more than one hundred feet tall. They reminded him of small mountains. He decided right then to get off the train, and at the next stop hired a carriage to take him back to the dunes. He spent the rest of the afternoon wandering among them, marveling at the curious features of their plant life. Close to the lake, he walked on bare sand beach, but as he trudged farther inland, he saw first clumps and then rolling green waves of marram, a species of beach grass. Farther from the shore, shrubs and flowering plants replaced the grasses, until they themselves were replaced by a young forest of short trees, and, behind that, an older, taller, more mature wood.

Cowles recognized a pattern in search of an explanation. Back at the University of Chicago, he decided to change his course of study from geology and paleobotany to plant ecology. For the next few summers, he regularly took the one-hour train ride from Chicago out to the Indiana lakeshore. He scrambled up and down the dunes, studying the interplay between the plants and the shifting sands beneath them. Through his research he developed what would come to be known as the space-for-time approach, or the *chronosequence*. Given the limits of the human life span, the impossibility of waiting centuries for trees to grow and prove or disprove his hypotheses, he needed a proxy for time. Space was one. To walk from the lake inland was to move back in time, he knew, from the young dunes to progressively older ones. The plant communities that marked the distance likewise represented temporal succession, with the dunes at the lake edge representing recent time and the forest representing earlier eras.

The marram, Cowles deduced, was the species that arrived first, setting root in the sand. It was able to resist the fierce winds, the blowing and drifting sands that occasionally buried it, and the heat of the summer sun. Once the marram established itself and proliferated, its root structure stabilized the dunes. It also provided shade and shelter from the wind, and when it died it released its nutrients, which contributed to soil development. Seeds from other species less suited to bare sand could then take root and grow. Eventually these species outcompeted the marram. They flourished until they in turn were outcompeted by another suite of species. This process of competition and replacement repeated itself until trees and mature forest grew up, signaling an end to the process.

From Cowles's observations, combined with the work of other biologists in the early 1900s, a general outline of succession began to take shape. Start with a bare plot of ground, with little to no soil. The initial colonizers have to be hardy and self-sufficient: mosses, lichens, annual plants like beach grass, or other species that can make do with scant water and nutrients. As these establish themselves in the first year or two, they stabilize the habitat and start to create soil, enriching it with organic material and nutrients like nitrogen and phosphorus, and increasing its capacity to retain water. The plot thereafter becomes more habitable for other plants, such as herbaceous perennials. When these have established themselves they outcompete the pioneers, being better able to take in the nourishment they need. After the perennials come the shrubs, and after them the trees, especially those that do well in open habitats. Once these trees have grown for a few decades, a final group of species, the more robust trees that can grow in the shadows of others, appear. Within a century or two they replace the first rank of trees. Nothing supplants them. After several hundred years, the forest matures into what is known as a climax community.

Cowles finished his dissertation in 1898. The article he published from it in 1899, "The Ecological Relations of the Vegetation on the Sand Dunes of Lake Michigan," became a classic paper in ecology, although he never meant his views on succession to become dogma. True, he had predicted that plant communities would tend toward a stable equilibrium, but he did not think such an equilibrium was ever reached. Communities exist, he believed, in states of continuous change. Something inevitably happens. A strong wind might knock a few of the old trees over. A wildfire might burn a forest to the ground. A volcano can lay waste to a landscape. The process then starts over, sometimes with a different outcome.

The wind, the wildfire, the volcano—each is an example of what ecologists call a *disturbance*, defined by one author as "any relatively discrete event in time (and space) that disrupts ecosystem, community, or population structures, and changes resources, substrate availability, or the physical environment." The term is slippery; biologists have devoted many years and studies to whittling other definitions that are subtly different yet similarly precise. But whatever its exact meaning, disturbance always involves a sudden and abrupt change, whether over a large or small area, drastically lowering the abundance of some species and opening up space in which others can compete. Disturbance takes what may have been a relatively stable system and introduces dynamism and patchiness. Space that one set of organisms has occupied after success in a competitive ritual is suddenly made free to all comers.

Given this, Franklin wondered what would happen at Mount St. Helens, where, across a space of 234 square miles, the ecosystem had been disrupted by a range of disturbances (debris avalanche, lateral blast, pyroclastic flows, tephra fall) of differing intensities. The blowdown forest, he knew now, was not an example of primary succession, defined by no soil or survivors anywhere: that term better described the Pumice Plain in front of the mountain. In the Blowdown Zone there was soil somewhere under all that ash, and the fireweeds he had seen showed that some organisms had survived. Classical theory therefore suggested that secondary succession would be marked not by a few lucky survivors sprinkled here and there, but rather by a flood of invaders from outside the disturbed area.

That was not quite what Franklin found. Most of his plots were still empty in September, but the few plants that had managed to grow over the summer had done so in interesting and distinct ways. Surprisingly, the clear-cuts had the most species and the highest overall plant coverage. Granted, the coverage in these areas was a little less than 4 percent on average, and most of the plants were the quick colonizers one would expect to find: fireweed, pearly everlasting, white hawkweed, thistle, bracken fern, thimbleberry, salmonberry—flowers and bushes that thrive in the full sun of open habitats and can regenerate from tiny pieces if conditions are at all suitable. The sorts of plants that thrive in clear-cuts, in other words. But they had not necessarily drifted in from elsewhere. They had taken over the plots before the eruption, after loggers had cut down all the trees and cleared out the other vegetation, as was the practice of the day. The reason they did comparatively well was that the stumps surrounding them, unlike fallen logs, did little to stop rain from washing the tephra away. This erosion had eased the plants' passage from the soil under the ash into the sunshine above.

In the blowdown forests, the average plant cover was much more modest: a mere 0.2 percent, which translated to about half a square meter out of a 250-square-meter plot. But this average concealed significant differences in coverage between the forests at different elevations. While the lowland plots, snowless in the spring, had almost no plants, the plots higher up that were blanketed in snow on the morning of May 18 had about the same number of species and coverage as the clear-cuts. But rather than weeds, the plants growing there were young trees and shrubs, including Pacific silver fir, mountain hemlock, and evergreen huckleberry. These species, Franklin knew, had made up the forest understory before the blast. When the snow fell in the late fall and formed deep drifts over the winter, their slight, springy trunks had bent under its weight. They spent the next few months pinned to the ground under its heavy mantle, which might be more than eight feet thick. This protected them when the blast cloud roared over them, leaving them untouched. Once the snowpack melted out in the spring and summer, they popped back up. "When you look around the basin now," Franklin had said at Meta Lake, "95 percent of the trees you see are those that survived in snowbanks."

For the next six summers, Franklin and his colleagues returned to the sites and watched the plots refill, noting ebbs and flows in the rates of growth. The clear-cuts might have had more plants in the beginning, but they maintained only a modest cover as the years passed. Meanwhile, both the scorched area and the snowless blowdown forests showed steady increases in both species diversity and cover, so that by 1986 their cover was nearly double that of the clear-cuts. Sites that were snow-covered during the eruption had nearly triple the cover of the clear-cuts. Often plants grew in the shade of downed logs, among their upturned roots. Franklin came to call these logs and other remnant structures "biological lifeboats" because of the way they protected and nurtured the new shoots.

More interesting were the differences in the plant communities between the habitats. Each had followed its own independent trajectory. The clear-cuts were still dominated by weedy species, but the plots in the blowdown forests, and especially those with snow, had species that had grown there before the eruption. Instead of new invaders coming in from the fringes of the devastated area, as succession theory predicted, old plants had sprouted from the middle. Sometimes it was just one or two individual survivors; sometimes it was big clumps.

"We expected invasion," Franklin says. "We saw something that mattered more: survival." This was a revelation. When studying the impacts of a disturbance, ecologists had never thought much about what had originally lived in the disturbed habitat. They were far more concerned—or preoccupied might be a better word—with what came after "time zero," when the disturbance hit. But maybe, Franklin was starting to see, there was no time zero. Maybe instead there were disjunct continuities. In what would become one of the enduring ecological lessons from Mount St. Helens, he started to think of survivors in general as the biological legacies of the pre-eruption landscape. These legacies served as links between the pre- and posteruption communities. They could be living or dead, organic or inorganic. "Essentially, all natural disturbances leave behind legacies of the predisturbance system," he says. "It shouldn't have surprised me that living things could survive the eruption, but it did."

———

To think of the eruption's effects in this way—as a function of surprise, rather than of a system obediently marching along to the dictates of theory—opened the way to other insights. One concerned the specific time and date of the eruption. That moment, 8:32 a.m. on Sunday, May 18, 1980, grew in idiosyncratic significance. What if Mount St. Helens had erupted twelve hours earlier, at 8:32 p.m.? Then many more animals, particularly small mammals, would have died. In the morning, they were in their dens and burrows. That would not have been the case at night. Or what if Mount St. Helens had erupted in the summer—in June, July, or August? Then the snowpack would have been gone, even at the higher elevations. In May, most amphibians were still in hibernation. In summer they would have been out and about, and so buried or incinerated. Fewer plants would have been spared in any form, because the soil would have been more thickly covered with ash and debris, and perhaps the top layers would have been so burned as to be sterile. The saplings and young trees that were safely buried under the snow would have been crushed by the big trees that were knocked over.

So the eruption, this singular event, was also rife with contingencies. Some were darker than others. What if Mount St. Helens had erupted at the same time the next morning, on Monday instead of Sunday? Then hundreds more people would probably have died. Much of the forested land around Mount St. Helens was owned by private timber companies, Weyerhaeuser first among them, and the forests were being actively logged. At 8:30 on a Monday morning, several hundred loggers would have been arriving for their shifts, the mountain ringing with the high whines of their chainsaws, the toots and chirps of whistles. The lateral blast would have killed them all.

Like the plants, the loggers were quick to return. Of the tens of thousands of acres of flattened trees, sixty-eight thousand acres had been on Weyerhaeuser's St. Helens Tree Farm; another sixty-four thousand acres were in the Gifford Pinchot National Forest. Federal, state, and private foresters alike looked at all the downed trees and saw little more than lost revenue. As one writer later noted in a magazine devoted to commercial forestry, "What nature had blown down, nature claimed."

The foresters were determined not to let all those dead trees go to waste; their outer bark might have been burned in the blast, but for the most part the wood underneath was in fine shape. Just days after the eruption, Franklin watched as the US Forest Service, the Washington State Department of Natural Resources, and Weyerhaeuser clamored to get into the Blowdown Zone. One week after Franklin's first Pulse started, on September 15, 1980, logging trucks began to roll into the northern portion of the Blowdown Zone, around the Green River, and to the area between the north and south forks of the Toutle River.

Salvaging volcano-felled timber was hard, dirty, and dangerous. The activity stirred up clouds of ash, forcing loggers to wear hospital masks in order to breathe. The ash dulled their equipment; cutters had to sharpen and resharpen their chainsaws after working only one or two trees. The loggers spoke in gloomy terms of working in a lifeless place, too much within sight of a volcano that could erupt again at any moment, the geologists' reassurances notwithstanding.

For the next two years, loggers salvaged as much commercially valuable timber as they could. During the months of peak extraction, as many as six hundred truckloads of logs were removed every day. In a parallel effort, in the spring of 1981, Weyerhaeuser employees began to replant the forests by hand, eventually putting in eighteen million seedlings over forty-five thousand acres. They had to dig a foot or so through the ash to reach the old soil, but the ash acted as a wonderful mulch. On eighteen thousand acres of federal land, the Forest Service added another nine million seedlings.

Coming to Mount St. Helens, Franklin and his colleagues from the Andrews had understood that they were not engaged in purely academic inquiry. They had the opportunity to lead the research effort in part because they were employees of the US Forest Service, and they were operating in a working national forest that just happened to be the site of a volcanic eruption. They had to consider not only their scientific interest in ecological succession, but also forest management practices on public and private land. But he and other plant ecologists observed the foresters' replanting efforts at first with bemusement and then something closer to horror. If the timber companies had their way, there would be nothing left to learn. "There was a sense among the scientists that some of this land needed to be preserved so we could watch it," Franklin says. "Some of it we should leave alone."

Along with other ecologists and interested groups, Franklin began to advocate for the formation of some sort of park or monument to protect a large portion of the blast area. Through their efforts, the Mount St. Helens National Volcanic Monument was created on August 26, 1982. Weyerhaeuser and Burlington Northern agreed to exchange roughly thirty-two thousand acres of blast-affected land inside the proposed monument boundary, much of which they had already salvaged for logs, for more than seven thousand acres a little farther down the North Fork Toutle River. In the end, the monument covered 110,000 acres, most of it north of Mount St. Helens.

———

For almost all of his career until 1980, Franklin had been focused on questions and ideas of how to maintain and cultivate healthy forest ecosystems, studying not only what those ecosystems looked like but also how they could be wisely used. At Mount St. Helens in 1980, the main disturbance was natural, volcanic, and acute, but in most other systems where Franklin had worked, the forces of disturbance were chronic and predominantly human. Federal and private foresters had thought of the woods as being continuously renewable. They could cut down all the trees and start again from nothing. Franklin argued that it was not so. Between clear-cut and old growth, between volcanic eruption and forest regeneration, lay several stages of rich and scientifically important biological change. The eruption had knocked over millions of board feet of timber, yes, but it had left a lot of other things behind, and those things were what would shape the future ecological community.

Insights from Franklin's work would inform thinking on contemporary forestry practices for years to come. But for Franklin, Swanson, and the scientists from the Andrews, Mount St. Helens would fade in importance. In the late 1980s, the "forest wars," disputes over the fate of old-growth forests throughout the Pacific Northwest, began in earnest, and the Andrews crew were centrally involved. For them, the mountain became one triangle among many on the time map on their wall, but its teachings would endure.

In stressing the importance of biological legacies, Franklin was trying to show loggers how to cut down trees the way a volcano does. At the same time, he was imparting another lesson, one larger and more philosophical and therefore harder for some to accept. After the eruption, people had felt an irresistible need to intervene, to try to put everything back to the way it had been, to erase the blast and its effects. Foresters believed they had the resources and the ingenuity to fix the landscape. If they could bring the trees back so they could cut them down again, then they could restore not only the ecology of the region, but also a proper sense of utilitarian dominion. They could show that humans need not live with such a naked reminder of the degree to which we are always at the mercy of inhuman forces.

4

THE SURVIVOR-HERO

W HEN THE FIRST TREMORS shook Mount St. Helens in March 1980, and clouds of steam and ash puffed out from the summit, and the northern slopes contorted and bulged as magma welled up beneath them—when it became clear, in other words, that something big was happening—Jerry Franklin began to reach out to other scientists he thought would be good to have around afterward. He wanted to prime their thinking about the questions they might want to ask.

One of the first people he called was a biology professor at Utah State University named Jim MacMahon. Franklin had met him a few years before, when the two had worked on a National Science Foundation project in the Soviet Union. Franklin had been the plant guy and MacMahon the animal guy. They had a good rapport, and Franklin hoped they could re-create that at Mount St. Helens.

What had struck Franklin about MacMahon was his boundless interests and energy, exceeding even Franklin's own. On accepting an award later in his career—one of several he received—MacMahon would describe himself as a "simple ecologist." It was the kind of modest immodesty that some successful academics like to employ. A snake chaser from an early age, MacMahon had become the curator of reptiles at the Dayton Museum of Natural History in Ohio when he was just fourteen; he held a similar position at Michigan State University at the age of eighteen. Shifting some within the field of herpetology, he earned his PhD from the University of Notre Dame in 1964 for work on the ecology of three species of salamanders. At Utah State, he published papers on almost every taxon that moved over the land in some fashion: arachnids, birds, insects, reptiles, amphibians, fungi, mammals. He was famous (or infamous) for the eighteen- and twenty-hour days he regularly put in, accomplishing in just one of those "what it takes most of us 2–3 times as long to do," one of his colleagues would later write.

MacMahon flew up to Mount St. Helens within a couple of weeks of the eruption to get the lay of the land. For him, as for other scientists, trips to the blast area were brief and sometimes harrowing. During one, the volcano erupted right under his helicopter when it was lifting off. He and the pilot felt the earth tremble, and they looked up just in time to see a pillar of ash burst out of the ground. The pilot banked hard the other way and they escaped unscathed, but MacMahon was shaken. "You were always taking a chance you would be in a bad area when the mountain went," he later said. "If you wanted to get in early, you had to do it."

For MacMahon, the prospective questions were so compelling that they brought an adrenaline rush, but he knew he could not study "all the bunches of surprises." By the start of the Pulse the following September, he had decided to work in the Blowdown Zone, documenting how small mammals—rodents, shrews, mustelids—responded to a volcanic eruption. The little work done on this topic elsewhere had been largely qualitative and treated as incidental to more important botanical questions. It was old, too; the most recent study was from the 1943 eruption of Parícutin, in Mexico, and had involved only a couple of biologists making a list of animals they stumbled across.

MacMahon was keen to see how small mammals might facilitate the spread of plants. He had a study species in mind, the northern pocket gopher. He was about to publish a monograph about pocket gopher bioenergetics and population dynamics, and he knew the species well. Since there would be so much to do, he brought a couple of his graduate students, along with a promising young undergraduate named Charlie Crisafulli.

On a late afternoon in early August more than thirty-five years later, Charlie Crisafulli is in a pickup, rattling down an old logging road in the Bean Creek drainage. Now a senior research ecologist with the US Forest Service, Crisafulli leans forward to squint through the dusty windshield. His gaze ping-pongs between the ruts and rocks in the road ahead and the adjacent hillside as it blurs by. He is searching for gopher mounds, but not just any gopher mounds. He has passed many and so far rejected each according to his own mysterious criteria. "Too old . . . Inactive . . . Nobody home . . . Last year's." He grins. "This is what we call roadside ecology," he says.

After an interval, Crisafulli sees a mound he likes. "There's a live one!" he says, braking sharply. He is out the door almost before the pickup has finished its recoil. From the bed he grabs a long metal pole and an odd contraption made out of a short piece of PVC pipe a couple of inches in diameter, with a complicated arrangement of wires and duct tape and other doodads affixed to it. (Is that a rat trap on top?) He sets this object down and considers the mound, pulls up the sleeves of his off-white T-shirt, tucks his long, graying hair behind an ear. "Let's see how deep this goes," he says, and starts to probe the mound with the metal pole.

Pocket gophers are solitary animals. A single one can dig a tunnel network that might cover an area of two thousand square feet, with multiple chambers ranging anywhere from six inches to six feet underground. "A digging gopher decreases the bulk density of the soil," Crisafulli says as he roots around. He has laid the pole aside and is on his knees now, plunging into the mound with his hands, first up to his forearm, then his elbow. "They have to clear out all that soil somehow, so they dig little spurs from the main tunnel and get rid of excess dirt that way. Which is how you get mounds." If a mound is brown, like this one, that means the gopher has been active within the past day or so. What Crisafulli is doing is called "digging down to the T," which is the spot where this spur meets the main tunnel. The T is where he will place his trap.

I stand back while Crisafulli throws himself into his work with what is clearly characteristic abandon. Once he has dug to the T, he stands up and brushes as much dirt as he can off his tall, lean frame. "Hand me that, will you?" he says, pointing to the PVC thing, which I understand to be the gopher trap. It is old—years old, decades maybe, an artifact from a bygone age of field biology. I learn that this particular model was designed in 1972 by two biologists from Texas Tech University. The entire apparatus is stuffed in a tunnel and buried. If all goes as intended, the gopher crawls into it and springs it, which immobilizes the gopher and keeps it unharmed.

Today Crisafulli is trying to catch a gopher so he can show it to some high school students from the Mount St. Helens Institute, a nonprofit organization that offers classes and guided walks around the blast area. The group will visit tomorrow, and while their impending arrival and the need for a live visual aid adds a certain urgency to the proceedings, it is not like the old days, Crisafulli says. "When you came out by helicopter and it was costing you six hundred bucks an hour, you'd better catch the fucking gopher."

Now he puts the trap in the end of the tunnel and wriggles it into position, testing a wire, making small adjustments all the while. His fine-tunings are born of frustrated experience. "The life of a professional gopher trapper isn't always easy," he says. "There's as much art to this as anything else." He has lost count of the number of times he set a trap and came back the next morning to find it sprung, but full of dirt instead of gopher. The gopher, detecting some anomaly, would back-fill the tunnel, packing the trap and rendering it useless while escaping scot-free. "That's the ultimate insult from the gopher to you," Crisafulli says. "It means the gopher was smarter than you."

Once he is satisfied with the trap's placement, he covers it with dirt, and then more dirt, and then, just to be sure, he plucks a leaf from a nearby huckleberry bush, gently tears it almost in half, and sets it over the trap's tripping mechanism. "There's nothing a gopher hates more than light, so you have to block every last little bit of it," he says. With that, he stands to assess his handiwork. "You're seeing a real blast from the past," he says, chuckling, when we get back in his truck to drive off to find another mound. "When I first came to Mount St. Helens, this was my whole life, trapping gophers all summer long."

———

Crisafulli did not know it at the time, but his arrival at Mount St. Helens in 1980 was the last stop of a personal journey westward. He had grown up in New York, near Albany, where he was raised on a big spread with six brothers and sisters. (His accent still comes through every so often, along with brief but fiery flashes of what he calls "my New York patience.") He spent as much time as he could in the outdoors as a kid. He loved to work outside, play outside, just be outside, especially in the Adirondacks. He stayed in New York for college, but after a couple of years decided he wanted to see some other part of the world. He looked west and chose Utah State University in Logan. The city was surrounded by mountains, and Crisafulli thought the skiing would be good. (It was.)

As an undergraduate Crisafulli had been interested in studying ecology, and especially the ways ecosystems responded to disturbance. At Utah State, he took several classes from MacMahon and worked on a few projects for him. When MacMahon asked, a few weeks after the eruption, if he wanted to go to Mount St. Helens, Crisafulli said yes without having to think about it too hard. Here was an opportunity to see the concepts he had studied and read about enacted outside, and on a tremendous scale.

This meeting between theory and practice came as a shock. When Crisafulli flew over the blast area for the first time, he beheld flattened forest, streams a running soup of ash and pumice, and Mount St. Helens, the cause of all the devastation, simmering and silent, if not yet still. The volcano showed Crisafulli the depth of his naïveté. He realized he knew nothing about disturbance, about what he had gotten himself into. "I saw the steaming, gaping crater and realized something incredibly profound had happened here," he says. "It was beyond all senses to comprehend the scale and the extent of change. It was exciting, but also chilling. I knew right away this was a mecca."

At the first Pulse in September, Crisafulli set out to survey the blast area for pocket gophers as part of MacMahon's crew. MacMahon had suspected gophers would have had a better chance of surviving the eruption than other small mammals because their tunnels would shield them from the heat, gases, and debris. On the morning of May 18, a digging pocket gopher might have sensed the shaking and felt some heavy thuds over its head, but to everything else it would probably have been oblivious. After the event, pocket gophers would also have been able to endure in ways that other small mammals could not. They feed on the buried bits of plants: the roots, the bulbs, the reaching tendrils called rhizomes. Even if ash and rock had covered the ground, the gophers would still have access to food, at least for a while.

MacMahon chose twelve study sites, most in the northeastern portion of the blast area, three to twelve miles from the crater. Surveys during the Pulse were quick affairs, and often unpleasant; if looking for a fresh gopher mound from a bouncing truck is hard and occasionally stomach churning, imagine trying to find one from a helicopter as it lurches and zooms along, a hundred feet above the ground. The good thing was that the mounds were relatively easy to spot, standing out like little brown truffles on the gray plains.

Although the northern pocket gopher is one of the most widespread of the North American gophers, ranging from northern Alberta and Saskatchewan south to central New Mexico, and from Washington to the eastern edge of South Dakota, it was not common at Mount St. Helens before 1980. Even so, MacMahon and his crews found evidence of posteruption gopher activity at three-quarters of their sites. Even areas otherwise devoid of life on the surface had gopher mounds lumping out of the ground. Their survival seemed to turn on the question of tephra depth: if the layer of ash and debris atop the ground was less than about a foot, a gopher had a decent chance of living to see the morning of May 19.

Beginning at the 1980 Pulse and for many years after, Crisafulli and MacMahon watched as surviving pocket gophers helped usher a little green into the blast area, their brown mounds and the areas around them sprouting new vegetation. All the things people hate about gophers in their backyards—the speed at which they can dig, their facility at turning over huge amounts of soil—were a boon for plants trying to grow on the unforgiving habitats around the volcano. With their ceaseless digging and movement through the soil, pocket gophers mixed up the fertile dirt that had been buried with the infertile ash above. The resulting mix was rich in carbon and nitrogen, and aerated, so much so that it had the consistency of commercial potting soil.

More importantly, since pocket gophers brought the old soil closer to the surface, new plants could form or reform associations with the mycorrhizal fungi that had been living in the soils beforehand. This symbiotic relationship enhances plants' ability to absorb nutrients and water through their roots. One ounce of old, gopher-processed soil held as many as two thousand fungal spores; in nearby soils, the count might be thirty. By mixing those spores into the ash, gophers turned it into a growth medium, rather than simply dead weight. Seeds that blew in and were fortunate enough to land on gopher mounds took root, and the mounds supported a much greater diversity of plants than open patches of ash immediately adjacent—patches that, but for the activity of the gophers, were otherwise identical. A range of plants took advantage of the gophers' labors: fireweed, huckleberry, lupine, sedges, brambles. Not only were there more species in the mounds, but they were also larger than specimens elsewhere and produced more seeds.

MacMahon loved the thought of this beady-eyed mammal tunneling through the soil, matched against the mountain and its titanic forces. In places where nothing apparently lived, pocket gophers moved about unseen, and where they moved, plants grew. As the years went by,

MacMahon would come to call the pocket gopher his "favorite beast," and said it was "the animal we should all get tattooed on our foreheads." But he tried not to get too carried away. "I do not mean to imply that gophers will be the main factor in the generation of the whole volcanically altered landscape," he wrote in 1982, after rhapsodizing at length on the pocket gopher's many ecological virtues. "Only that like all organisms, they have an influence, no matter how small."

———

Crisafulli ends up setting eight traps. When he checks them the next morning, three are unmolested, three are back-filled ("Damn!"), and two hold northern pocket gophers. He lets one gopher go and puts the other in a fish tank with some dirt and lupine leaves and lettuce to keep it occupied and reasonably content. "You want to see the fur fly, you put two male or two female pocket gophers in a small, contained space," he says. "I'm telling you, nature red in tooth and claw!"

The students arrive around 10 a.m. in a big white van. Most seem to be in their early teens, an age Crisafulli calls "fun but dangerous." He leads them to the patch where he captured the pocket gopher, waits for everyone to gather, and then brings out the fish tank. "Who's ready for a show?" he asks. Wearing leather gardening gloves "so he won't chew my fingers off," he reaches in and plucks out the gopher, which has been nibbling on the lupine leaves. This one is small, a juvenile. His thick fur, or pelage, is a mix of brown and gray. His front paws are pink, short, and muscular. Their sharp, protruding claws give him the ability to move through the dirt with the ease of a swimmer moving through water. His hind legs are flat; their main purpose is to shift out of the way the dirt that the front paws have loosened. His brow is flattened, suggesting stubbornness, and his oversize incisors protrude past his lips, which can close behind them when he is digging. His nose is in constant motion as he *sniff-sniff-sniffs* the unfamiliar air. His black eyes are so small as to seem incidental. Crisafulli uses a pencil to show off the bulging cheek pouches that give the pocket gopher its name. In these the gopher stashes seeds and other foods that he finds while excavating his tunnels.

The kids ooh and aah. A few get their phones out. While they snap pictures, Crisafulli recites the attributes of the northern pocket gophers of the Blowdown Zone: how they are the blast area's classic survivor; how they can turn 25 to 30 percent of the ground in a single territory; how they were once uncommon here, but are now abundant and increasing in number, and have become more broadly distributed than ever before; how the volcano, by turning the forest into what pocket gophers saw as a giant meadow, made this place "gopher heaven."

I sit on the roadside and listen. This part of the Bean Creek drainage, outside the monument boundaries, is one of the areas the Forest Service replanted with conifers—mainly noble fir—after the eruption. The skinny trees grow in thick, regimented rows, bringing to mind a tree farm, but a lot of small animals scurry about nonetheless. A golden-mantled ground squirrel runs under Crisafulli's truck, stops, runs out again. A short distance away, a chipmunk chitters from the safety of a log, vanishing in a blink when a kid turns to look at it. Were Crisafulli to catch one of these other small mammals, the kids would no doubt find them just as fascinating, but because they do not have the same role in shaping the landscape as the pocket gopher, their stories are somehow less essential.

Crisafulli brings his talk to a close; the pocket gopher has given enough of his time for the kids' benefit. "Back you go, buddy," he says, and sets him on the ground.

"Aren't you going to put him back near his tunnel?" one of the kids asks.

"No need," Crisafulli says. "Watch."

The students watch. The pocket gopher twitches, perhaps summoning the gumption to make a dash for freedom across the open ground, but then Crisafulli gently places his gloved hand over him. "Just got to point him back to his home," he says. "Remind him where he comes from." At this, the pocket gopher noses the dirt instead, turns back to peer at Crisafulli, chews on a nearby leaf. He sniffs around some more, nibbles the vegetation. Apparently he is no longer fazed by the fact that we are all staring at him. "Look how he's eating the root nodules," Crisafulli says. "Those are full of nitrogen. Nice and nutritious."

Some of the air of anticipation starts to leak from the kids. Where they were rapt, now they twitch and fidget. They seem to have realized that while the northern pocket gopher is one of the mountain's ecological celebrities, it is still just a small rodent, and they are growing a little bored staring at him as he goes about his small rodent business, snuffling around in a nearsighted way. But after a couple of minutes the pocket gopher hunkers down on a spot and starts to dig. His movements are rapid, practiced, focused. He digs and digs and digs. This is what he was born to do and he is good at it. Working with his massive foreclaws, he seems to sink into the earth.

Crisafulli plucks up a small digital camera and snaps a few photos. "Nice," he murmurs. How many pictures of northern pocket gophers must he have taken over the past three decades? Hundreds, at least. Yet here he is, clicking away as if it were the first time he has ever seen one. But he has to hurry, for the gopher is rapidly disappearing. In seconds his head is out of view. Within a minute he has vanished almost entirely, his presence revealed only by the pulsing dirt left in his wake. He returns to the surface every so often to push out piles of dirt like a little bulldozer. Then he stops coming to the surface at all. The only evidence of his activity is the fresh brown mound of dirt and the group of students who are again staring at the ground, rapt.

"Whoa," one kid murmurs. "That was so fast."

"I told you," Crisafulli says, grinning. "Watch."

———

At the end of the day, after all the kids have left, Crisafulli drives back to his summer base of operations. It is also outside the monument boundary, a couple of miles from Bean Creek, along a narrow old logging track called National Forest Road 2560, which branches off from Forest Road 99. After a while 2560 widens some, and on the left are a pair of big white canvas wall tents. In front of the tents are piles of gear: dip nets, crates, boots, buckets, a pickax or two. Smaller tents belonging to Crisafulli's crew peep out from among the trees. The spot is known informally as Ecology Camp, or more informally still as Charlie's Camp after Crisafulli established it in 2005.

Crisafulli brings his pickup to a stop and lopes over to the biggest wall tent to start preparing dinner. "You're in for a treat," one of his crew tells me as everyone settles in to chop vegetables. Tonight's menu is spaghetti, chicken parmesan, a big green salad, and a couple of bottles of red wine, with chips and homemade salsa to tide us over while Crisafulli cooks. The chicken is one from Crisafulli's own flock, and all the vegetables for the salsa and the salad are from the garden at his three-acre property outside Yacolt, about an hour north of Portland. The wine is of his own vintage, made from grapes grown in eastern Washington. Crisafulli eats very little that he has not grown, caught, or shot himself. In a good year, he might harvest more than three hundred pounds of potatoes and can dozens of gallons of tomatoes. "Buying food, it just doesn't taste the same," he says.

Charlie's Camp has been Crisafulli's home away from home for more than a decade, although he also uses other camps as circumstances and studies require. He has been at Mount St. Helens continuously since 1989 and estimates he has spent some three thousand nights on or around the mountain—far more than anyone else, perhaps more than all other scientists combined. It is a precise calculation, continuously updated. "This is my thirty-seventh year, and if I spend about eighty nights a year here, well, you do the math," he says. It is hard to think of a single project here that Crisafulli is not somehow involved with, has not contributed to in some way, or at least has not had strong opinions about. "Mount St. Helens exposes your weaknesses," he says, and his weakness is Mount St. Helens. For his crew, the thought of Crisafulli retiring, even as he nears retirement age, has become a running joke. How could he tear himself away from this place? There is too much still to learn, too much happening, too many old questions that still need answering, too many new questions that the answers to the old ones will provoke.

Over dinner I get a small hint of this continuous unfolding when Crisafulli shares a heretical little secret: the northern pocket gopher may have become the blast area's classic survivor tale, but the way most people think of the pocket gopher is outdated. "In the beginning, for probably the first decade or so, pocket gophers were good for plant succession," he says. "That's pretty well documented. But what do pocket gophers like most in a landscape?"

"I don't know," I say.

"Meadows," Crisafulli says. "They like big open areas. They don't like forests. There aren't enough calories for them in a forest. So what do you do if you're a pocket gopher?" He waits for an answer I cannot provide before providing it himself. "You do whatever you can to keep the trees from coming in." Pocket gophers have actually been suppressing plant growth in recent years. He guesses there might be hundreds or even thousands of miles of tunnels in the blast area, and this tunneling is itself a kind of chronic disturbance, keeping some types of plants from becoming established. By repeatedly turning over the earth, the gophers are slowing succession to suit their own ends.

"So the gopher goes from being a survivor-hero of the Blowdown Zone to kind of a villain," I say.

"Well, I wouldn't go that far," Crisafulli says. "It's just an animal doing what an animal does. Which is certainly reasonable. But the point is, these things are always a lot more complicated than they're made out to be."

———

A couple of hours later, after the dishes have been washed and stacked to dry and Crisafulli and his crew have excused themselves and gone to their tents, I get up to go as well. The days start early here: Crisafulli sometimes rises at five in the morning to take photos of the mountain or other curiosities in the favorable light, and then everyone else heads to the Pumice Plain to check the scads of small-mammal traps they set out the evening before.

I should sleep, too, but I am not yet ready to turn in. I decide to go for a walk to see Mount St. Helens. It is hard to get more than a glimpse of the mountain from Charlie's Camp, even though it sits only a few miles to the southwest. All the firs the Forest Service planted here decades ago have now grown so tall and thick in their orderly rows that they obscure it. (Crisafulli has set up his tent in a spot that enjoys an unobstructed view of Mount Hood.) To get a clear view of the Lady, as Crisafulli sometimes calls the mountain, I have to hike about a mile or so back up the road to a big, open lot. The night is quiet except for the stirring wind and gravelly crunch of my steps. Stars and a bright moon glitter among broken clouds, and the air is deliciously cold.

Franklin, MacMahon, Swanson, others—Crisafulli has outlasted them all. When they decided to let go of various lines of inquiry, he kept pursuing them, adding his own all the while. (Swanson once told me, "Without Charlie, maybe 10 percent of everything that's been done here gets done.") He is invested in the mountain, in what is said about the mountain, in how the mountain is thought about. This investment leaves him leery of most popular accounts of it. For him they are incomplete; or, worse, they become an excuse for people to stop looking.

"Promise me you're going to talk about more than just pocket gophers," he had said earlier in the evening. "Pocket gophers and prairie lupine. Sometimes I feel like that's all anyone wants to talk about."

"I promise," I said.

"You've got to think about more than the pocket gopher," he said.

"I will."

"You think the story has ended, but it hasn't," he said.

No, I suppose it has not, and never will, at least until the next eruption. I reach the lot and clamber ten or twenty yards up a gravel mound at its edge. On the other side, the slope drops all the way down to Bean Creek, the rushing of which I can barely hear, but from the top, Mount

St. Helens rises above the folds of its foothills. Its crater opens to the north, angled slightly away from where I stand. During the day you might see dust and ash waft from the serrated rim. Within the crater are the layered remnants of past eruptions, rough etchings in gray and brown. These form an amphitheater around the new dome, which has been growing since 1980.

I zip my jacket up to my throat and jam my hands in my pockets and take in the tableau. Seen during the day, the maw of the mountain is certainly remarkable, but Mount St. Helens actually looks more impressive now, as a silhouette. With the stars overarching it and the lights of Portland illuminating it from behind, it loses the spectacle of its dimensions, the chaos of its guts. Blacker than the sky, it is simply a rumpled form in the dark. It leans heavily from left to right as if sloughing into the west, and the void of its settled mass blends in with the hills over which it normally towers, as it becomes one with the landscape and the life—the lives—it has so dramatically reshaped.

5

TO RECOVER OR NOT TO RECOVER

IN 1981, in the midst of all the other work they were doing in the
Blowdown Zone, Charlie Crisafulli and Jim MacMahon set out for
the Pumice Plain to place a few transects. This was a kind of side project: they wanted to begin surveys for birds and small mammals. They
hardly expected to find any. The main lessons from the Blowdown Zone
might be about how plants and animals living in the zone survived and
reshaped their communities, but on the Pumice Plain there would be
no uplifting tales of sprouting plants or rodents poking their noses out
from under piles of debris weeks after the eruption. These plains were
new land, sterile land, land made up of compacted pumice 120 feet deep
on average. Everything that had lived here before the eruption—every
tree, flower, bug, mouse, or elk—had been vaporized, buried, cooked, or
otherwise killed.

Crisafulli and MacMachon's search for transect sites had them riding
in a helicopter as it hugged the ground, low and slow. Such flights over
more than three thousand acres of blinding white terrain were not,
as Crisafulli says, "good for the stomach," but in due course he and
MacMahon had laid several lines across a wide swath of the Pumice
Plain. The results from their first surveys were what they expected—
zeroes—but they continued the work the next year, and one day in June,
when they were walking to one of their transects, they spotted a small
patch of purple on the ground ahead.

"What's that?" MacMahon said. He and Crisafulli crunched over the pumice toward it. They found a single adult prairie lupine, about five inches tall. Its flowers were a delicate purple atop an erect stalk, poised over a burst of small, palmate leaves, themselves such a light blue-green it suggested teal. A ring of seedlings surrounded it, like disciples attending a sage in the wilderness.

Crisafulli and MacMahon could hardly believe what they were seeing. The little group of flowers was small, about twelve inches in diameter, surrounded by dacite, a type of igneous rock, and pumice. Making its presence even more astonishing, the lupine had to have been growing for at least a year to have produced seedlings. How had it made its way all the way out here, a lifeless area four miles from the crater? Had a bird eaten the seed and pooped it out while flying overhead? Transport aside, how had the seed managed to take root when there was no soil?

Without knowing the answers, Crisafulli and MacMahon did what came naturally: they documented their finding. The following spring, in 1983, they came back to the lupine and measured out a rectangle 168 square meters in area, with the plant at the center. They hammered a few stakes around the perimeter and then strung twine around the stakes to cordon off the founding plant so no one would step on it. It was the first vegetation plot on the Pumice Plain.

———

The art of explaining a volcano can rest as much on the language as the science, but the first time ecologists had seen Mount St. Helens after the eruption, they had been speechless. It was as if life itself had gone quiet, shouted down by geology. But life is always speaking, however softly, and even while the mountain was in the throes of its various upheavals, organisms were already finding their way back to it.

The lupines Crisafulli and MacMahon found were not the first organisms to reach the Pumice Plain. At any one moment, biologists tell us, at least half of all the insects and spiders in the world are aloft in some fashion. Rescue crews at Mount St. Helens reported seeing flies and yellowjackets in the blast area within a day of the eruption. By the summer of 1981, while Crisafulli and MacMahon were laying out their bird and mammal transects, a team of ecologists from the University of Washington was monitoring spiders as they parachuted down to the Pumice Plain. They later calculated that for every one hundred square meters of ground, eighty-four spiders touched down per day.

Those spiders were part of a phenomenon known as the arthropod rain. (The phylum Arthropoda includes both spiders and insects.) The first to land met a quick end: the pumice was so hot that their bodies were likely incinerated on contact. As the ground cooled, the fine particles blown about by the winds acted as a powdery insecticide. Ash abraded the waxy coatings of their cuticles, or exoskeletons, and they desiccated rapidly. Lab tests showed that most arthropods exposed to Mount St. Helens ash died of dehydration within twenty-four hours.

Even after the ash had settled, conditions remained fatally harsh. There was no food, no water, no shelter from the summer sun. Still the arthropods came, drifting in, alighting, and dying by the thousands. With them came plant seeds, small pieces of lichen, and other organic matter. During the summer, five to fifteen milligrams of this material fell from the sky on every square meter of exposed ground every twenty-four hours. Fifteen milligrams is 5/10,000 of an ounce. Admittedly this does not sound like much, but algebra helps give a proper sense of scale. The Pumice Plain is about six square miles in area, or fifteen square kilometers, or fifteen million square meters. Fifteen milligrams per square meter thus becomes 225 kilograms (496 pounds) of organic material blowing in per day. Over a period of one hundred summer days, that becomes 22,500 kilograms (49,600 pounds) of organic matter and nutrients settling on the Pumice Plain before the first snows arrive. That is more than 23 US tons.

Eventually all that natural fertilizer began to have an effect. Even if the arthropods were not alive and eating, their bodies could be scavenged, and the first insect to reproduce on the Pumice Plain was a scavenger: a carabid beetle called *Bembidion improvidens,* of which a single larva was found in 1982. More beetles followed. By 1983, several carabid species had breeding populations. Meanwhile, the number of plants known to be growing on the Pumice Plain stood somewhere between zero and Crisafulli's cluster of prairie lupines.

Before Mount St. Helens erupted, terrestrial ecologists were not trained to think of a biotic community starting from anything other than plants. Now here was one assembled of beetles that were able to persist without vegetation. "An absence of plants," two ecologists would later write, "does not necessarily mean an absence of resident animal populations." But that did not mean plants were not also on their way.

———

For the rest of the summer of 1983, Crisafulli watched the lupines grow. From the thousands of plant seeds that fell to the Pumice Plain, the prairie lupine had to be among the last species anyone expected to take root first. Lupines do not have the profile of an early colonizer. Their seeds are smooth and heavy and about the size of a lentil, not fluffy and light and easily wind-carried like the fireweed's. Unlike grass seeds, they lack barbs to catch on the pelt of a passing elk. They are contained within hairy pods that dry out over the summer and then pop open, ejecting the seeds only about a yard or so. Also, although the species was known to occur at Mount St. Helens before the eruption, it had been found in subalpine meadows, not in the desertlike conditions of the Pumice Plain.

Still, the presence of the prairie lupine made an odd kind of sense. Lupines thrive in nutrient-poor habitats. Their roots have little nodules that house bacteria, and these can draw or "fix" nitrogen from the air, turning it into ammonia. With these "little factories," as Crisafulli calls the root nodules, lupines can make their own food. In return, lupines provide the bacteria with simple sugars; being a good host is the key to any successful mutualism. A lupine's small leaflets move to track the sun's progress across the sky to capture solar energy. When the air is too dry, the leaves fold up to conserve moisture. Their taproots can dig deep through rough ground to reach water and have a skin like toughened bark. Those heavy seeds, poor voyagers though they may be, are durable and capable of lying dormant for years before they sprout.

By the end of 1983, the lupine patch had expanded to two feet in diameter. When Crisafulli arrived at Mount St. Helens in the spring of 1984, the original lupine and its seedlings had enriched the area around them with enough nutrients to support a few other species: fireweed, pearly everlasting, and some of the other usual suspects. Crisafulli kept track of them all. He built a squat platform out of plywood so he could hover over the plot without harming its inhabitants. A year later, he counted more than twenty-four thousand plants, including yarrow, rough bentgrass, beardtongue, sedges, and forbs. In 1989, the plot had more than 164,000 plants. They had burst through their borders and were flowing across the Pumice Plain in waves of subtle color.

———

There can be an eagerness to look at Mount St. Helens and the colors spreading across its contemporary landscape and speak of resilience, or the capacity of a place to recover from a great disturbance. Plants and animals thought destroyed were not. Others came back more quickly than anyone had anticipated. A biotic community has steadily reassembled. Does this mean that Mount St. Helens has "recovered"?

Everywhere they looked, Crisafulli and other scientists were seeing the strain the events at Mount St. Helens put on the concept of recovery: how they were helping to revise ideas about what it looks like, or whether it is even an appropriate term to use. In addition to the lupines and spiders and beetles, for example, there were also amphibians, fifteen species of which had been found at Mount St. Helens before the eruption.

Given amphibians' known sensitivity to even the smallest environmental shifts—species all over the world are disappearing as a result

of habitat loss, climate change, and disease—no frogs, toads, or salamanders were expected to have survived the eruption. This was another
incorrect working hypothesis. Although no amphibians survived in the
debris avalanche or the Pumice Plain, when Crisafulli surveyed a series
of lakes, ponds, and streams in the Blowdown Zone in the summer of
1980, he found eleven species.

One was the western toad, a species endangered throughout much of
its range. Like other survivors, it had benefited from the eruption's tim-
ing. Because toads were hibernating in dens beneath the snow-covered
ground in mid-May, they were not subject to the eruption's most devastating effects. By 1981, toads were breeding at seven of the ten lakes where
Crisafulli had found them before. Every July, their toadlets emerged,
hopping on land by the hundreds of thousands. Each was delicate brown
and the size of a dime. The ground seemed to seethe as they clambered
over each other, their aggregations a tangle of skinny limbs.

Crisafulli kept following the western toad and its kin in the Blowdown Zone, finding more amphibian species when they appeared,
tracking them as they traveled across the blast area. He found one toad
he had captured and marked at one site at another lake nearly three
miles away. With the elimination of its predators, the western toad was
thriving under the open sun. The several thousand adults thought to
occupy Mount St. Helens constituted the highest population density ever
recorded for the species. But it would not be accurate to say the western
toad has recovered; its success has far exceeded anything that might be
called recovery.

The western toad, the prairie lupine, the pocket gopher—these show
why, more than three decades on, Crisafulli makes it a point never to say
anything has "recovered" at Mount St. Helens. To make that claim would
be to imply, first of all, that the community has returned to a previous
state of being—one considered standard, or static. More erroneously,
recovery is premised on some notion of a terminus, an end. In this, the
term undervalues the dynamism of the ecosystem at Mount St. Helens, both in this moment and in moments to come. "This is an active

volcano," Crisafulli says. "It perpetuates a cycle of renewal." Life is here in wonderful and unexpected ways not in spite of the eruption, he knows, but *because of* the eruption.

———

Over the next two decades, Crisafulli watched as the prairie lupines spread quickly over the Pumice Plain. They started to go through cycles of boom and bust, leaping forward, dying back, expanding again. The cause of those cycles was mysterious—there are many ways for a plant to die—but two hypotheses arose. The first was that insects were killing the lupines. Several species of beetles had arrived on the Pumice Plain and were feasting on those long, woody roots. The other hypothesis was that the lupines were facilitating their own demise. By adding nitrogen to the soil and then dying back, the lupines left more welcoming spaces for plants that could not make their own nitrogen but were in other respects better at competing for space and nutrients.

Crisafulli observed all of this. The lupines were little earth movers, little earth builders, physically trapping and gathering sand and ash blown about by the wind. Minute mounds formed where they grew, and these helped the ground retain water. They became islands of fertility in the sterile plain. When the plants died, other species, like hairy cat's ear, were able to take advantage of the lupines' modest organic and hydrological legacies. Spiders crept among the little leaves, while bees went from blossom to blossom. The progression showed the importance of biotic interactions: from pumice and ash to prairie lupine, to fireweed and pearly everlasting, to yarrow and bentgrass and sedges and hairy cat's ear, to insects, to birds like the horned lark, to small mammals like the long-tailed vole. Organisms depend on each other. Nothing can live alone for long.

Sometimes when he could steal a moment from his other Pumice Plain projects, Crisafulli ducked away to visit the original lupine plot and see what was new. He liked to walk among generations of that founding lupine's offspring, and all the other plants and creatures they had helped to usher in. Doing so gave him a sense of interconnectedness and satisfaction, something verging on contentment. *Where else but at Mount St. Helens?* he thought.

Later the Forest Service had a sign made to commemorate the plot. The sign is still there, off to the side of the Truman Trail where it crosses the Pumice Plain. Some of the original metal stakes still stand, ancient and rusted, but several PVC stakes have toppled over where water has washed them out. They lie on their sides like fallen trees, aligned away from the mountain.

The sign itself—more of a placard, really—is bleached and weathered. A plastic cover meant to protect the message is so sun-blasted that it is cracked like safety glass. The sign depicts a young man crouching and gazing intently at something on the ground. This figure wears a baseball cap backward. Maybe he is meant to be Crisafulli, although he does not look tall enough. Around him are blocks of text, like the verses of a poem, although time, the elements, and all the cracks have conspired to erase most of the words, leaving only this cryptic message to those of us just passing by.

> A single prairie lupine found
> on the Pumice Plain enticed
> scientists to establish a
> research site.
> This species thrives at this
> elevation of 3,500 feet because
> conditions here mimic the
> environment
> above --- 500 feet.
>
> An armored seed
> A torrential rain
> A crack in rock
>
> ---- --- --- -- -- --- ----

A purple flower -- --- ---- gray
A scientist discovers the scene
A plant --- --- ---

---- --- ---- -- --- --

--- -- --- -- --- -- ----

--- --- -- ---- anniversary

1982 ----

---- --- --- ---- ---

--- --- ---- mossy ----

--- -- ---- --- -- ---- --

--------- --- ---- -

--- --- ---- ------

how ---- --- ---- ---

---- ---- --- ---- --- ----

--- and ---- ---- ----- -

--- ---- ---- ---

This --- ---- --- ----

how lupines --- ----- ----

to the returning forest

Above the text is what may be a title, an appeal, or a directive, one that
strikes me as odd given the context of this scene.

DO NOT DISTURB
PLEASE

6

LINES OF SUCCESSION

To GET FROM the parking lot at Windy Ridge out to the Plains of Abraham, you can go one of two ways. The first is to take the Truman Trail (#207) two miles to where it meets the Abraham Trail (#216D), and then follow that for a couple of miles as it ascends a ridge above the Smith Creek drainage. This route is short but steep. The second is to continue along the Truman Trail down to the Windy Trail (#216E), climb to the Loowit Trail (#216), and then head up to Windy Pass before dropping to the plains. This route is longer and also steep. The question of which to take turns on your viewing preferences. Do you wish, as you huff and puff, to look out over the roadless forests of the Dark Divide toward Mount Adams and a more conventional wilderness landscape? Or do you want to walk in and among Mount St. Helens's curious features for as long as you can?

Cynthia Chang has opted for the former. A plant ecologist from the University of Washington at Bothell, she steps lightly up the unsteady log ladder on the Abraham Trail, even with a backpack full of gear. "What a view!" she says. With her is her student, Laurel Baum. She is taller than Chang, and her pace is steadier—more of a plod. The reason for that becomes clear when we reach the plains and Baum sets down her backpack. It settles on the ground with a solid *clunk*. Chang is immediately suspicious. "Laurel," she asks, "what's in there?"

"Nothing," Baum says. Then she allows: "I brought along some of the extra rebar."

"How much?"

A beat. "All of it."

Chang is aghast. "*All of it?*" she says.

Baum shrugs.

"Like, all thirty pounds of it?"

Baum shrugs again. "I didn't want you to have to carry it," she says. With an almost apologetic air she begins to pull bundle after bundle of eighteen-inch-long rebar stakes from her backpack.

"Laurel, that's way too much for you," Chang says as the rebar piles up. "Please don't do that again." Then she grins. "Still, as long as we've got it all . . ."

Chang has come to the Plains of Abraham today in search of a set of old research plots. She has their GPS coordinates, and she hopes that if she can find the plot boundaries, she can replace the old metal stakes marking them with the new rebar stakes. Doing so will ensure the plots are findable, she says, "for the next hundred years." But the coordinates are more approximate than she anticipated, and the old stakes not quite as durable. After a few hours of sometimes aimless wandering, we have uncovered only a few. Chang is undaunted. "We'll be back tomorrow," she says to Baum, who is stashing the rest of the rebar next to a boulder. "We can come faster because we won't be carrying so much."

We decide to hike back to Windy Ridge by way of Windy Pass. It has been hot all day, but now it must be at least 100°F. The sky is wide, the high July sun a white ball of fire. The pumice reflects the sunlight up from the ground, so we are seared both from above and from below. Mount St. Helens, almost completely snowless at this time of year, shows itself for what it is: a great mound of rock and dust and ash that casts no shade. Its shape wavers and pulses; this might be due to the heat or something more worrisomely physiological.

I look back. Even after three decades there is only a light smattering of green. Few places around Mount St. Helens are as stark as the Plains of Abraham, but Chang says barrenness is innate to them, rather than due to the eruption. Their name similarly flouts assumption. Although it evokes a biblical austerity—this seems a good place to plead with the God of the Old Testament, to offer sacrifice—the plains are actually named after a series of lush green fields in Quebec City, Canada, which themselves are named after a Scottish farmer, Abraham Martin, who ran livestock on them in the seventeenth century. Someone whose own name has since been lost came here and saw these flats and thought of a city park in Quebec and its Scottish farmer, and the rest of us are left to square that vision with our own.

At last we reach the pass. Behind us lie the plains; before us extends the much larger Pumice Plain. Spirit Lake fronts it like a doormat, with the shorter, bare peaks of the Mount Margaret Backcountry beyond. The wind rushes up and over us, unobstructed. I sit for a moment to catch my breath. Near my feet, a spray of prairie lupines shivers in the wind. I look up and see that they are shivering along with hundreds of their kin—no, thousands of them, cluster upon cluster of prairie lupines carpeting the hillside.

"Look at all the lupines," I say.

"I know," Chang says. "Pretty, aren't they?"

"Yes." Pretty, and also abrupt. This mass of lupines has marched all the way up to Windy Pass, but not over it. The line where they stop is so neatly demarcated that it does not seem biological but rather a border enforced by some other means. "Why haven't they made it to the Plains of Abraham?" I ask.

"I'm not sure," Chang says. "But you can see how well they're doing here." Yes, they are. The individual plants have merged into a purple tint that extends far down the slope, mixing with other colors (red, yellow, white), rippling in the wind.

———

The plots Chang and Baum are looking for were established in 1989 by a professor from the University of Washington named Roger del Moral. Like most people drawn to the volcano and its post-1980 ecologies, del Moral had started his career looking at other things, but when Mount St. Helens began to stir in 1980, one of del Moral's colleagues sent a note around the department: "If it does erupt, what are we going to do?"

Del Moral spent much of April making plans as best as he could. The time was marked with strange omens. In the middle of May, he had been scheduled to give a workshop on national forest management in Kentucky. He was reluctant to leave, but he had committed to going, and the earthquakes jolting the mountain had quieted. Before he went, Jerry Franklin called him from Corvallis. At the end of their conversation he asked del Moral when he thought Mount St. Helens might blow. "May 17," del Moral said. "You can write it down."

Del Moral left for Kentucky, where he stayed with some old friends. Hanging on their wall was a Sierra Club calendar filled with iconic American wilderness scenes. The photo for May was of Mount St. Helens. There was the mountain in all of its saturated-color glory: the perfect peak, the dark forests, the lake—the Mount Fuji of North America. As del Moral gazed at it, Carol Baskin, one of his hosts, came up to him. "Was Mount St. Helens going to erupt?" she asked. Del Moral thought of the immense bulge on the northern flank, now expanding by several feet per day. Government geologists were on TV hemming and hawing about chances and likelihoods, but del Moral felt no such compunction. He was far from home. Why bother to equivocate? "Sure, Carol, real soon," he said. "And it's going to be big."

A couple of days later, on a Sunday morning, del Moral boarded his flight home to Seattle. Somewhere over Montana, the pilot announced that Mount St. Helens was erupting, and they would have to make a detour. The plane swung south and then turned to the Pacific Ocean to approach Seattle from the west. Del Moral craned to see out one of the windows. Massive clouds of ash were pouring out of the mountain, swallowing everything to the east. *Oh, my God*, del Moral thought. The next day, when he went into his office, his answering machine flashed with a message. It was from Jerry Baskin, Carol's husband. "Sir," he said, "you are a prophet in the state of Kentucky."

Del Moral was first able to visit the blast area that July, joining Franklin and a few others on a helicopter tour of possible field sites spread around the blast area. The temperature that day was supposed to reach the mid-nineties, and waiting to board the helicopter, del Moral balked at having to wear the hot, poorly ventilated flame-retardant jumpsuit. If the helicopter crashed in the blast area, he asked one of the crew, would the suit really save him? "No," the man replied, "but it might make it easier for search and rescue to find your body."

With that in mind, off they went. Everywhere the helicopter landed, del Moral jumped out, took a few pictures, and gathered a bucketful of whatever substances lay on the ground, to be tested back in his lab as growth media for seeds. The day was fun, fascinating, and miserable. Sometimes when he hunched against the wind, his face white from the ash and dust, his throat parched, his hair and mustache stiff as straw, he thought back to his hosts' calendar and the colorful picture of Mount St. Helens. Now, two months later, the volcano had a much simpler palette: black and gray. He wondered why he had bothered to bring color film.

When it was time to select a place to work, del Moral decided he was not all that interested in the Pumice Plain. It was, to his taste, a bit *too* sterile, and would likely stay that way for years. The pumiceous deposits were inhospitable to plants. The ground was unstable. Wind would blow the ash around, the pumice would shift and grind, and mudflows and other floods were bound to sweep through every spring. Even if a seed somehow managed to land, the plant would likely get crushed or washed away before it could grow. Research in such habitats would have to wait a few years.

Del Moral chose to begin his work on the lahars and areas affected by tephra on the southern side of Mount St. Helens. He set up a few plots at a place called Butte Camp, and some more close by at Pine Creek, a little to the east. The aesthetics of his sites struck him as interesting. The mountain towered above them, but the crater was invisible. On these south ridges, outside the blast area proper, Mount St. Helens did not have the overt volcanic aspect for which it was now so famous. It looked instead more like the rest of its cousins in the Cascade Range: peaked and imposing, while also somewhat lumpy and inert, but sitting atop forces people often forgot were prone to agitation.

—————

Like Franklin, who was working in the Blowdown Zone, del Moral was eager to ask basic questions about disturbance and succession: what it was, and just as important, what it was not. But whereas Franklin was mainly concerned with secondary succession—the return of a plant community from its shattered remnants—del Moral was more interested in primary succession: the rise of a community after all the plants and soil have been destroyed.

More than eighty years after Henry Chandler Cowles had jumped off his train at the Indiana dunes, succession was still a vibrant field of ecological study, his work and theories having inspired generations of scientists. One of the first and most prominent was Frederic Clements. Born in Lincoln, Nebraska, in 1874, Clements earned his PhD at the University of Nebraska, where he stayed to become a professor of botany. Unlike Cowles, Clements did not wish to be associated with a single place like the dunes. He traveled widely during his career, spending the winters in Arizona and California, doing research both outdoors and in greenhouses. In the summers, he traveled to a field station up in the mountains of Colorado. His preferred habitats were also more physically stable; the grasslands and forests he studied were less disposed than sand dunes to messy and unpredictable shifts.

Like Cowles and many other biologists in the nineteenth and early twentieth centuries, Clements paid close attention to developments in geology and looked for ways to apply its findings and theories to ecological processes. One idea he found especially intriguing was the organismal metaphor, proposed by a geographer and geologist from Harvard University named William Norris Davis. In 1899, the same year Cowles published his first paper on succession in the dunes, Davis began to outline his ideas of the geological cycle—or, as it would come to be known, the cycle of erosion. Landforms once created, he wrote, went through an orderly progression, being worn down through the eons from uplifted slabs of rock to more rounded, gentle plains. The stages were discrete and recognizable, and could be seen almost anywhere: in arid river systems, in islands bordered by coral reefs, and high in glacier-sculpted mountains. (Curiously, Davis seems to have had little use for volcanoes.) He likened his cycle to the development of a human being. As with a person, so the land could be young, could mature, could advance to old age.

Clements found much to like in Davis's organismal metaphor. Like Cowles, he believed that plant communities could change over time in nonrandom and predictable ways. Through Davis, he became attracted to the idea of regarding plant communities holistically. "The motive force in succession," he wrote, "*i.e.*, in the development of the formation as an organism, is to be found in the responses or functions of the group of individuals, just as the power of growth in the individual lies in the responses or functions of various organs."

Clements believed that climate and habitat, rather than interactions between the species, did the most to dictate what species would survive where. Although he accepted that competition played a role, he thought plants mostly vied against their own kind. Tree species 1 might compete with tree species 2 but less so with shrub species 1, which was busy competing with shrub species 2. Groups of species were thus linked together into units of succession, or *seres*: tree species 1, shrub species 1, and grass species 1 (or sere 1, as Clements defined it) thrived for a time, but eventually gave way to tree species 2, shrub species 2, and grass species 2 (sere 2). This process repeated until the community consisted of the most dominant tree, shrub, and grass: this he called the climax community, which was itself a kind of metaorganism, or superorganism.

Here, Clements departed from Cowles, who had not believed that the equilibrium implied by a climax community was ever truly achieved; the world was too dynamic a place, and conditions were always changing. Clements argued that, left alone, a climax community could last for millions of years. It was an endpoint. So powerful was its pull that it was for all intents and purposes inevitable. If an ecosystem in a climax state was ever disturbed, he wrote, all the species that had characterized the climax state would return in their former abundances. A place that hosted a mature oak forest as a climax community, for example, could only ever host a mature oak forest as a climax community, and never anything else.

In 1916, Clements published *Plant Succession: An Analysis of the Development of Vegetation.* "Succession," he wrote near the beginning, "is preeminently a process the progress of which is expressed in certain initial and intermediate structures or stages, but is finally recorded in the structure of the climax formation." The book gained a large and committed following among plant ecologists, who found in it a useful conceptual template for their own studies. Its influence lasted well into the 1960s, and elements of it still circulate. But some ecologists were less persuaded by Clements's grand organismal view of plant communities. One, the British botanist Arthur Tansley, did not even like calling a community a superorganism. In a 1935 paper that he dedicated to Cowles, Tansley coined the term *ecosystem* and proposed it as a replacement.

Another of Clements's most persistent critics was a plant geographer and systematist named Henry Gleason, who worked at the New York Botanical Garden in the Bronx. First as an undergraduate at the University of Illinois, and then as a doctoral student at Columbia University, Gleason had also read Cowles and been fascinated. When he later read Clements, he was intrigued as well. Eight years Clements's junior, he accepted many of Clements's concepts and employed several of his terms. In the field, he even used one of Clements's books, *Research Methods in Ecology*—the first ecological textbook published in the United States.

What Gleason objected to most strongly in Clements was what he saw as a tendency to idealize the plant community as a construct. Yes, a person could go outside and see plants grouped together in ways that appeared stable and uniform in a given place, but that did not mean those plants associated together as neatly and inevitably as Clements claimed they did. Clements encouraged ecologists to take a more comprehensive view of plant community development. Gleason urged them to look instead at shorter time scales, which revealed a series of messy, dynamic arrangements. Plants responded to other plants, but there were no leagues within or among species. Succession was the outcome of individual plant behaviors and of what Gleason called "accidents of dispersal." What ecologists deemed a community, he argued, was often a coincidental gathering shaped by a wide range of factors. "Many carefully planned series of observations have shown that, within the extent of a single plant society, the individual plants are distributed at random," Gleason wrote in 1936, "or in other words, by chance."

In 1917, Gleason published "The Structure and Development of the Plant Association." He followed this in 1926 with a paper titled "The Individualistic Concept of the Plant Association," which he later refined and republished in 1939. In these papers and elsewhere, he argued that communities were hardly organisms, let alone superorganisms. They were just many plants occupying the same areas, each responding to its own needs. "Every species of plant is a law unto itself," he wrote, "the distribution of which in space depends upon its individual peculiarities of migration and environmental requirements." But Clements ultimately did not find these arguments compelling. They were too reductionist, too chaotic, too inelegant. Clements by nature eschewed disorder, both ecological and personal; a classmate had said of him that he "had no redeeming vices." His dismissal of Gleason's ideas led to a widespread coolness toward Gleason's work, prompting a frustrated Gleason to say he was something of an "ecological outlaw." Years later his work was reread by a more sympathetic audience, and the Ecological Society of America officially adjudged Gleason an eminent ecologist, but by then he had left ecology, choosing to devote his time and energy to plant taxonomy.

It was in a field that still simmered with conceptual tensions between the holism of Clements and the individualistic model of Gleason that del Moral began his work in the lahars, trying to uncover the succession mechanisms that dictated which species might show up where, and in what order. What would Mount St. Helens shed on the topic: light, or merely more heat?

As the years passed del Moral found it hard to extract the sorts of clear, broad messages that make ecologists giddy. Instead he confronted a world of provisos. Local conditions could be important, things as ordinary as annual weather variations. The summers of 1980 and 1981 were unusually wet. Damaged plants in some of his plots were able to persist, and seedling survival rates were high. Then in 1984 and 1985 the summers were unusually dry. Seedlings established themselves in much lower numbers. "Check the forecast," however, did not sing as ecological theory.

Also, the plants del Moral was surveying did not all seem to have read the same ecology textbooks. Some plots had more of the wind-dispersed species that one would expect to see, like fireweed or pearly everlasting, but at one of his sites, some of the earliest species to appear were more typically associated with climax communities. The most important factor in their success was that they had reached the site ahead of other species. Finally, features of the landscape could shape the initial composition of a plant community as much as nutrients, weather, or fortune did. The gentle rise of a ridge could block seeds from reaching open plots, effectively isolating sites that were just three hundred feet apart. But again, the quirks of local topography did not constitute a theory.

Above all, succession was slow. Species might arrive in the plots and become established, but their cover, or the percentage of ground they occupied in a plot, often stayed low for years. Del Moral thought this was due to the harsh environment. With a few exceptions, most of the earlier studies of succession had been done in sand dunes, grasslands, and forests—temperate habitats at low elevations that were much more welcoming for a variety of plants. Mount St. Helens was neither cool nor temperate nor especially welcoming, either for plants or for people.

If the mountain's southern flank was proving to be an ecological jumble, the stories del Moral was hearing from the Pumice Plain about lupines and other species made even less sense. Finally, in 1984, the temptation to see what was happening in places even more bleak than his own sites became too great, and he decided to set up some permanent plots there, too. "Only rarely have terrestrial plant ecologists been able to observe the colonization of a pristine landscape," he would later write. "A better understanding of the 'rules' by which individuals and species form communities should lead to a better understanding of the forces that structure mature communities."

The rules he found there were even fewer than he had seen among the lahars. The plant community that was assembling on the Pumice Plain appeared to be largely random, driven by rare dispersal events. In one area, he studied the potholes that dimpled the ground, thought to have been formed when blocks of ice entrained deep in the pumice deposits melted. Most of the potholes were not very large—a little more than three hundred square feet in area and eight inches deep—but as little sinks in an otherwise flat expanse, they made wonderful seed traps. Del Moral sampled 111 of them. Rather than share common species, each had its own floral community, like a private, curated garden. The plants at one pothole told him little about what he might find at another close by. Dispersal and succession, he was seeing, were a lot more about what was actually there than what succession theory predicted should be there.

"Community structure in mature vegetation is often assumed to result from deterministic links between plants and their environment," del Moral wrote in 1999. "Many ecologists have recognized the importance of both historical and stochastic factors. However, the search for 'assembly rules' suggests that deterministic factors could strongly affect species composition." In the event of an (apparent) absence of rules, researchers were as likely to blame themselves ("sampling error") or some mysterious force ("unmeasured variables") as they were to question the rules that underpinned their thinking. But what if the lack of rules was at first the rule? Other expectations ecologists largely accepted as successional gospel had not been supported at Mount St. Helens. Mosses, lichens, and cyanobacteria, the classic pioneer species according to theory, were almost nowhere to be found in the area for the first six years. Only after flowering plants were in place did they start to appear at all; and then, rather than facilitate growth, they seemed to suppress it.

These patterns, or their absence, were even more pronounced in the Plains of Abraham, where del Moral set up plots in 1988. The plains had never been a friendly environment for plants, sitting in the rain shadow of the mountain. Although they were spared the debris avalanche, a heat blast had seared away all vegetation above the ground. The Muddy River lahar then scraped away all the plants and soils. Hot pyroclastic flows spilled over the crater rim both on May 18 and during subsequent eruptions months later, covering and re-covering the ground with pumice. Tephra fell from the Plinian column over the top of them, forming great, grapefruit-sized clumps of wet ash.

"Primary succession on the Plains of Abraham has not followed many rules suggested by earlier studies," del Moral would write. "Physical amelioration and chance have determined much of the early pattern. . . . The result is a chaotic invasion pattern dictated by idiosyncratic, if not completely random, events, as well as the number of available germinable seeds." Succession did not recapitulate phylogeny; mosses were not John the Baptist, preparing the way. There were plants, but no plant community, at least not yet. As del Moral would sometimes say, "It was total anarchy out there."

The question, when he thought about how this all related to succession theory, became one of applicability. Mount St. Helens resisted the paradigm proposed by Clements, but did that point to flaws in the primary succession model or say more about Mount St. Helens? Maybe it did not matter. In graduate school, del Moral's advisor, the eminent botanist C. H. Muller, had been a passionate Gleasonian, antideterministic to his core, with a personal dislike of Clements, whom he derided as "one of the Eastern Powers." Muller had had no use for those received dogmas. Vegetation communities developed not in stages but along a spectrum, their changes continuous. If discrete communities existed at all, then they did so mostly as a bookkeeping exercise. That lack of order was what del Moral was seeing on the Pumice Plain and the Plains of Abraham. "The luck of the draw," he would write, "has never been as evident in ecology as on Mount St. Helens."

———

Over in the Blowdown Zone, Franklin had talked of biological legacies. On the Pumice Plain, del Moral was starting to think about legacies too, albeit in a different way. By 2010, he had been monitoring primary succession around Mount St. Helens for thirty years. His career had been defined by that work in ways he could not have imagined. But he had had enough. He did not feel like watching plants creep around for another forty or fifty years. In this he was not alone. Many of the original researchers who had remained at Mount St. Helens were getting older. Apart from Crisafulli, who would probably stay until he had to be carted away in a box, they all faced a difficult question: How were they to bequeath their long-term studies to the next generation of scientists?

Such studies are the gold standard of ecology, but a long time by human standards is rarely a long time ecologically. Yet most ecological studies had been carried out by a single person, or at most a small group. Even groups of scientists who worked together, as at Mount St. Helens, were often only loose affiliations. The data might reflect the character and inclinations of the scientists who gathered them; and human memory is brief, gauzy, subject to creative restructuring. Things that seemed self-evident to one scientist may be baffling or incomprehensible to the one who follows, and these disconnects can shape what is remembered and what is forgotten, what is preserved, what is let go.

Del Moral did not want his data to wither. He had spent years making close, careful observations. Certainly they held more lessons than he and his students had yet unearthed. He decided to offer all he had to the wider world. In 2010, he published a short announcement in the journal *Ecology* titled "Thirty Years of Permanent Vegetation Plots, Mount St. Helens, Washington." He directed interested parties to an online archive where he had outlined why the mountain was such an excellent place to study primary succession. He catalogued all his data, his grids and permanent plots, his methods. He included pictures of his field sites, showing a little of how the vegetation had changed over the years, or had not. He mentioned the sixty papers his work had produced and suggested there was more to be done. "The data sets compiled here are publicly available data," he wrote. "Permission to use these data will be granted upon request by Roger del Moral." Then he waited for someone—anyone—to get in touch.

———

In 2010, Cynthia Chang was almost done with her PhD in ecology at Yale University and in search of what to do next. One day while eating lunch she was paging through a recent issue of *Ecology* when she came upon del Moral's announcement and read about all the data he was offering. *What a resource!* she thought. *What a fantastic study system!* She wrote a proposal to the National Science Foundation requesting funding for a postdoctoral position at the University of Washington. While she was waiting to hear back, she accepted another position at the University of Florida and moved to Gainesville, but then she learned that her Mount St. Helens proposal would be funded. Excited, she cut her time in Gainesville short, packed her things, and moved across the country.

Chang had not even been born when Mount St. Helens erupted. It was a place she had read about in books, first as a kid and later as a student. Although she had regarded the mountain as a classic example of succession, she was not an out-and-out successional ecologist. For her dissertation she had worked on plant diversity in prairies, spending the high summer at a long-term research site in Kansas, crawling for hours across ladders arranged over plots so as not to harm the prairie, counting blades of grass. The tall grass had whished around her as she worked her way down through its layers, touching every leaf and stem, identifying all the species. Shortly after she began, she had discovered she was allergic to grass. She had persisted because, as she later said, she was question-driven rather than organism-driven.

The questions that drove Chang had to do with the mechanisms that drive the nature and structure of plant communities. In this she found herself at the intersection between older work on succession and newer theories of plant community assembly. Although the two fields dealt in many of the same processes—dispersal, biotic interactions, the ways environmental conditions determine the presence or absence of a species—ecologists tended to treat them as distinct. Where succession and community assembly differed most was in their relationship to time. Ecologists who worked on community assembly often did not consider time as a factor, particularly the time after a disturbance. The way they looked at plant communities was ahistorical. In asking why a community was the way it was, they were more likely to consider the regional species pool or the life-history traits of its members. An ecologist guided by succession theory, however, would want first to know when the last major disturbance had been, where the community was along its postdisturbance trajectory, and whether any legacies were left from the predisturbance plant community.

Chang was working to refine the successional conceptual framework by taking into account the factors and mechanisms that predominated in community assembly studies. Succession studies, in turn, could bring an appreciation of how those factors and mechanisms might vary in their influence at different stages over time. Consider a patch of ground at Mount St. Helens stripped of its old vegetation and ripe for occupation. What species would reach it? To answer that question one first had to know the regional species pool: every plant in the vicinity. To that pool would then be applied what she called a dispersal filter: the factors that determined whether or not a species might show up. A plant's own inherent dispersal ability might be high, for instance, as with fireweed. Or the species might already be close to the site, like the prairie lupine discovered by MacMahon and Cristafulli, so that even if it did not have the lightest, fluffiest seeds, it did not have far to travel. Luck also played a role. A seed might be trapped in the tread of someone's boot a hundred miles away and deposited when the owner decided to take a hike at Mount St. Helens.

The dispersal filter whittled the regional species pool down to the list of potential colonizers: those species that had physically reached the site. But reaching the site did not guarantee establishment. Now an environmental filter came into play: the degree to which the species' traits were suited to the site's conditions. If the site was open and dry, then species that needed a lot of water or shade were unlikely to flourish. The environmental filter whittled the potential colonizers down to the actual colonizers: those that could survive and germinate at the site. Lastly came the filter of biotic interactions. Did a species help other species grow, acting as a facilitator for later arrivals? Or did it inhibit other species' growth and so come to dominate the site, creating space only when it died? Did a beetle or elk like to eat it, so much so that they could prevent it from spreading, or even eradicate it? Once all these filters had been applied—the dispersal, the environmental, and the biotic interactions, all acting at different points in time—the species that persisted in their various abundances made up a site's local community.

Chang's approach of combining theories from both succession and community assembly also freed succession from its overreliance on linearity. The traditional schematics that trooped dutifully from an initial disturbance to weeds to shrubs to the big trees of the climax community were simplistic even by the standards of conceptual models. It was not what happened in real life, in which communities were often subject to frequent disturbances both small and large. True, at any one time or in any one place, a volcanic eruption was not terribly likely. Even Mount

St. Helens, as active as it was, erupted only every 140 years on average. But significant disturbances, like the forest fires that swept through the western states every summer, or the hurricanes that slammed into the southeastern US and the Caribbean several times per year, were hardly rare. By placing Mount St. Helens within that suite of disturbances, Chang could free it from being merely an example of volcano ecology. Its old data would be given new life.

———

In April 2012, Chang arrived in Seattle and settled down with del Moral's data set. She brought to it a statistical sophistication increasingly de rigueur in ecology. With new techniques she could probe the data until ever more subtle patterns emerged. When she analyzed thirty years' of plant growth in del Moral's plots, from the lahars to the scours to the barren sites on the Pumice Plain and the Plains of Abraham, the patterns were, she saw, quite subtle. No single criterion could characterize the community response across the habitats. Different sites were subject to their own stressors. On the lahars, for instance, isolation from potential colonists slowed recovery. The scoured sites had achieved maximum plant cover faster than the lahars and the Pumice Plain, but their poor soils limited species diversity. All in all, the mountain was simply a tough place for plants to grow, and would likely remain so for decades.

Chang finished her postdoctoral work in 2014 and soon after was hired as an assistant professor at the University of Washington's Bothell campus. At the Pulse the following summer, her first, she helped start an ambitious project with a group of the younger ecologists who were interested, as she was, in continuing to sample original plots from around the blast area. Their aim was to take the decades of data from the Blowdown Zone, the Pumice Plain, and the Plains of Abraham, among other places, and compare them all to see if their plant communities were all developing in similar ways. Given the diversity of the disturbance processes, they wondered, how had the communities changed through time? Were there detectable trajectories? Were they stabilizing at all, or were there still a lot of shifts as species arrived and disappeared?

No one had compared the different zones in this way before. Chang and her colleagues first looked at their species richness, which was simply a count of the number of species per zone. One of classical succession's most durable predictions is that species richness should increase for a while after a disturbance and then level off. That was what they found across the zones, although richness in the Pumice Plain and the Plains of Abraham was actually beginning to decline a little.

Chang next looked at the change of species relative to overall species richness. Perhaps their absolute numbers might have stabilized, but was that because there was a high degree of turnover, with additions and subtractions canceling each other out, or was the community actually stable? Here, some surprising patterns emerged. In the Pumice Plain and the Plains of Abraham, richness was due to stability: a group of species had arrived, established, and endured. In the Blowdown Zone, however, the opposite was true. There was a greater degree of turnover. A lot of species were still moving in, even thirty years after the eruption.

Using an analytical method called nonmetric multidimensional scaling, or NMDS—in essence a measure of how similar a plant community is from one time period to the next—Chang took measurements of plant diversity from 1980, 1989, 2000, and 2010. She had predicted that the Pumice Plain and the Plains of Abraham would be the least similar from decade to decade, because they had the most open habitats and the greatest amount of space for new species to occupy. But that was not what she found. Instead, it was the Blowdown Zone that was still changing the most.

All of this told her that at many places around the blast area, the plant community was starting to become stable in some ways. The dispersal filter had narrowed the species, the environmental filter had narrowed them further, and now biotic interactions between the remaining species were increasing in importance. Some species, like the prairie lupine on the Pumice Plain, facilitated the growth of other species by improving the soil or providing shelter. Others, like willow trees, were dying back because of attacks from a species of beetle called the willow stem borer. The species larvae bored into the stems of willow (as its name implied), working their way from willow patch to willow patch and, in the words of one ecologist, keeping succession in a state of "chronic reset."

The big question for Chang is what will happen to the Pumice Plain in the future. She hypothesizes that its vegetation community still has at least one more period of rapid change and upheaval in store, and this will be marked by the arrival and settlement of one final group of plants: trees.

––––––

A year after her first trip to the Plains of Abraham, Chang is once again hiking across some of the blast area's more barren spaces, this time on the Truman Trail (#207) from the Johnston Ridge Observatory down to the Pumice Plain. Her students are again in tow, and again they are carrying a lot of rebar, but instead of Baum, who graduated last year, this year it is Daviel O'Neill and Camilo Acosta who plod.

"We're here," Chang says when she reaches the east side of the Pumice Plain after a few miles. O'Neill and Acosta set down their packs, which settle to the ground with the solid and familiar *clunks*. O'Neill and Acosta stretch their backs. "I feel like I'm floating," Acosta says.

Chang laughs while she scans the landscape. She is looking for young conifers, which are fairly easy to spot on the Pumice Plain's open expanse. Most are short, more like shrubs than nascent trees. "There's a good one!" she says. She walks up to a noble fir that is about as tall as she is, steps back, considers it. It has the fresh green of a new tree and sways slightly in the wind. "It looks cute," she says to Acosta and O'Neill. The two chuckle. "In science," Chang says in what I think of as her professor voice, "we can make decisions based on cuteness at times."

O'Neill and Acosta start to pull out the rebar while Chang writes some notes in her field book. Prior to the eruption, the timberline on Mount St. Helens was at a little over four thousand feet. This was unusually low—more than one thousand feet lower than at Mount Adams nearby, and two thousand feet lower than at Mount Rainier. Repeated volcanic activity most likely held the trees at bay. They marched up the slopes, and then the mountain erupted and knocked them back down. Until May 18, 1980, conifers had again been advancing steadily, and now, more than three decades after that latest setback, they are trying again. The landscape is dotted with them: firs, mostly, and some stray pines, none more than ten or fifteen feet tall.

Chang wants to learn how all these trees affect the ground they grow on. "One of the things about the early plant work is that it's all obser-vation," she says. "There hasn't been much in the way of experiment, which is how you really tease out mechanisms." Her plan is to shape her plots like plus signs. At the end of one three-meter-long arm will be a living tree; at the end of another, a patch of unmolested ground to serve as a control. On the other two arms will be additions to mimic the tree's effects, parsed as Chang conceives of them. "Trees can add two basic things to the ground," she says: "shade and nutrients." One arm will thus have a black sheet that covers roughly the same area as the lowest level of branches, blocking the sun; at the end of the last arm, Chang will add modest amounts of carbon, to mimic leaf litter. She will then track the plant community as it develops in small plots along each arm.

O'Neill and Acosta start hammering rebar stakes into the ground, while Chang measures out bisecting transect lines. "Sometimes I wish I was a forest ecologist," she says, fanning herself with her sun hat. "There's no shade here!" But after twenty minutes she and O'Neill and Acosta have the plot set up.

"It looks good," Chang says, and O'Neill and Acosta project an air of relief. One plot down, thirty-nine to go. Chang hopes that elk will not chew through the ropes that hold the shade cloth. Elk, she hears, can be the bane of biologists on the Pumice Plain. They eat rope, ribbons, plastic flagging. "Every time you touch something you leave a little bit of salt on it," Chang says. "Elk love that. They smell something salty, they want to try a bite, and they don't care if it's your research." But she is early in her career and has the time to refine her methods to make them sufficiently unappetizing. "I've got at least another thirty years of working life," she says. "So now it's my turn to ask how succession is playing out."

7

THE CONCRETE FOREST

O N A BRIGHT morning in June, I am in a forest surrounded by fallen trees. These are a common feature around Mount St. Helens, but the difference here is that I am thirty-five miles northeast of the mountain, which is nowhere to be seen, and the trees have fallen for any number of reasons, be it age or wind or rot, and at any number of times, rather than from a single cause on a single day nearly forty years ago.

"You can see this isn't the usual blast-zone moonscape people are always going on about," Don Zobel says. He is wandering amid the trunks in a bright yellow rain slicker. The sun might be out, but to get here he had to push through a thick understory still dripping from last night's rain. It was like getting slapped in the face over and over with a wet mop.

Zobel finds a trunk to his liking and sits on its spongy bark. He takes off his raincoat and retrieves a clipboard from a backpack. Through thick glasses he peers at the top page. A retired botany professor from Oregon State University, he has had a vision problem for nearly twenty years that prevents him from seeing plants in diagnostic detail, but he can still collect data. "The main player in the plot last year was vame," he says to Dylan Fischer. He pronounces it *vay-me*, for *Vaccinium membranaceum*, or big huckleberry. He looks down the page. "There was also a lot of trace stuff."

"Right," Fischer says. Several decades younger than Zobel, Fischer is a biology professor from the Evergreen State College in Olympia. He takes a square made of white PVC that is one meter on a side and places it next to a small pink flag. (The ground is festooned with these flags, marking the one-meter intervals of several long transects.) To read the plot, as

99

botanists say, he does not squat next to it as others do but rather bends from his hips, keeping his back straight. He calls this his "veg yoga." He holds the position for a couple of minutes, fingering leaves and stems, murmuring to himself. "There is so much here," he says. "You won't see plots with this many species in any other study at Mount St. Helens."

The forest is heavily peopled today. Joe Antos, a retired biologist from the University of Victoria in British Columbia, Canada, has been calling out plant names to one of Fischer's students a few yards away. On hearing Zobel say "vay-me," he takes a moment to opine on the relative merits of all the berry pies he has made over the years. *V. membranaceum* is the tastiest, in his view, but the competition is keen. "Huckleberries taste different depending on the species," he explains, "so we have been scientifically obliged to experiment."

Uniquely in the research community of Mount St. Helens, Zobel, Antos, and Fischer work far outside the monument, among some of the most ancient trees in the Gifford Pinchot National Forest. With firs and hemlocks and cedars up to six hundred years old, this part of the forest was far enough from the mountain to escape its full wrath, but it was still touched significantly, if subtly, by tephra.

———

On May 18, 1980, the skies over Oregon and Washington were as clear as could be hoped for on a spring morning in the Pacific Northwest, and the eruption of Mount St. Helens was visible to any satellite that happened to be in high Earth orbit overhead. One of these, a government weather satellite called the Geostationary Operational Environmental Satellite-3, or GOES-3, snapped a picture of the event every thirty minutes. Because of its schedule, the first photo is from 8:50 a.m. (Would that Mount St. Helens had collapsed at 8:20 a.m. instead of 8:32!) By then, the swiftest destructive processes were over. The debris avalanche had ground to a stop, and the remnants of the lateral blast cloud were settling, the gray deposits covering the fallen trees like a burial shroud.

One process, however, was just beginning: the Plinian column. At 8:37 a.m., the first cloud of ash and pumice—tephra—had started to billow from the volcano's new crater. The satellite photo from 8:50 shows it blooming out of southern Washington like a giant crown of black broccoli. It is almost at its full height, having risen fifteen miles into the sky. Its leading edge is forty-five miles wide; its total eventual mass has been estimated at five hundred million tons. In the next photo, from 9:20 a.m., the plume has climbed a few thousand feet higher and expanded to seventy-five miles across. A faint shock wave of moisture called a skirt cloud can be seen racing away from it like a ripple across a pond. By 9:50 a.m., the skirt cloud has reached Puget Sound, and the plume is dispersing, blown east-northeast by the prevailing winds.

For the next seven and a half hours, GOES-3 tracked the plume's progress. By 5:20 p.m., it had widened to smear over much of eastern Washington and northern Oregon, the Idaho Panhandle, southwestern Montana, and the northwestern tip of Wyoming. It was well launched on its trajectory across the United States and, eventually, the entire Northern Hemisphere.

For people that lived in its path, the plume arrived like something out of an apocalypse. The sky darkened; the air temperature dropped and then rose. Birds stopped singing. The sun guttered like a candle when the plume passed over, then seemed to vanish. Street lights flickered on, even though it was the middle of the day. Red and green bolts of lightning flashed through the clouds, thunder boomed, and tephra fell from the sky like a fine, dry rain—several inches of it in places. It piled in drifts. Roads and highways throughout eastern Washington were closed due to ashfall. As many as ten thousand motorists were stranded, caught in the whirling ash; an estimated five hundred thousand people were told not to leave their homes.

It was an event beyond human recall and understanding. People outside the immediate vicinity of Mount St. Helens had assumed they would be safe should the mountain erupt. Government scientists assured them they had little to fear from ashfall. Now, as ash filled the sky, some people wept, some prayed, some filled their bathtubs with water to drink, some were stoic. "If this is the end of the world," one woman in Yakima told her daughter, "the hell with it. I'm ready."

———

Don Zobel was at church in Corvallis on the morning of May 18. He is punctual by nature, and the service started at 8:30, so it was not until later, when the congregants were chatting and drinking coffee, that someone arriving for a later service asked, "Have you all heard about Mount St. Helens?"

Zobel and his wife, Priscilla, had not. They rushed home and turned on the Sunday news programs. Breathless broadcasters were standing outside and gesturing to the spectacle behind them. Log-choked mud-flows crashed down the Toutle River at incredible speeds. Grainy videos from wobbly aircraft showed the mountain spewing massive amounts of ash. Zobel drifted over to his couch and sat down, watching without saying much. It was as if he had traded one biblical event for another.

Later that afternoon, Zobel had to leave for a spring get-together for plant ecologists from Oregon State and the Andrews Forest. Antos was there—he had been Zobel's graduate student since 1978—and so was Jerry Franklin. As the gathering was breaking up, Franklin mentioned that he was putting a group together to work at Mount St. Helens. Both Zobel and Antos said they were interested.

Later, Antos came to Zobel's house so that they could discuss the wisdom (or peril) of switching his thesis topic. He had been doing a project on Alaska yellow cedars in the southern part of their range, from Mount Rainier down to Northern California. Several of his plots had been in the blast area. They were sure to be affected, perhaps severely enough to scuttle the whole project. But what might he study at Mount St. Helens instead? While both Zobel and Antos recognized the eruption as a once-in-a-lifetime research opportunity, Zobel was sensitive to Antos's position as a student. Since almost all the experienced researchers would want to work in the blast area, it might be tough for a student to get a foothold.

They decided it made the most sense for Antos to work outside the blast area proper. Zobel suggested they study the effects of tephra on plants. He had taken students on field trips to lava flows and other tephra deposits and had an interest in what he calls "volcanically induced vegetation." Studying Mount St. Helens tephra would have distinct advantages. For one thing, since tephra fall had not laid waste to the forests like the other ejecta, they would probably be able to reach their sites without helicopters, perhaps even by driving. Moreover, although tephra was the least spectacular of the disturbances, it was the most far-reaching. The eruption was known mostly for the violence it wreaked on the local landscape, but the tephra was mild and ubiquitous, and so at risk of being overlooked.

Zobel and Antos first visited Mount St. Helens on June 15, driving out by themselves on Highway 12, approaching as close as cars were allowed to go. Although the tephra deposit was pretty thin there, the changes to the forest were still remarkable. Tephra clung to the trees, giving them a gray cast. When a plant physiologist from the University of Washington later measured the temperature of Pacific silver fir needles on branches embedded in clumps of tephra, it was more than 30°F warmer than needles from which tephra had been cleared.

Because Zobel had to leave for a trip to the East Coast, Antos had to set up the sites on his own. He and Zobel wanted sites that would capture both the gradient of the disturbance, from shallow tephra to deep, and the natural varieties of the habitats covered by the tephra, some of which had many species and some of which did not. In keeping with a Forest Service safety requirement, the sites also had to be no more than a seven-minute walk from a car.

After driving miles and miles of ash-covered logging roads and poring over Forest Service maps, Antos found places he thought would work well: two sites thirteen miles from the crater, where the tephra was at least five inches deep; and two sites thirty-six miles away, with tephra about two inches deep. At each distance, one site was species rich, and the other species poor. All were in old-growth subalpine forest.

By looking at the condition of the tephra, Antos could tell that the two species-rich sites had still been covered with snow during the eruption, although most of the snow had now melted. The snow cover would be something else to keep in mind.

Antos started laying out transects and putting in plots in July. Where most of the other researchers working in the blast area were content to call the eruption itself the experiment, he set up a controlled experiment, clearing some plots of the tephra deposits. These plots would act as controls, showing as much as possible the state of the forest had Mount St. Helens not erupted. The question was how to clear the tephra without damaging the delicate plants. Where it was deep he could dig it up, but where it was shallow, or where he was trying to get it off the plants themselves, he had to be more creative. Sometimes he blew on the plants to knock the tephra off or spent hours with a toothbrush, gently scrubbing the leaves and shoots.

The work was sometimes slow and tedious. A few times, in a gambit born of equal parts industry and frustration, Antos brought out a generator and a vacuum cleaner to clear tephra off the ground. That worked surprisingly well, except that hauling the heavy generator around was a pain. But at least access to his sites was not a problem, and he did not have to jockey with other researchers for helicopter time. After more than a month of getting rained on and then drying out, the top crust of tephra on the logging roads had become so hard Antos could drive over it in his pickup without even breaking through. He took to saying he worked in the concrete forest.

———

Once the plots were put in, Antos watched to see how the buried understory would change over time. He was interested especially in the factors that influenced those changes: the depth of the tephra, the presence of snow, the type and age of the plants, and so on.

Lots of things began to happen in slightly different ways, he saw. The understory community resisted a streamlined narrative. There would be no pithy summary, no easy tale. "If this instance is representative of vegetation responses to disturbance," Zobel and Antos wrote in a paper summarizing their first decade of research, "generalizations about vegetation change will remain difficult to identify."

Still, they were ecologists in the classical style, so they had to try, and some consistent, if complex, patterns emerged. The forest understory, often thought of as a collective entity, has many components, and these were responding to the tephra in different ways. Bryophytes—nonvascular plants, like liverworts and mosses—did poorly everywhere, whether the tephra was deep or shallow. "The moss layer got creamed," was how Antos put it to me. But for some flowering plants, burial in tephra actually stimulated growth, so long as the tephra was less than two inches deep. Others survived in a state of near quiescence, often for three or more years, and then sent up shoots through the eroded tephra crust. In tephra more than five inches deep, however, flowering plants did not do so well. Some were lucky enough to grow in the refuge of a downed log and so were spared the worst effects, but most perished, unable to break through the hard surface crust.

For the small trees and shrubs—the largest members of the understory—the depth of the tephra crust seemed irrelevant to their survival, but snow cover was another matter. In the Blowdown Zone, Franklin had observed that snow was a savior for both plants and animals, acting as a heat shield. In the concrete forest, snow was a killer. Tephra had landed atop it, and when the snow melted, the wet tephra formed a heavy paste. Rather than eroding as it might in the rain, it dried into a crust and settled down like a heavy slab. Less than two inches of tephra could severely damage even a large huckleberry shrub because the shrubs had been lying prostrate on the ground under the snow. In a normal year they would spring up fresh when the snow melted, but the tephra pinned them down. Mock azalea and oval-leaf huckleberry numbers declined.

Big huckleberry, once one of the most common species on the plots, was wiped out almost completely.

Damage did not always spell death, though. In the end, few species were eliminated completely from the whole understory community, and few new species arrived that had not been there before. Sites with shallow tephra and less snow had higher overall plant cover; by year 10, the number of species had returned to pre-eruption levels, even if cover was still lagging behind. But in the sites with deeper tephra and snow cover, understory cover had not returned to its former levels even after three decades.

Zobel and Antos studied their plots closely for the first four years. As the patterns started to stabilize, the frequency of their visits declined, and they came less often over the next two decades. By the early 2000s, Zobel's worsening vision meant he could no longer drive, although his wife sometimes drove him. Antos, meanwhile, was keeping busy in Victoria, where he studied old-growth forests and had a harder time getting away. Funds for their work had never been bounteous or consistent. If the project was to survive them, it was clear, as Zobel says, "that some succession was in order."

Unlike Franklin, whose students had inconsistently sampled his plots after his interests led him elsewhere in the mid-1980s, or Roger del Moral, who offered up his data sets to the wider world, Zobel and Antos decided to recruit a protégé. In 2005, at that year's Pulse, they announced that they were looking for someone to take over their work. One person expressed an interest, but nothing came of it. Five years later, after not hearing from anyone, they did a more dedicated search, combing through websites of colleges and universities in the Pacific Northwest, looking for young faculty who might be open to the work. Again, nothing came of it. Finally, at a research symposium in 2010, Zobel ran into the first biologist who expressed interest in the project. Was the offer still available, he asked? Zobel said it was.

The biologist was Dylan Fischer, who had done his undergraduate degree at Oregon State; he had even taken a botany class from Zobel.

After working as a backcountry ranger, he had gone on to earn his PhD from Northern Arizona University, and in 2005 had started teaching at Evergreen State College, where his research focused on the ways plants recover from disturbance and how they behave in restored landscapes.

When Zobel and Antos took Fischer out to their sites, he was struck by how valuable their work had been as an experiment within an experiment. "Every square meter you look at, you know exactly what happened to it going back to 1980," he says. "Each plant operates like a character in a drama: six hundred plots, six hundred stories." This project could not be allowed to disappear. Zobel and Antos had done a tremendous job as preservationists. They had even saved a lot of old equipment for Fischer to use. "I think Don is still using pencils he used when he was a grad student at Duke," he says.

Fischer also recognized a chance to develop his own research. He saw questions Zobel and Antos had been aware of but had not explored, about such things as soil formation and nutrient content. In part this was due to the tyranny of the eruption. In 1980, it dominated not only the landscape but also scientific thinking. When Zobel and Antos began their work, they were looking at how plants survived in soils covered with tephra, when tephra was inescapable. When Fischer came, he saw a green, intact forest that looked much like other forests. The effects of the eruption were no longer immediately obvious: the forest had absorbed them. A new community was assembling, not so much responding to the eruption as adapting to the new conditions. "When this project started, the story was about the eruption, but now it is really about time," Fischer says. "And the story is not close to being over—I want to keep it going for a while."

————

The next morning, when Antos, Fischer and the others leave, Zobel suggests that the two of us visit a site closer to Mount St. Helens. We drive down Forest Road 25 for several miles until we reach the turnoff for Elk Pass. After bouncing down an even smaller spur for a couple of miles,

Zobel says we can walk the rest of the way. The gravel road is overgrown with grass; it must not get much vehicle traffic.

The sky is clear and the view opens east, toward Mount Adams. After a few minutes, Zobel spies some landmark—a depression in the undergrowth—and leaves the road to head into the forest. Soon we have reached site DR (deep tephra/species rich). The ground is cool in the shade of the forest canopy. Rows of pink flags and white stakes peep up amid the understory. The trees tower over us, vast in both space and time.

Next to the transects Zobel walks quietly, talks quietly. Tall and stooping, his steps deliberate, he is primed to notice things on the ground. He recalls almost every detail and nuance of the site—how a difference in slope affected this plot here but not the one next to it, how slight changes in the soil chemistry mattered to that plot over there. I listen and know I will not remember 10 percent of what he says.

I ask about Fischer. This year marks a formal transition, when Zobel and Antos's work will become his, and the two of them will stop coming so much, or perhaps at all. Is it hard for them to give up the project after all this time?

"Dylan is great," Zobel says. In passing off the project, he and Antos had been careful to ensure that Fischer knew how to identify all the plants. They walked him through all the definitions they had been using. But Fischer is already starting to speak in his own language and use his own tools of inquiry. Early in the collaboration, he used statistical analyses to identify some trends Zobel and Antos had not thought even to look for. Ecology has changed; Fischer's is a different knowledge from theirs, and that is the point.

We have strayed from the site, moved deeper into the trees. "Look at the forest floor here," Zobel says. "If you did not know what to look for, you might not even know there had been an eruption. But dig down a little. See what you find."

I squat down. The ground is crunchy from all the fallen conifer needles. Since we are just thirteen miles from the crater, I do not have to dig deep to reach the tephra. A couple of inches beneath the brown dirt, I come to a band of gray that is several inches thick. Scooping out a little of it, I turn it in my fingers. It is wet and gritty, like soil in waiting. Something of a cottage industry, I have read, has grown up around this stuff. You can buy a couple of ounces of Mount St. Helens ash online for a few bucks. Those with more upscale tastes can look for jewelry made from helenite, also known as Mount St. Helens obsidian. Helenite was discovered when workers with Weyerhaeuser, while using acetylene torches, noticed that the tephra nearby melted into a brilliant green glass. (The green comes from chromium and copper mixed with the silica.) Jewelers fashioned it into rings, earrings, and pendants. Some of the higher-end pieces might go for two hundred dollars.

Here in the forest, the tephra has a different value as a new layer in the Earth's thin skin. Already it is being incorporated under the leaf litter—sticks, twigs, and needles dropped by the trees above. (Mor humus, Zobel calls it.) The litter presses down on the tephra as the tephra once pressed on the plants, mixing it with lower layers of old soil, turning all of it into new soil, new life. "In other parts of the country, soil comes from the ground, like rock weathering," Zobel says. "Here in the Cascade Range, it falls from the sky." By this he means it falls from the shrubs, from the trees, from the volcanoes.

I stand up, brush my hands off on my pants, and look around at all the trees, silent and softly lit. Being among them is like being in the Andrews, or some other old forest not marked by Mount St. Helens and its convulsions, and I mention this to Zobel. "Yes," he says. "But also no." Everywhere is marked in some way by some mountain, he notes; tephra surrounds us. In addition to the layers from the 1980 eruption of Mount St. Helens, there are layers of tephra from eruptions of Mount Rainier, Mount Baker, Glacier Peak, and even Mount Mazama, which collapsed on itself several thousand years ago to form Crater Lake. Layer upon layer, age upon age, these peaks and their eruptions added to the land, changed it, shaped it. Dig down deep enough to reach bedrock, and you will find an ecological history of Cascadia that has been written more than a little by its volcanoes.

PART THREE

OF LOGS
AND LAKES

8

A BLACK STEW OF BACTERIA

O F ALL THE EVENTS in the eruption of Mount St. Helens, one of the most fascinating to imagine is the moment when the first block of the debris avalanche slammed into Spirit Lake with such force that the entire basin emptied, and more than fifty billion gallons of water were thrown up the surrounding hillsides. Some of the water may have splashed the summit of Mount Margaret and the little bronze survey disk. Then it rushed back down, sweeping away the snow and soil on the ground, every animal from a shrew to a bull elk, and tens of thousands of trees that the lateral blast cloud had knocked down seconds before. All of this debris crashed into the basin, churning and tossing.

Later in the afternoon, when the pyroclastic flows began, waves of pumice surged down into the lake. As the ash plume billowed past, more than a foot of tephra settled over the mess. The next day, the water's surface was so choked with logs and tephra that when rescuers flew over it, they thought the lake had boiled away in the heat, or perhaps been completely buried. "Spirit Lake Gone," read a banner headline in the *Oregonian* on May 20. But Spirit Lake was still there, if smothered.

In the months that followed, the snow melted and the soil and ash settled to the lake bottom, but the logs floated on the surface as a great mat, initially covering almost half of the lake. Many sank as the years passed, and the mat now covers closer to one-fifth of the surface. Yet it is still such a distinctive feature of Spirit Lake that from the Pumice Plain, or up in the Mount Margaret Backcountry, you watch it the way you might watch the clouds. It mimics their slow shape shifting, and in this offers an object lesson in the nature of entropy. A strong westerly wind, common here, can herd all the logs into one of the lake's northern arms and hold them there, but on calm days the logs are free to drift.

Once on just such a day I was hopping across logs piled at the end of the Harmony Falls trail, on the lake's eastern shore. (The falls are gone, buried somewhere deep beneath the ground, along with the crushed remains of a lodge.) I had wandered out over the lake as far as I dared, and sat down to take off my shoes and cool my feet in the water. The lake is not very deep here, and the black shadows cast on the bottom by the floating sticks and branches were like artful brushstrokes. I was admiring their curious calligraphy when an enormous log sidled up. I had not been paying attention, had not seen it coming, but suddenly it was right there, nudging against my toes. Its knots and branch stubs stuck out of the water like the snout and eyes of some enormous crocodilian. I hastily withdrew my feet, put on my shoes, and got up to leave. As I made my way back to land, I turned around to eye my pursuer, but the log had already drifted away to rejoin the mat.

Spirit Lake is thought to be about 3,500 years old. Its formation marks a distinctive stage in Mount St. Helens's eruptive history, which doubly serves as the boundary between what geologists call Old Mount St. Helens and Modern Mount St. Helens. The old mountain was less a single peak than a cluster of domes composed primarily of dacite and silicic andesite rocks. Then, beginning in the Spirit Lake stage, the mountain's eruptive output changed. The material it spat shifted from primarily silicic to mafic rocks rich in magnesium and iron. (*Mafic* is a portmanteau of *magnesium* and *ferric*.) The mountain's appearance changed as well. A single cone started to replace the cluster, growing taller and taller over the next few thousand years until it became the peak that persists to the present day, albeit with one notable recent alteration.

Geologists further divide the Spirit Lake stage into six eruptive periods. The first, the Smith Creek period, is itself divided into three volcanic episodes, each characterized by its own distinct layer of tephra. The first episode was, by geological standards, brief and uneventful. A series of small eruptions produced a thin but widespread layer of pumice, which geologists call layer Yb, and then a much thicker, rockier layer, Yd. The mountain then lay dormant for several hundred years until a second, much more explosive eruption began. Thought to be the mountain's biggest eruption, it was about four times the size of the 1980 event in terms of both force and ejecta. Several hundred square miles of what is now the United States and Canada were covered with a thick, coarse layer of tephra (layer Yn). Pyroclastic flows ran down the mountain's flanks, leaving a yellowish pumice, and the new dome began to form, although for several centuries it looked in profile like a lumpy pile of mashed potatoes.

Soon after this eruption came the third episode of the Smith Creek period, which left a layer of tephra again characterized by rocky fragments more than pumice (layer Ye). Lahars traveled more than twenty-five miles down the valley of the North Fork Toutle River, creating the dam that led to the formation of Spirit Lake. Another dormant interval followed, this one lasting at most about three centuries. The start of the Pine Creek eruptive period came next, from 3,000 until 2,500 years ago. In this period, several lava domes grew and collapsed, and lahars further added to the North Fork's valley floor, raising the fan that held the new lake. Although the lake experienced a few catastrophic breaches that sent walls of water down the North Fork Toutle, its configuration thereafter stayed largely unchanged, while the summit of the mountain became higher and more conical in shape.

In 1979 the biology of Spirit Lake resembled that of most alpine lakes in the Cascade Range. Sitting in what one limnologist has called "a deep hole," its waters were cold and clear, its sides steep, its bottom muddy. It was larger than most lakes in the range, with a surface area of about 520 hectares (1,300 acres) and an average depth of nearly 40 meters (120 feet); its eastern arm in places was more than 55 meters (180 feet) deep. Its drainage basin was small relative to its size and heavily forested, mostly with old conifer trees, which meant that few nutrients were free to flow down to the lake. Nitrogen and phosphorus levels were low, and plants covered less than 1 percent of the bottom. The only limnological survey of the lake, completed in 1937, offered just one brief aside about phytoplankton or aquatic invertebrates, mentioning "diatoms, greens, and yellow-browns," and "one species of rotifer and a few copepods." All of these had been caught in a net towed through the water for about five minutes.

————

When the aquatic ecologist Jim Sedell arrived at Spirit Lake in June of 1980 as the head of the team that would study it, he came as one who knew the joy of running waters. He was thirty-five, bearded, balding a little bit, and he wore big glasses, which gave him an earnest look. He had grown up in Redmond, a small town in the middle of Oregon, and spent summers in the Cascades near his home, fishing for trout in the alpine lakes or for salmon on the Metolius River. In 1965, he held the last chinook salmon caught on the Metolius before the Round Butte Dam was completed on the Deschutes, of which the Metolius was a tributary. The experience had showed him how waters could change themselves or be changed at the whims of external forces.

Sedell wanted to be a lawyer when he left for college. He studied philosophy and political science at Willamette University, but when he needed a break, he and a friend would drive from Salem out to the coast at Lincoln City. They spent the low tides hunched over the tide pools. His friend was majoring in biology and knew the names of everything—the algae draped over the stones, the skulking crabs and brightly colored nudibranchs, the darting sculpins. Sedell watched and reveled in the Pacific's steady pounding. *Boy*, he thought, *this beats a law library!*

In his remaining time in college, Sedell started taking courses in biology and statistics. After he finished his degree, he wrote to the heads of graduate programs across the country. He informed them (or, rather, confessed) that he was a liberal arts student but had taken such-and-such science classes. If he applied, what were his chances of getting in? (He did not want to waste twenty or thirty bucks on the application fee if there was no point.) Most professors said he need not bother, but two places—the University of Nebraska and the University of Pittsburgh—were willing to consider his application.

Sedell decided to go to Pittsburgh. He had never been to the East Coast, and to a lifelong westerner, living in the exotic psychic territory of Back East seemed like a big deal. Unsure once there whether to study animals or plants, he fell in with a stream ecologist. He took to the research, so much so that when his adviser left for a job at Michigan State University, Sedell followed, commuting between Pittsburgh and East Lansing to avoid having to retake his qualifying exams at Michigan. He ended up writing his thesis on the ecology and natural history of two species of caddis flies and received his PhD in 1971.

After Sedell finished his degree, Jerry Franklin hired him to come back to Oregon as a postdoctoral researcher at the Andrews Forest. This was during the first few years of the International Biological Programme, and Franklin needed an aquatic ecologist to join what Sedell called his "scruffy crew of early-seventies longhairs" to look at the relationship between forests and water. Until then, the broken branches or thick tree trunks that lay across the creeks and streams had been considered nothing more than a nuisance for loggers. Forest and water were separate domains, until Sedell and the Stream Team showed otherwise with their study of stream health throughout the Lookout Creek drainage. The broken trees and woody debris were vital for the ecosystem in a number of ways. In biological terms, they gave refuge to juvenile salmon, resident amphibians, and invertebrates. In physical terms, they altered current flows, shaded the water and kept it cool, and added nutrients to it. Water was the richer for wood.

Sedell enjoyed the work and the interdisciplinary ethos of the Andrews, the way ideas could come in from anywhere. At first he had sometimes felt like a misfit among the other scientists. "I wasn't trained like all of you were," he would lament to Fred Swanson. "No," Swanson said. "You weren't constrained. Your thought processes are very free." Franklin said Sedell was irreplaceable and uncontrollable. "Jim!" he would sometimes plead. "You gotta quit telling crazy fairy tales! At least call them hypotheses!"

For all of the intellectual satisfaction he derived from his post-doctoral work, Sedell found it financially constraining. He and his wife had a young child, and his salary was not enough to support them. He wanted a job that was a little less liquid, a little more stable. In 1977, the Weyerhaeuser Company offered him a job managing their aquatic research team for three times the money. Franklin warned him against it. He said Sedell had three years at most before he would be worthless as a scientist. Sedell went to work for the commercial forestry giant anyway, but while he was there, Franklin kept sending him research proposals to review so that he could keep abreast of what his old colleagues were up to.

Sedell stayed at Weyerhaeuser for a couple of years, until it became clear that carrying water for loggers was not his cup of tea. He was still arguing about the best ways to manage streams, but his team was small and they lacked, as he later put it, "a single, compelling landscape to rally around." He worried that he was losing his bearings in some fundamental way, and he was looking to leave when a series of small earthquakes started to jolt one of the mountains up in southwestern Washington. Shortly after, Franklin called Sedell to say he was putting together a group to study Mount St. Helens once it erupted. Would he be willing to come back to where he belonged?

Given Sedell's history with the Stream Team, Franklin and Swanson thought he would be a good choice to coordinate research on Mount St. Helens's lakes and streams. The biggest and best-known of the lakes was Spirit Lake, but bodies of water of varying size and significance surrounded the mountain. There were some a few miles north, in the lee of Mount Margaret—smaller lakes like Boot Lake, Grizzly Lake,

Obscurity Lake, and Shovel Lake. Meta Lake was just a couple of miles south of those, and Ryan Lake a few miles northeast. Clearwater Creek was that area's big drainage, fed by Smith Creek and Bean Creek. To the northwest were Coldwater Creek and Castle Creek, both of which joined the North Fork Toutle.

The problem, Sedell soon discovered, was that, lovely as all these lakes and creeks and streams were, almost no data about them were available. They had been managed as purely recreational spaces for camping, boating, and fishing. The only study of Spirit Lake dated from 1974, when a couple of scientists from the USGS had gathered basic data on its depth and water chemistry. Other scientists were confronting similar predicaments in their preparations to study both water and forests. Until it began to buck and heave, Mount St. Helens had been seen as a beautiful but not terribly interesting mountain. No biologists had done any substantial research on or around it. The few studies that had been carried out were mostly quick inventories of plants and animals, but its ecological community was thought to be pretty similar to that of other mountains in the area.

In part this dearth of attention was due to Mount St. Helens's sitting at the intersection of so many jurisdictions. The landscape consisted of patches of national forest, state forest, private timberland and tree farms. Lodges, scout camps, and public campgrounds and cabins lined the shores of Spirit Lake and other nearby lakes. People came to Mount St. Helens to cut trees, hunt elk, fish for trout, relax in the shade, or bake in the sun, but not to study. Mount Rainier, so much bigger and so close at hand and, by the standards of the day, so dramatically pristine—the mountain had been the center of a national park since 1899—was much more attractive as a research site.

Sedell had to figure out how best to negotiate that scholarly lassitude. Everyone assumed the mountain would erupt soon, and the posteruption work would have to be informed by knowledge about its pre-eruption state. He hastily organized a number of quick trips in late April, during which he and his crew dashed out to collect water samples from twenty of the lakes. He knew the effort was incomplete and slapdash, but it was the best he could do, and it was better than nothing. Then he went back to Corvallis to wait for Mount St. Helens to do what it would.

———

After the eruption, a couple of weeks passed before Sedell and his team were allowed to fly to Spirit Lake. When they did, they got out of the helicopter on the Pumice Plain and gawked. Spirit Lake lay before them like a pool of oil in an otherwise ash-gray landscape. Sedell could not help but smile grimly to himself. How absurd those crystal-pure water samples back in the lab now seemed! They were not samples so much as relics from a lake that no longer existed. Spirit Lake was gone, just as the *Oregonian* had said.

What was in its place? No one had any idea. When Sedell knelt at the shore, he could see no more than a few inches below the dark, clouded surface. Logs and pumice floated in the steaming water. The temperature was close to 100°F, warmer than a human body, and the air was rank with sulfur, methane, turpentine, and other noxious fumes. To the north, the hills had been stripped to a raw, diagonal swath of bedrock, showing the scouring reach of that great wave.

On the flight out Sedell had told himself over and over, like a mantra, that Spirit Lake would be nothing like those mountain lakes of his youth, but he was still unprepared for the full brunt of the shock. Growing up among mountains, he had supposed them to be permanent, but Mount St. Helens was gutted. To be a witness in a place so desolate was almost a physical sensation. He had no reference points to help him to orient his thoughts. Nothing was even remotely familiar. He felt dizzy, even a little nauseated.

Somehow he and his team were going to have to make sense of this. He felt a sense of renewed purpose. He wanted to look at everything about Spirit Lake: its biology, its chemistry, its biochemistry. All he needed to get started was some samples. He had brought along an inflatable yellow raft in which he had planned to paddle out a little way from shore to reach deeper water. With all the floating logs, that no longer struck him as such a good idea, and in any case, when he put the raft in the water it sprang a leak. Now he was in a bind. He hated to waste an expensive helicopter ride, so he grabbed some vials and waded waist-deep into the lake. It smelled and felt like a pulp-mill lagoon. He scooped water into the vials and waded back out. "Okay, let's get out of here," he said, and he and his team flew off. Within two days, his temperature spiked and he quaked with chills, but he had his samples.

Sedell and his crew visited Spirit Lake from June through September and the first Pulse. Like the land, the lake was alive with surprises. Nausea gave way to a kind of wonder, and the intellectual challenges of the work were absorbing. They quickly determined that, as on the Pumice Plain, the eruption had sterilized the lake. Its native phytoplankton and zooplankton were gone, the former starved for light in the black, stinking water, the latter starved for oxygen.

The blackness was a sign that the lake was enriched with tremendous amounts of nutrients from all the soil and animal carcasses and logs the wave had dragged into it. The blast cloud had not only knocked down the trees, it had also charred them. This charring freed the organic matter and chemical compounds stored in their living tissues, which had washed into the basin. Sedell and his crew saw some of the highest concentrations of dissolved chemicals anyone had ever recorded in a freshwater system. The level of manganese was 815 times higher than it had been prior to the eruption, the level of phosphates 248 times higher, iron 193 times, and chloride 85 times. There was 60 times as much dissolved organic carbon, and higher concentrations of suspended particulate carbon (that is, floating bits and pieces of bark or soil). The water was more acidic than previously, dropping from its previous near-neutral pH of 7.35 to 6.21—the equivalent of human urine.

What organisms could possibly thrive in this environment? Sedell enlisted John Baross from Oregon State to help him find out. An oceanographer, Baross did not seem the obvious choice to study a mountain lake, but he specialized in extremophiles: microbes that live near hot ocean vents or in extremely salty places. He also spent a good deal of his spare time speculating about what life might look like on other planets. This was a perfect background for studying the alien landscape of Mount St. Helens and its curdling cesspool, Spirit Lake.

Sedell and the lake team showed that the biological dynamics of Spirit Lake were the complete reverse of those on the land surrounding it. The land was barren. There was nothing in the Pumice Plain except some dead spiders and beetles, and one year later, a single flowering plant. In the Blowdown Zone, although Franklin, MacMahon, Crisafulli, and others thrilled to the discovery of individual plant and animal survivors, they still spoke of occupancy rates in tenths of a percent, or at most 4 or 6 percent. Spirit Lake stank with life. In the absence of organisms that derived their energy from photosynthesis, such as phytoplankton and algae, chemosynthetic bacteria reigned, drawing energy from the rich chemical soup of the lake waters. By late June, just a few drops of water held five million microbes. For weeks the lake veritably bubbled with their activity.

The community underwent rapid shifts as different groups of bacteria worked their way through different energy sources, flourishing for a time and then dying back. The first to thrive were microbes that feasted on carbon-based compounds. These quickly decomposed and oxidized much of the organic matter in the lake. Through their activity they depleted the lake's supply of dissolved oxygen. By July, the lake was anoxic, save for the top few feet, where wind stirred in minute amounts of oxygen from the air. The only microbes capable of surviving in such conditions are anaerobic bacteria and protozoans, among other more primitive life-forms. But those that could live lived well. Other types of bacteria increased through the summer and fall, oxidizing the iron, manganese, and sulfur ions the volcano had dumped into the lake in bulk. Methanogens reduced carbon dioxide to methane, which bubbled to the surface as a gas. Baross estimated that every gallon of water contained more than one quadrillion bacteria. The densities were the highest ever recorded in the field.

Some of these species were of interest for more than academic reasons. Like Sedell, more than two dozen other scientists who worked around the lake suffered from a mysterious, flu-like illness, as did a visiting photographer from *National Geographic* magazine. Their symptoms were a temperature, a cough, and a general feeling of weakness. They took to calling their collective ailments Red Zone fever. It became a joke, a badge of honor, to be physically sickened by the mountain. This ailment was eventually suggested to be a mild form of infection by *Legionella*, the genus of bacteria that causes Legionnaires' disease. Spirit Lake's warm, turbid water was an excellent incubator for *Legionella*, and seven *Legionella* species were found in it, including two previously undescribed strains. These were isolated and named *Legionella sainthelensi* and *L. spiritensis* to commemorate their origins.

———

When the first Pulse ended, Sedell's intensive involvement at Spirit Lake ended with it. Years later he would have a hard time saying why he left. Maybe it was the Red Zone fever, or maybe it was because the place was impossible to reach without a helicopter, and he liked to feel more at home at his study sites. For the next couple of years, a few members of the lakes team flew out to take samples when they had the free time and the resources, but those visits were sporadic; they had collected most of the data they needed in that first summer.

Sedell himself was drawn back to the fast, cold, cleaner waters of the Andrews Forest. Mount St. Helens had let him test some theories about what ecological recovery would look like and the processes he would find in disturbed habitats. It was time to immerse himself once again in old-growth forests and the question of how their management affected streams and, in turn, salmon. Like Franklin, he became a central figure in the Pacific Northwest forest wars, helping, as the representative fish biologist, to develop what would become the Northwest Forest Plan. He participated in the Pacific Northwest Forest Summit in Portland in April

1993. Besuited and clean-shaven, no longer a longhair, he sat one chair away from Vice President Al Gore, with Jerry Franklin between them. He spoke of the importance of forest watersheds to salmon, arguing that when you manage a forest, you are also managing the fish. President Bill Clinton later sent him a letter thanking him for his testimony.

After the Northwest Forest Plan was adopted in 1994, Sedell's career followed the track of an adept and upwardly mobile public administrator. He left the Andrews to become the director of Wildlife, Fish, Water, and Air Research at the US Forest Service, a position that obligated him to move for a time to Washington, DC. A couple of years after that, he was asked to direct the Forest Service's Pacific Southwest Research Station in California. In that role he was in charge of forests and projects in California, Hawaii, and throughout the Pacific, with a staff of more than four hundred. He was good at the job, working to implement what he considered positive change. He helped to establish an experimental forest reserve in Hawaii, one much like the Andrews in spirit if not in species, and considered this one of his finest accomplishments.

Sedell did not visit Mount St. Helens again until 2005, when he came back for that year's Pulse. It was an emotional return. To see the mountain again was almost as much a revelation as it had been twenty-five years before. He realized how much he missed mucking around the blast area, reveling in the strangeness of the lakes. At one lake north of Spirit Lake, the water had been so full of sediment that it had the consistency of tar; he was almost able to walk on the gummy surface. At another, he had scrambled over masses of fallen old-growth logs to see the lake underneath, almost as though it was looking back at him. He remembered the colors. One small lake was light brown from all the organic nutrients; another was green from ash deposited in it.

After just two decades, everything had changed. In 1980, the land had been bleak and it was the lakes that were alive, but now their older relationship was closer to being restored. All the lakes were clear and blue, even Spirit Lake. Their shores were thickly greened not just with nascent vegetation but with small trees. Could he have foreseen this on his first visit? Hardly. But that was what had made it so wonderful.

Sedell died of cancer a few years after his final visit to Mount St. Helens, at the age of sixty-eight. His colleagues remembered him as one of the most energetic and innovative stream ecologists they had ever known. A catalyst's catalyst, they had called him. "Drive, nuggets!" he had cried to his crews, pumping his fists, and drive they had. He had urged them all to work with the larger narratives of the mountain in mind. "What's the story?" he often asked, encouraging everyone to gather the strands of their inchoate impressions and spin them into a cogent tale. If some of the exactness was lost, that was fine. It was better to be exciting, because there was a story at the volcano, and they were the only ones telling it, so they had not only to get it correct, but also to make it true.

9

THE TUNNEL

JIM SEDELL AND his team may have been able to describe the state of Spirit Lake within a few months of the eruption, but the lake was not at all close to being settled. The debris avalanche had raised its surface by almost two hundred feet; the deepest sediments of its new bottom were at a higher elevation than its old surface had been. The lake had also nearly doubled in area and now covered more than 2,200 acres, or about four square miles, spreading out like an amoeba to swallow up land. Because of this it was shallower—110 feet deep at most—with large, lurking shoals of debris. The first surveyors to try to map its new contours described their efforts as "uncertain." How could they be otherwise, with the interred remains of Mount St. Helens shifting underwater, or piling up on the northernmost shores?

The changing features of Spirit Lake added to greater uncertainties. Its old outlet through the North Fork Toutle had been plugged. When the first winter storms arrived in late October, they brought rain and snow in abundance, and the lake began to rise. By the spring of 1981, the surface was thirty-nine feet higher than it had been the year before, and the lake's volume had increased almost 30 percent. The following spring, the volume had increased another 40 percent, and the surface had risen another 24 feet, to 3,458 feet in elevation. The top of the debris pile that dammed the lake was only 74 feet away. The debris dam had an average thickness of 276 feet, but it ranged from less than 30 feet in places to well over 500 feet through the heart of the lake's old channel. The dam was made of boulders, rocks, gravel, and sand from the mountain's north flank, with tephra mixed in from the ash plume. All of this was perilously compacted and prone to erosion.

In this new landscape, the rising of Spirit Lake spurred that oldest of human urges: to stand athwart an inexorable natural force and tell it to stop. Personnel from the US Army Corps of Engineers had been warily watching Spirit Lake even as they were kept busy elsewhere, clearing the Toutle and Cowlitz Rivers of logs and mud to lessen the flood risk, and sucking up silt from the Columbia River, where commercial ship traffic had been brought to a standstill for several months. Now they worried that Spirit Lake would overtop the debris dam. Their models predicted that the lake would be just fifty feet below the dam's crest in 1983 if annual rains were at normal levels; if it rained just a little more than usual, the lake would rise to within forty feet of the crest.

Geological precedents were not encouraging. Since its formation more than three thousand years before, Spirit Lake had periodically breached its natural dams, draining suddenly and violently, and then slowly refilling in the centuries that followed. Such an event in the distant past was interesting for academics to ponder, but were the dam to fail now, the towns of Toutle and Toledo down on the Cowlitz could be swamped by a lahar bigger than the ones caused by the eruption. Engineers wrote ominously of a wall of mud more than forty feet tall crashing down at seventy miles per hour. No one knew precisely what the damage would be, but it was sure to be catastrophic.

To prevent such a disaster, in November 1982 Corps engineers set out to build a pumping station on the south shore of Spirit Lake. It was to be the largest human intervention into the heart of the blast area, and the first since the new national volcanic monument had been designated a couple of months before. Scientists had hoped that the mountain's natural processes and features would have been allowed to continue unimpeded by human activity, but one could not be a zealot about such things, so workers hauled in mobile offices and bulldozers and cleared a landing pad for a helicopter. They drove twenty massive diesel-powered water pumps by truck across the Pumice Plain and floated them on a barge 150 feet long. Heavy logs from the log mat were chained together end to end to form a boom that would protect the pumps. A pipeline more than three thousand feet long was installed to carry the water to the North Fork Toutle. Once all the pumps were operational, they sucked more than eighty thousand gallons of water per minute from the lake.

"The likelihood of a breakout is very, very small," Hugh Fowler, the Washington director of emergency services, told the *New York Times*. "We have Army Corps of Engineers pumping to thank for that." But this fix, everyone also understood, was not permanent. Corps engineers knew they had two choices in the long term: they could either dig a new channel through the debris avalanche and let Spirit Lake drain that way, or they could excavate a long tunnel under one of the rocky ridges that bordered the lake. Digging a channel through the debris dam threatened to destabilize it further, so they opted for a tunnel. The next question was which way to dig it. Should they bore under Windy Ridge and divert the lake east, so that water would drop down to Clearwater Creek and ultimately flow into the Lewis River? Or should they send the water west, under the recently rechristened Harry's Ridge? (It was named after Harry Truman, the cantankerous proprietor of the Mount St. Helens Lodge who had refused to evacuate and was killed in the eruption.) Then the lake would leave through the North Fork, as it had before.

Political challenges exacerbated the engineering ones. By 1982, word had spread of Sedell's findings on the diverse community of bacteria in Spirit Lake's soupy waters. In addition to the *Legionella*, researchers had detected another pathogen, *Klebsiella pneumoniae*, which causes a range of diseases, from severe pneumonia to gastroenteritis to urinary tract infections. Also, lest anyone forget—and few had—the water contained a range of toxic chemical pollutants and heavy metals left behind from the eruption. Who could say what else might be lurking in the lake? (While no one was aware of it at the time, *Naegleria fowleri* would be found in the lake in a 1987 survey. *N. fowleri* is an amoeba that infects the human brain and causes primary amoebic meningoencephalitis, or PAM. The species is known colloquially as the brain-eating amoeba.)

No township was eager to receive Spirit Lake's grim effluent. Communities east and west of Mount St. Helens jostled with one another. "You take the water now," the westside officials said. "No, *you* keep taking it," the eastside officials responded. Corps managers knew that whichever way they sent the hazardous lake water, they would have to assure restive communities that no one would turn strange colors or come down with awful diseases. In January 1983, soon after pumping had begun, they asked one of their limnologists, Doug Larson, to figure out how to convince everyone that Spirit Lake was safe.

———

Doug Larson was a tall fellow originally from Illinois. He had earned his PhD from Oregon State University for work on a system of lakes around Crater Lake, and he later spent years at loggerheads with national park administrators there over leaky septic tanks and possible sewage contamination of the lake's crystalline waters. For his doggedness in the face of bureaucratic inertia, he reckons, he became something of an enemy of the people, in those parts at least. It would not be the last time.

Larson visited Spirit Lake with Jim Sedell's crew during the first Pulse in 1980, although not as part of their team. He liked the scientists from the Andrews well enough, but he was skeptical of their broader research motives. He felt the Forest Service folks had come to Mount St. Helens in search of a threshold of acceptable destruction: to discover how much people could do to the land and get away with. The plant and animal survivors they had found only reinforced an institutional predilection to believe that landscapes could absorb a lot of punishment and still recover.

Now, charged with collecting samples from the lake every few weeks and analyzing them, Larson demurred. A few bottles of water, he told his supervisors, were hardly enough to reveal Spirit Lake's dynamic physical, chemical, and biological properties. What was needed was a proper limnological workup to identify emerging chemical or biological hazards before they became real problems. He would have to come to the lake year-round, not just during the summer months as Sedell's team had done. It was not merely a question of his professional desires, he said—it was a question of ensuring that the Corps complied with federal directives. "Yielding to these directives," he would later write, "the Corps finally approved the program in April 1983."

Having extracted concessions from one federal behemoth, he faced down another. Although he received no money from the Forest Service, the agency, in its capacity as caretaker of the new national monument, had jurisdiction over how he pursued his work. This led to occasional friction. During his first year at Spirit Lake, Larson decided he needed a semipermanent lab structure. With all the dust blowing around, his water chemistry protocols were impossible to adhere to en plein air. He went to his supervisors at the Corps and got their permission to install a field lab on the Pumice Plain. Shortly afterward, a helicopter flew a small Quonset hut to the lake's south shore. Larson built up a low earth berm around it and added six hundred sandbags to anchor it. Filling and refilling sandbags would become his main pastime. He started to ask any visitors to bring ten full sandbags with them. Sandbags were the currency, the price of admission. "No sandbags, no helicopter boarding pass," he would say.

Forest Service managers complained that Larson's hut was an eyesore. The point of the monument, they argued, was to preserve the volcanic landscape as an aesthetic space as well as a research space. He was asked to paint the hut to make it visually inconspicuous. Camouflage it, he was told. Fine, Larson said. Complying with the letter of the Forest Service directive, he painted the hut in US Army regulation colors meant for forested terrain—a livery of greens and browns that was visible for miles across the gray plains.

The need for a drainage tunnel and Larson's scientific ambitions led to a shift in the research trajectory at Spirit Lake. Sedell's team had dwelt primarily on the lake's chemistry and bacteriology—the things that were, bizarrely, there. Larson wanted to learn more about what was not there: the phytoplankton, zooplankton, and algae that might come back, that would indicate the lake had returned to a state one might call normal. This is not to say no one had been looking for phytoplankton before, only that very few were around to be detected. Where John Baross's bacterial numbers could be expressed in quadrillions of cells per drop of water, a survey in August 1980 had yielded precisely 259 phytoplankton per ounce of water. Another sample taken later in October found 260 phytoplankton. Spirit Lake was still dark and bubbling and anoxic—hardly the optimal home for organisms that need light and oxygen.

Over the next two years, bacteria had continued to proliferate, while the number of phytoplankton somehow became, as one biologist characterized it, "even more pathetic." Single samples taken in 1981 and 1982 both yielded fewer than one single cell per ounce of water, but change was coming. A pair of samples in July of 1982 showed three types of zooplankton: rotifers, copepods, and cladocerans. There were close to six hundred cladocerans per ounce of water—not a quadrillion, but not zero, either.

What was responsible for this slightest of revivals, Larson inferred, was the twofold effect of rain and snow. Precipitation not only raised the lake level but also diluted the water. As the concentrations of organic matter decreased, the water cleared, and light could reach deeper into it. Before the eruption, Spirit Lake's water had been almost preternaturally pellucid. Water clarity is measured with a Secchi disk, a device named for the Italian astronomer who invented it in 1865. Eight inches in diameter and patterned black and white, the Secchi disk is tossed over the side of a boat and sunk until it is no longer visible—a point called the Secchi depth. In the mid-1970s, Secchi depths at Spirit Lake ranged from thirty-five feet to forty-six feet. (Water clarity can vary with the seasons.) When Sedell's group dropped their Secchi disk into the lake on June 30, 1980, it vanished only few inches from the surface. But when Larson dropped the Secchi disk into the lake in 1983, it was visible nearly thirteen feet deep. With the water like this, the light-loving organisms might return.

All the while, the pumps kept extracting water, helping the lake water turn over. The log mat, still drifting over the lake surface, made studying Spirit Lake a real challenge. Larson had thought Sedell and his team were nuts for trying to use rubber rafts to get around. He would not be so foolish. He told the Corps he needed a real boat, one sturdy enough to endure the occasional collision with a submerged trunk. He was given an aged fiberglass cabin cruiser, which lasted less than a month before a log cracked its hull. Larson filed a complaint and asked for a more suitable vessel. A steel-hulled boat called *Traveler* was helicoptered out. *Traveler* was twenty-six feet long, with a metal cage that encased its propeller and rudder. It had been designed to survey rivers in the Midwest, where it had performed admirably. Larson was assured that *Traveler* was the most robust, leakproof, and unsinkable boat in the Corps' fleet.

By his own admission, Larson was hard on *Traveler*. He bounced off logs during his regular circuits of the lake and was obliged from time to time to ram through the log raft. *Thump, thump, thump* went the logs against the leakproof hull. By October the hull had developed such a collection of minute fissures that Larson had to pump water for more than half an hour every time he wanted to take *Traveler* out.

In spite of this regular punishment, *Traveler* was hardier than the cabin cruiser, and Larson was getting a lot of work done. Then, one day in November, he was out when the wind shifted. Within ten minutes, logs blew in from elsewhere on the lake and surrounded him. *Thump, thump, thump* went the logs against *Traveler*. Then came a new sound: *crack, crack*. Then *gurgle, gurgle, gurgle*. *Traveler* started to settle at the stern and list to port. The lake was more than ninety feet deep where Larson was, and the water 46°F—cold enough to induce hypothermia within minutes were he to abandon ship. He radioed his Corps colleagues at the pump station to ask for help. With their helicopter hovering nearby to pluck him from the lake if need be, Larson piloted through the log mat to open water and gunned the engine. The contest of horsepower and buoyancy with gravity ended in what might best be called a draw when the unsinkable *Traveler* got stuck in the lake bottom a few yards from shore. Larson jumped out and waded the rest of the way to safety.

Traveler would travel no more. In April 1984, the boat was helicoptered out of Spirit Lake and decommissioned. A couple of months after that, Corps engineers brought in a rotary tunneling machine they called the Mole. (Given the locale, Gopher might have been a more appropriate nickname.) The Mole began to bore under Harry's Ridge on the lake's western shore, opening a way for the lake to drain into the North Fork Toutle River. Thirteen months later, on May 6, 1985, the Spirit Lake Outlet Tunnel was completed and opened. It was more than 8,500 feet long and 11 feet in diameter, with a negative slope of 1.063 percent. A regulating headgate in the lake prevented logs and other debris from clogging its intake, and it sent water to the South Fork Coldwater Creek at a peak flow of over four thousand gallons per minute. From there the water rushed on to join the North Fork. The surface of Spirit Lake would stay at 3,440 feet in elevation, give or take a few feet.

The project cost $13 million, but the tunnel had been bored through a complicated matrix of volcanic bedrock. Some of it was mostly volcanic tuff that was twenty-six to thirty-seven million years old. Atop the tuff were the remains of basalt and basaltic andesite lava flows. These were not stable rocks. Within the ridge, geologists had identified twelve faults and shear zones, five of them major, along the tunnel's plotted path. These would likely buckle and squeeze and twist the tunnel in the decades to come. Corps engineers had been aware of all of this, but the lake was rising, and they had to hurry. They would have to deal with problems as they came up.

––––

From 1983 through 1985, Larson had visited Spirit Lake more than one hundred times, but with the tunnel done and the water quality getting better, institutional priorities changed. The Corps no longer felt his intensive study was necessary. The money that had kept him afloat was diverted elsewhere.

Larson asked if he could keep coming. He had watched the lake go through what he would later describe as a "biological renaissance," from stinking bilge to its former clearness. He had found and identified 138 species of phytoplankton. The photosynthetic foundation of the food web was back in place. In 1980 and 1981, Sedell's team had debated how long it would be before the lake looked anything like it used to. In one paper they had speculated it would take one to two decades at least, but they had underestimated the lake's recuperative capacity. It took six years. A new Spirit Lake was rising, one that was a rough approximation of the old lake, but no one would be there to watch it like Larson had.

In a last gambit, Larson tried to convince the Forest Service to let him at least keep his research outpost. Maybe he could come out and work at it when he had days off, or during his vacations. Monument managers said no, and in 1986, the hut was taken down and helicoptered out.

Larson was happy with what he had managed to do even as he regretted work not done, such as studying nutrient cycling and figuring out a nutrient budget for the lake. But conditions had been awful, the work too haphazard, the lake too fraught with perils. Sometimes he had envied the ecologists who worked on the nearby land. They did not have to navigate the logs!

For the next nineteen years, Larson visited Spirit Lake whenever he could. In 1989, he found thousands of copepods and cladocerans in the water column. The first plants appeared: charophytes and Eurasian milfoil, an invasive species. (It had probably hitched a ride to the lake on ducks.) Small freshwater snails crawled along the milfoil.

Years later, he went back to the site of his old field hut and found it overgrown with tall cattails. The green was everywhere, covering a nice brown mud. He felt a slight pang now that all traces of his work had been erased, but it was nice to know the plants had taken over his space. They were, he thought, a most effective camouflage.

10

THE LOG MAT

JIM GAWEL, AN environmental chemist, squints from the stern of a small boat as it bobs just off Spirit Lake's southern shore. His hand rests on the handle of a puttering outboard motor. Sunny wavelets twinkle back at him, but he is unmoved by their cheer. "The logs aren't out yet," he says.

Ken Burkart, his student and field assistant, nods as he moves some boxes around. "Yeah," he says. "Yet."

"Hmm," Gawel says. The southwest wind last night was strong, and the logs were bunched up in the lake's northeastern arm, with a few strays scattered elsewhere. Now the wind has died to a light breeze. The logs from here look like a white film atop the water, but Gawel can see that the main mat is already breaking up. "Well, we'll do what we can," he says, and twists the outboard's throttle. The motor's putter climbs to a high whine. Gawel points the boat away from shore to the right, toward a pocket of the lake known as Duck Bay. As the boat slops along, he sits slouched in thought, his long legs arranged around piles of equipment. His short, sandy hair peeps out from under his ball cap and fidgets in the wind. He has a lot to do and an uncertain amount of time in which to do it.

About a quarter of a mile ahead, tucked in the shadow of Windy Ridge, four white domes that look like small tents sit on the lake. Two are paired; the other two sit alone among small groups of logs that form almost a perfect square. The farthest dome floats next to two large logs that jut out of the lake at forty-five-degree angles. As the boat pulls up to this arrangement, Gawel glances back at the log mat, although from this vantage a hillside conceals almost all of it. "Logs," he says, and chuckles. "Always such a pain in the ass."

Gawel is a professor at the University of Washington in Tacoma. Around 2004, he had just taken the job and was casting about for projects when he met Charlie Crisafulli, who was looking for someone to carry on the research at Spirit Lake. Doug Larson had officially retired from the Army Corps of Engineers in 1993. Although he had made occasional trips in the years since, he had lately started to spend more time adding to the vast model railroad empire in his basement when he was not writing barbed critiques about the Corps in magazines.

Crisafulli did not want Spirit Lake to go unstudied. The year before, he had gone out to gather data on water chemistry, phytoplankton, zooplankton, and amphibians, but he could not do everything himself; he was stretched thin enough. He invited Gawel to the Pulse scheduled for the summer of 2005. It would be a big one, Crisafulli promised—the twenty-fifth anniversary after the eruption, with lots of people talking about lots of projects. Surely Gawel could find something that interested him.

Gawel went to the Pulse and had a grand old time. By day he toured Mount St. Helens and the blast area and Spirit Lake. By night he sat in a camp chair in front of a big fire at Tower Rock, drinking beer and listening to stories. He thought about what he could add to the posteruption research. Studying Spirit Lake would be a new gambit for him. He was an experienced climber and spent a lot of time in the mountains, but he had never studied an alpine lake. For his PhD work at the Massachusetts Institute of Technology, he had focused on dirtier water: the waterways of Boston, laden with arsenic and heavy metals. "Nasty, nasty rivers," he says of them. "Ones that I would not dare set foot in." But as he basked in the warmth of the fire and loosely attended the chatter of the other scientists, he decided he could stand to diversify. It might also be nice to work in clean water for a change.

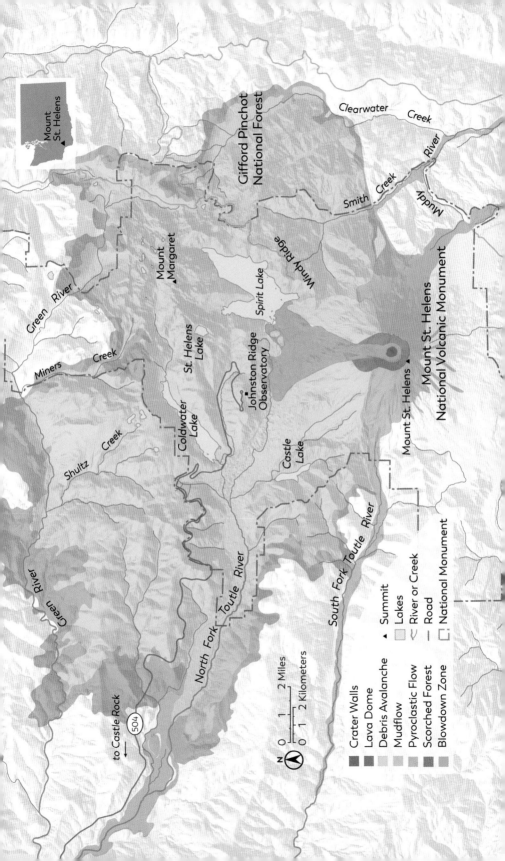

Mount St. Helens

to Castle Rock
504

Green River

North Fork Toutle River

South Fork Toutle River

Shultz Creek

Green River

Miners Creek

Coldwater Lake

St. Helens Lake

Johnston Ridge Observatory

Castle Lake

Mount Margaret

Spirit Lake

Windy Ridge

Gifford Pinchot National Forest

Clearwater Creek

Smith Creek

Muddy River

Mount St. Helens

Mount St. Helens National Volcanic Monument

N

0   1   2 Miles
0   1   2 Kilometers

▲ Summit
Lakes
Ⅴ River or Creek
— Road
⌐ ¬ National Monument

Crater Walls
Lava Dome
Debris Avalanche
Mudflow
Pyroclastic Flow
Scorched Forest
Blowdown Zone

Above: Mount St. Helens and Spirit Lake in 1968, twelve years before the eruption. The mountain then was 9,677 feet in elevation and surrounded by conifer forests, while Spirit Lake was a popular summer vacation destination, with cabins and lodges dotting its shore. Photograph courtesy of the US Forest Service.

Opposite: Mount St. Helens erupting on the afternoon of May 18, 1980. Pumice and ash billow from the new crater, while mudflows spill down the mountain's slopes. Photograph by Austin Post, courtesy of the US Geological Survey.

The Pumice Plain in front of Mount St. Helens in September 1980. Created by pyroclastic flows, the pumice was up to 120 feet deep in places. Plant and animal colonization would take longer here than in the other disturbance zones. Photograph by Lyn Topinka, courtesy of the US Geological Survey.

Fallen trees flattened during the lateral blast litter the Blowdown Zone near Mount St. Helens. The eruption left a complex mosaic of disturbance zones that covered more than 230 square miles around the mountain. Photograph by James Hughes, courtesy of the US Forest Service.

Fred Swanson makes a note after measuring the depth of the blast deposit near
Mount St. Helens. A geologist with the US Forest Service, Swanson was one of the
first scientists to visit the blast area after the eruption and ultimately helped pave
the way for ecologists to see it shortly thereafter. Photograph by James Hughes,
courtesy of the US Forest Service.

The debris avalanche deposits spread out from Mount St. Helens, as seen in September 1980. These were formed when the summit collapsed at the start of the eruption and extend fourteen miles down the valley of the North Fork Toutle River. Photograph by R. L. Schuster, courtesy of the US Geological Survey.

Ash covers fallen trees in part of the Blowdown Zone. After the debris avalanche came to rest and the lateral blast cloud raced over the land, several inches of ash and pumice drifted down from the Plinian column over the landscape for the next several hours. Photograph courtesy of the US Forest Service.

Top: Fireweed above Spirit Lake. Ecologists visiting the blast area for the first time after the eruption expected to find nothing but devastation, but small fireweed shoots were already poking up through the ash. Photograph courtesy of the US Forest Service.

Above left: Ecologist Jim Sedell from Oregon State University clambers over fallen trees to get water samples from a lake in the blast area after the eruption. Photograph by Sarah Greene, courtesy of the H. J. Andrews Experimental Forest research program.

Above right: Bob Lucas (front) and John Weinheimer measure rainbow trout caught during a survey of Spirit Lake in 2000. The two state biologists first detected trout in the lake in 1993. Who introduced the fish is unknown. Photograph courtesy of Charlie Crisafulli.

A patch of prairie lupine near Windy Pass, just northeast of Mount St. Helens. Prairie lupine was the first species of plant known to colonize the Pumice Plain, its traits uniquely suited to the hot, dry habitat. Photograph by the author.

Top: The southern arm of Spirit Lake as seen from Windy Ridge in 1985. During the eruption, thousands of fallen trees were washed into the lake by a giant wave, creating an enormous log mat. Photograph by Ted Quackenbush, Wikimedia.

Bottom: The log mat at Spirit Lake in 2012. Initially, the mat covered about 40 percent of the lake's surface. Many logs have since sunk to the bottom, but the mat still covers about 25 percent of the surface. Photograph by Stephan Schulz, Wikimedia.

Left: US Forest Service biologist Charlie Crisafulli holds a northern pocket gopher he caught in the Bean Creek drainage near Mount St. Helens. Crisafulli has been studying the ecological response of animals and plants to the eruption since 1980. Photograph by the author.

Below: A northern pocket gopher peers out of a tunnel. Pocket gophers managed to survive the eruption in their burrows, shielded from the most devastating effects. Their subsequent digging helped mix the inorganic blast deposits with buried soils, spurring plant growth. Photograph courtesy of Charlie Crisafulli.

Mount St. Helens as seen from the outer edge of the Blowdown Zone. After the eruption, the lateral blast cloud left a fringe of dead trees, seared by its heat but left standing. Photograph courtesy of the US Forest Service.

Top: The North Fork Toutle River, seen from the east looking toward Mount St. Helens. More than with other rivers, the eruption dramatically changed the North Fork, producing billions of cubic yards of sediment that decades later continues to be washed into the river and transported downstream. Photograph courtesy of the US Geological Survey.

Bottom: A herd of bull elk on the Pumice Plain. More than 1,500 elk are estimated to have been killed in the eruption, along with thousands of other large mammals. Elk are highly mobile, though, and were soon making tentative forays into the blast area. Their movements helped break up the blast deposits, making it easier for plants to grow. Photograph courtesy of Charlie Crisafulli.

Above: Mount St. Helens seen from the west over the debris avalanche deposits in the early spring. This area of the debris avalanche, known as the hummocks, has dozens of ponds that host scores of amphibians and aquatic invertebrates. Photograph by the author.

Next page: Mount St. Helens in midsummer, view of the crater from the summit of Mount Margaret, with Spirit Lake in the foreground, nearly forty years after the 1980 eruption. Photograph by the author.

The Spirit Lake Gawel first beheld in 2005 was in the midst of its reversion to its earlier physical state. The black, frothing dreck Sedell had jumped into had been steadily replaced with the water Larson had struggled to boat across, once again cold and for the most part clear. But the biology of Spirit Lake was on a different path. In the last paper Larson published, he had shown that chlorophyll *a* levels were as much as two orders of magnitude greater than they had been in 1974. (Scientists use chlorophyll *a* as a proxy for primary productivity.) The lake was no longer oligotrophic, with few plants but abundant oxygen. It had become eutrophic, richer in nutrients, and so capable of supporting a wider cast of life, its bottom thick with plants.

This developing biological richness gave Gawel a place to start. One of the first things he wanted to do was put together hydrologic and nutrient budgets for the entire lake system, adding up what goes in, what goes out, and what stays. This would entail calculating every input, from the streams and groundwater and rains and snowmelt that fed the lake to the nutrients that drifted down out of the sky. All those inputs he would weigh against the water that drained out via the Corps of Engineers' tunnel and the phytoplankton, zooplankton, insects, amphibians, fish (although Spirit Lake had been fishless until the early 1990s, when rainbow trout mysteriously appeared), and other living things in the water, all of which represented nutrient outputs and reservoirs.

Beginning in 2008, Gawel began to document and diagram Spirit Lake's various flows and fluxes. The work introduced him to what he calls "adventure science." Adventure science meant schlepping heavy gear, like air tanks, for miles down narrow, brushy trails so he could scuba dive and do plant surveys. Adventure science meant reaching the end of the trail, finding out the tanks were not needed, and having to turn right around and haul them back up to the road. Adventure science, Gawel says, might best be summed up as "Things go wrong." He has since appended a corollary: "Duct tape or electrical tape can fix almost any problem."

To his title of environmental engineer and chemist, Gawel now added *ecological accountant*. He consulted a nationwide modeling study to determine how much atmospheric nitrogen was entering the lake each year (nutrient input). He measured the flows of the creeks and streams that ran to Spirit Lake from Mount St. Helens, the Pumice Plain, and the Mount Margaret Backcountry (nutrient input). He suspended small sediment traps from the lake bottom to sample the materials sinking from the surface (nutrient output). He and his students boated around the lake towing mesh nets to catch phytoplankton and zooplankton (nutrient reservoirs). They put out insect traps to see what bugs were emerging (nutrient output). They worked with Crisafulli, who crept on hands and knees over the shoreline looking for salamanders, frogs, and toads once they had metamorphosed and crawled or hopped onto the land (nutrient output). Crisafulli also was monitoring the rainbow trout (nutrient reservoir).

When Gawel had corralled all the values he thought he needed, he was dismayed to find they did not quite add up. The actual levels of phosphorus and nitrogen in the lake were much higher than he could account for. Some other source was contributing nutrients, but Gawel could not for the life of him figure out what it was. *I'm an engineer and a chemist*, he would grouse to himself, *and here I am having to worry about biology!* But Spirit Lake was as beautiful as it was occasionally frustrating.

Flummoxed, Gawel went to a conference to present his findings. He sketched the dynamics of the lake so far as he could tell and took the audience through his methods and results. Then he explained his dilemma: the mystery of the surplus nutrients. Where were they coming from? He said he would welcome any ideas and opened the floor to questions.

Someone raised a hand. "What about the log mat?" the person asked.

"What about it?" Gawel said.

"Well," the person said, "don't you think all those logs are probably covered with biofilm?"

Gawel thought for a moment. "Yeah," he said. "Yeah, I bet they are." Inwardly he thought, *Well, shit.*

Gawel had been going out of his way to avoid the logs. They had already shown a knack for smashing his instruments and sending them in pieces to the depths. Also, he had heard enough stories of Larson getting trapped by logs and nearly crushed. The logs struck him as a sinister force: abiotic, bleached white, drifting, dead. But now he considered them. Why would the undersides of tens of thousands of big trunks, so waterlogged after three decades that they could not even roll over, *not* be slick with the green, sticky slime of bacteria, fungi, and other microorganisms that make up biofilm? All the signs had been there, right under his nose. In the summers the log mat was often confined to the northeastern corner of the lake. Jostled by the winds, the logs rubbed and ground together. The northeastern corner was where he had found some of the highest concentrations of phosphorus. In that grinding, biofilm must be getting scraped off the logs and sinking to the lake bottom.

Resolving to study the logs was a lot easier than doing it. To access them when they were penned in one of the lake's northern arms was out of the question. There were no trails to those parts of the lake. Even if he could get down there somehow, wading among the logs and trying to attach things to them would be far too dangerous. He might as well save himself the trouble and just snap his own femurs. Maybe if he could take a boat out on the lake and catch a couple of isolated logs, he could work with them that way. He waited until the wind was low and the water calm and the logs adrift, and then he boated out. He felt like a jackal, or some other small, unwisely ambitious predator trying to isolate an enormous, weakened water buffalo from a herd of its violent compatriots.

Gawel had two gaps to fill to balance his nutrient budget. First, he needed to know how much biofilm was on the logs (nutrient reservoir); and second, how much biofilm fell off the logs and settled to the lake bottom (nutrient input). For the first question, he paddled out to some of the bigger logs, selected several at random, rocked them until they flipped over—which turned out to be incredibly hard to do—and cut out two-inch squares. From these squares he found that the undersides of the logs were positively fuzzy with biofilm. He took each square back to his lab, analyzed it, and was able to extrapolate a value for the entire log mat.

The second question was trickier. For this Gawel wanted to attach a small water bottle under a log to act as a sediment trap. Capturing a log and stringing the bottle under it would be easy enough, but then he had to set the log free and find a way to get the bottle back after a week or two. This proposition was much more dicey.

Gawel paddled out and found three candidate logs. From each he strung a water bottle and a bright orange flag on a pole, the kind cyclists use to increase their visibility in traffic. The poles were nearly five feet tall. Surely the flags would be visible from almost anywhere, and he would have no trouble finding the logs and tracking their progress around the lake. But the logs, as is their way, did not cooperate. After Gawel affixed his flags and pushed the logs away, they were swallowed up in the log mat. When he hiked to the lake a few days later and scanned what he could see of the mat with binoculars, his flags were nowhere to be found.

Gawel despaired at ever finding his logs again, but a month later, he was down on the south shore when he happened to see a bleached and tattered flag fluttering from a log in the middle of the lake. He paddled out and was able to retrieve his water bottle from underneath the log. Over the next few weeks the other two flags also reappeared, and he was able to collect those traps, too. All were full of green scum.

The log mat made up at least part of his mysterious nutrient source. The logs were dead, yet they were adding a significant quantity of biofilm. That realization stirred Gawel's curiosity further. He could calculate the amount of biofilm produced and shed by individual logs, but how did the logs collectively affect the lake? Perhaps the whole was greater still than the sum of its parts. He would need to return to his engineering roots to explore the question. He still had an engineer's love of tinkering and jerry-rigging. If working on the log mat in its entirety was out of the question, he would wrangle free-floating logs over to a corner of the lake and chain them together. He would make a log mat of his very own. How hard could it be?

Log Mat East—the little log mat Gawel and Burkart are visiting today—is made up of thirteen logs: nine large trunks surrounded by four even larger ones that form a square pen around them, linked at the corners with chains that weigh thirty pounds apiece. "Gathering them was no picnic," Gawel says. On windless days, when the logs dispersed according to the random patterns of Brownian motion, he kayaked out with a heavy cable and a battery-powered drill. When he found a likely log, he drilled a hole in it, attached an eyebolt, and wrangled it over to Duck Bay. He collected the logs until he had two sixteen-foot-square mats. The labor was pure adventure science. "Somehow, whenever you're building a log mat and wouldn't mind having some logs around," he says, "there aren't any logs anywhere near you."

Gawel can now ask questions about how insects are using his log mat and how much biofilm it generates. Among their several tasks today, he and Burkart also have to come up with a way to help the log mat survive the winter, when all the roads are closed and no one can reach Spirit Lake except by a twelve-mile snowshoe trek. At present it is chained to two big trunks that stick out of the lake, two of several such trees that were hurled through the air during the eruption. When they knifed into the lake, they plunged into the muddy bottom with such force that they stuck and stayed upright.

Gawel does not fear the main log mat crushing his creation in Duck Bay. "I don't think the mat ever really makes it down to this corner of the lake that much," he says. The bigger worry is how his mat will withstand the seasonal rises and falls in lake levels, buffered though they may be by the tunnel. "I'm assuming if we chain it with enough slack to the trunk"—he thumps the entrained log with his fist—"it should be here next spring." He grins. "Knock on wood, right?"

Sitting in the middle of the log mat is the small tent, a bug trap called a BugDorm. ("That's its official name," Gawel says. "It's legit.") With its black bottom half and white upper, the BugDorm entices bugs as they emerge from the water to fly to its apex, where their doom awaits in the form of a small bottle of alcohol. Gawel and Burkart put the tents out yesterday—the one here, one on Log Mat West, and the two anchored over open water—and they have to empty them today so they can count the contents and identify the species. "We used to leave them out for three days," Gawel says, "but the wind would blow them over and sink them, and then we'd lose the whole sample."

Gawel also wants to set out some little ceramic flowerpots at different depths to check biofilm growth rates under the mat. As he and Burkart measure out string, from somewhere on the Pumice Plain comes a high, loud screech. Burkart stops what he is doing. "What was that?" he asks.

"An elk bugling," Gawel says. "The bulls are gathering their harems." An answering bugle comes from the backcountry behind us, thinner and quieter for the distance. The first elk bugles back: *Skweeeeeeeeee-ump! Skweeeeeeeeee-ump!* Theirs is an eerie duet. Gawel spies the first bull on the plain and points out the herd, which has at least nine females. "They'll do this all day," he says. "You'll get used to it. Sometimes—"

"Jim," Burkart interrupts, pointing to Gawel's shoulder. "Spider."

"Gah," Gawel says. "They're just everywhere, always ballooning in." He frowns at a spot near his clavicle. Scrambling toward his exposed neck is a small spider. Gawel lets it crawl onto his index finger. "Off you go," he says, and flicks it over to the log mat. "I was going to say that sometimes this place can look pretty dead," he finishes while the spider lands and scuttles away. "But there's a lot going on." He has seen river otters sunning themselves on Log Mat West, and ospreys diving for fish. Caspian terns fly over every so often, sometimes at night. Several times when he has boated out he has surprised a bald eagle perched on the jammed log. Every year, the expanding willow thickets make the south shore a little greener.

Gawel and Burkart are still at work when the first logs drift into view. "Here they come," Burkart says. We can see only the tops of the larger ones and cannot tell whether smaller logs are floating with them. Their slow, swirling movements have a languid menace.

"That's our cue," Gawel says. Given the way the lake water circulates, the logs most likely will not drift over here, but they could make the return boat trip a little more exciting than it needs to be. Gawel yanks the outboard awake while Burkart loads up their equipment. They have set up what they can. Someday the last of these logs will sink and join the thousands of others, and Spirit Lake will go back to being an open lake, without all of its strange floating sentinels. But in the meantime there is no sense in tempting fate. Gawel pilots the boat away from his little mat so he can avoid the much larger one, and points the bow toward the shore. The logs are dead. Long live the logs.

FISH IN A FISHLESS LAKE

O NE OF JERRY FRANKLIN's favorite stories from the early days at Mount St. Helens is of a morning in July 1980, when he and Fred Swanson were flying around the blast area. Franklin asked the helicopter pilot to stop at Meta Lake. From the air the lake was a vivid patch of blue among a thatched mess of gray, but Franklin knew that the lake basin had been under about eight feet of snow when Mount St. Helens erupted. His working hypothesis was that the snowbank might have helped some of the smaller plants survive. (This working hypothesis, unlike some of his others, turned out to be supported.)

The pilot swung over to the lake, found a spot near it, and set down. Franklin and Swanson got out and waited for the clouds of ash to settle before tramping off through the fallen trees. The going was hard but also enlivening, the gray dappled with the green of short shrubs and young trees that had sprung up from under the snow's protective blanket. *Look at all those survivors!* Franklin thought. He could hardly wait to start sampling.

A couple of hours later, he and Swanson clambered back to the helicopter. The rule was that it had to stay with them all day in case the mountain "got any ideas," as Franklin would say. In addition to the pilot, a firefighter was also required to be along. "It was a waste of a seat," Franklin says, "but the government wanted to make sure none of us academics walked into the rotors." What that meant in practical terms was that while Franklin and Swanson were out and about, the pilot and firefighter had to occupy themselves as they saw fit.

On this trip, Franklin and Swanson returned to find the pilot and firefighter holding a bucket and looking pleased with themselves.

"What have you guys been up to?" Franklin asked.

"We were fishing," the pilot said.

"What? Fishing?" Franklin said. "No way."

"Yes, sir," the pilot said.

"Well, did you catch anything?" Franklin asked.

"Yes, sir," the pilot said.

"Show me," Franklin said. Ever the empiricist, he refused to believe claims without evidence.

The pilot grinned and held out the bucket. In the bottom were several small brook trout. Franklin gaped at the trout. The trout gaped at Franklin. "Give us a minute," Franklin said. He and Swanson walked down to the lakeshore. The water was dark and turbid, but when they looked they could see live crayfish scuttling over the bottom, and aquatic insects flitting about. The snow had not shielded just the shrubs and young trees from the blast cloud, they realized. The snow- and ice-covered lake was protected as well. The trout had probably been unaware of the violent happenings right over their heads, although they might have darted for the safety of the shadows when they felt the deep rumble beneath them.

Back at the helicopter, the pilot started the engines. The rotors began their slow, preparatory revolutions. Franklin climbed in and buckled up, gazing out the window as they lifted off, lost in thought. Fish in the blast area! What else would they find?

———

I am thinking of Franklin's account while I scramble down the Pumice Plain to Spirit Lake. As surprising as the survival of the brook trout had been, their initial presence in Meta Lake in the first place was just as remarkable. Fish rarely swim to high alpine lakes in the American West on their own, especially when, like brook trout, they are native to the eastern US and Canada. The trout caught by the helicopter crew were survivors from state stocking operations that dated back at least to the 1930s. In 1976 and 1979, biologists with the Washington Department of Game (now the Department of Fish and Wildlife) had airdropped, or "planted," 1,945 trout fry into the lake. A few months after Franklin and Swanson visited, a pair of state biologists paddled out in a raft and set a gill net baited with canned tuna. When they came back the next day and pulled in the net, they had caught thirty-five small brook trout.

Striding along ahead of me today is Charlie Crisafulli. He is bantering with Kate Culhane, Nina Ferrari, and Tara Blackman. Culhane and Ferrari, both in their early twenties, are Crisafulli's field crew this summer. Blackman, who is in her early thirties, has led Crisafulli's crews for the past six or seven years. She is, after Crisafulli, the old hand in these parts. The mid-September afternoon is sunny and unseasonably warm, and everyone is in good spirits. The four have spent the past couple of months ranging all over the blast area, capturing small mammals, counting birds at dawn, and measuring vegetation, among other grueling pursuits. Now they are about to spend a comparatively restful hour or so on one of Crisafulli's more idiosyncratic projects: monitoring the return of fish to a lake the eruption had rendered fishless.

Because of the natural barriers between them and neighboring rivers, few of the thirty-seven lakes around Mount St. Helens had fish prior to European settlement in the late nineteenth century. One that did was Spirit Lake. Great runs of coho salmon, sea-run coastal cutthroat trout, and steelhead swam from the Pacific Ocean to the Columbia River, up the Cowlitz and then the Toutle, and eventually into its North Fork. Other fish probably lived in the lake as well, but no one is certain, since few surveys were done before 1980, and none was comprehensive.

The one survey that could be called reasonably complete was the one from 1937 that Jim Sedell had mined for its scant information on phytoplankton and zooplankton. That survey had been less about finding fish than assessing Spirit Lake's suitability for additional fish stocking. State biologists had been planting rainbows in the lake since 1913, but they never seemed to reach the hoped-for length and girth. The survey suggested why: because the lake was oligotrophic, the trout did not have much to eat. The surveyor, Harlan Guy, concluded that Spirit Lake could support about a pound of fish per acre per year. Given the size of an average rainbow trout and the area Spirit Lake covered at the time, this added up to six hundred fish or so. Undeterred, state biologists planted forty thousand rainbow trout every year from 1951 to 1979. Absent certain geological developments, they probably would have planted rainbows in 1980, too.

———

Crisafulli, Blackman, Culhane, Ferrari, and I make our way through the willow thicket that fronts the shore of Spirit Lake, emerging near Duck Bay. In the middle of it floats Jim Gawel's Log Mat East. Larger logs are scattered around, both in the water and on land. Some have washed so high up the banks that they are crushing the willows. I ask Crisafulli how this is possible; the Spirit Lake Outlet Tunnel presumably drains the lake at a fairly constant rate. Crisafulli grimaces. During their most recent inspection, engineers with the Army Corps had discovered that the tunnel floor was heaving in one or two spots, shrinking its diameter from its usual eleven feet to seven feet. If it shrank too much more, the tunnel might not be able to keep the lake at a safe level during a big rain event, so in January 2016, the Corps had closed the tunnel to repair it. During that short time, Spirit Lake rose about eighteen feet. Logs floated up among the living trees. When the repairs were complete and the tunnel reopened, the lake drained back to its appointed level of 3,440 feet so fast that the logs were left marooned.

The tunnel incident spooked the Corps. Large gears in the bulky machinery of the federal government had begun to turn, to crank and smoke. There was talk of major repairs, or possibly drilling a second tunnel. Meetings were being held. A report had been commissioned from the National Academies of Sciences, Engineering, and Medicine. It was hard to say what would be decided, but Crisafulli was not optimistic. "The tunnel repairs were quite the shot across the bow," he says. "And knowing the Corps . . ." He trails off and shrugs. Perhaps an unmolested research space is not as sacrosanct as he likes to think it is, or should be.

Blackman, meanwhile, has found the sampling gear cached next to one of the logs. We each take a pole, tie a barbless hook on a line, and spread ourselves along the lakeshore.

"Do you go fishing a lot?" I ask.

"No, we never go fishing," Crisafulli says. "What we're doing is called 'hook-and-line sampling.'" He fiddles with his lure. "It's kind of a touchy subject."

Twenty or so yards away, Blackman smiles to herself and casts her line.

————

When Jim Sedell first came to Spirit Lake and peered into its murk, it was evident that every single fish that might have been in the lake was dead. That was not true of all the lakes in the area. Throughout the summers of 1981 and 1982, state biologists visited eighteen lakes formerly stocked with rainbow, cutthroat, and brook trout. They found surviving fish in twelve of them. Most were stunted and in poor condition, but their mere presence was heartening. It was as if the decision to stock the lakes was somehow validated by the trout's luck and hardy constitution. They belonged in the landscape as much as the fireweed, the pocket gopher, or the lupine, having lived through the most devastating insults and traumas Mount St. Helens could inflict.

No one bothered to look for fish in Spirit Lake at first, but as the water cleared, the levels of oxygen rose, and plants appeared, state biologists came out to do the occasional, hopeful survey. They were always skunked. A gill net set in the middle of the lake in June 1983 caught nothing. Doug Larson never saw a single fish on any of his visits through 1986. Even though a couple of surveys in later years also turned up nothing, biologists were not yet ready to consign Spirit Lake to a state of perpetual fishlessness. The lake had had fish before; therefore it should have fish again. Larson and others argued against it. Spirit Lake should be allowed to recover naturally, they said. The lack of intervention was not only the lake's greatest scientific asset but was also in keeping with both the spirit and the letter of the monument designation from 1982.

State biologists reluctantly agreed not to think about planting trout until 1987 at the earliest, but that commitment did little to quell wistful thoughts about fisheries in Mount St. Helens's largest and most famous body of water. In 1993, on what they thought was yet another pointless survey, a pair of state biologists named Bob Lucas and John Weinheimer boated out and set a gill net baited with canned fish. When they came back the next day, ensnared in the net was a single adult male rainbow trout. The fish was more than ten inches long and weighed a pound. Lucas and Weinheimer named the trout Harry, after the local Harry Truman.

The next summer, the two returned and set another gill net. This time they caught a single adult female rainbow trout. She was more than seventeen inches long and weighed almost two pounds. Lucas and Weinheimer named her Harriet.

No surveys were done in 1995 or 1996, but in August of 1997, a Forest Service employee caught another female rainbow trout in a gill net, thirteen inches long and weighing a "plump pound." The worker was so thrilled she let out a whoop and kissed the fish. She named her Helen.

In 2000, Lucas and Weinheimer decided to resurvey two dozen lakes where fish had been found in 1980 and 1981. Although most lakes still had fish, four did not. The effort took them two years. When they finally came to survey Spirit Lake in 2002, they approached it with some trepidation. Its yield to date was one fish per year. Maybe those first two or three trout had died without spawning. Their worries were misplaced. "The first cast into Spirit Lake appeared to have hooked bottom," they would write, "but when a huge rainbow exploded on the surface, we knew Spirit Lake had finally turned the corner."

That one huge rainbow was more than two feet long and weighed almost seven pounds. Lucas and Weinheimer later caught thirty-two more rainbows with gill nets or hook-and-line sampling. For a high mountain lake, the rainbows were monstrous, lunker trout. They averaged almost two feet in size and weighed about four pounds. They were all at least two years old, which meant they had to be spawning somewhere, whether deep in the lake or in one of its tributary streams, although no one could find any fry.

The establishment and apparently increasing number of rainbow trout in Spirit Lake came as great news to the state biologists, even as the trout's origins remained a mystery. Crisafulli compared their genetics with tissues from rainbows that had been planted before the eruption, but they did not match. These trout had come from someplace else. Theories were proffered. Perhaps the trout were hatchery fish? Or maybe they had managed to survive in one of the tributary streams? That seemed unlikely. Maybe a couple of rainbows had lived in St. Helens Lake, which is deep and cold and drains into Spirit Lake from the Mount Margaret Backcountry? But no one had seen rainbows in that lake for many years. Maybe they came from Coldwater Lake, which the state had stocked with thirty thousand rainbows, and had swum up through South Coldwater Creek and into Spirit Lake by way of the tunnel? Even more unlikely.

Stories began to circulate, rumors with more than a whiff of conspiracy. Crisafulli heard from several people over the years who claimed to know a guy who knew a guy who swore up and down that the rainbows had been planted by Corps engineers while they were boring the Spirit Lake tunnel in the 1980s. Lucas, who had achieved minor renown as the person who caught Harry in 1993, received an anonymous phone call one night in the late 1990s from a person who claimed to be responsible. "I'm the one who planted that fish," the caller said, and then hung up.

———

Blackman, Culhane, Ferrari, and I cast and reel, cast and reel, while Crisafulli walks up and down the shore. Sometimes he stops to make a cast or two, but more often his attention is drawn to other biotic stimuli. Now he is bent over the lake, staring into the clumps of vegetation near the shore. Almost all of it—the water crowfoot, the hornwort, the various pondweeds—is new to the ecosystem, a consequence of the lake's higher nutrient levels and new shape; extensive shoaling along the shore has created a shallow littoral zone, where sunlight can reach the bottom. Rooted plants have flourished here and provide great refugia for fish. "Look! Look at all these fry!" Crisafulli calls out. "There are so many fry in here!" He has never seen such an abundance of young trout in this part of the lake, and this close to shore. "There must be thousands!"

Along the shore, lines start to go taut. Crisafulli had said the trout here are "bitey," and in short order Blackman has hauled one in. Then Culhane catches one. These are quickly measured, weighed, and tagged and released back into the lake. A few minutes later Blackman catches another trout, and Ferrari catches one. I have still caught nothing, have not gotten even so much as a nibble from what are purported to be among the fattest, easiest trout in the world to catch. It is not a good feeling.

I decide I need a way to reach the deeper water where these fish presumably lurk. I wade into the lake and clamber up on one of the big logs whose butt is caught on the shore. I work my way to its other end, stand on the wedge of dry, sun-bleached wood, and cast my line. The hook sails through the air and lands between two logs drifting past. I start to reel my line in, my mind drifting with the sibilant *whizzzzzz*, when suddenly the line jerks. Good lord, I finally got one! I pull the rod to coax the fish toward me, reel a little, pull the rod, reel a little. The resistance is strong, the line twangy. It disappears into the lake some twenty yards from me. Maybe the trout darted to hide in the safety of the vegetation? I reel, but now the line feels like it is about to snap. This trout must be enormous! Then I notice one of the logs moving.

I give the pole a tentative tug. The log wobbles in response. Great. Thus begins a delicate negotiation, for I need the hook back; Crisafulli told me in no uncertain terms that these hooks do not grow on trees. But the hook is embedded in the log, and the log is cumbersomely intent on its own course. We begin a slow dance, the log and I, wherein I tug the line, the log turns a little and drifts toward me, the line feels like it is about to give, I stop tugging.

They say fishing teaches patience. I am doing my best to learn. Finally, when the log is close, I tug more vigorously. The log on which I stand tilts forward ever so slightly and rolls a little—not much, but just enough so that when I step back to regain my balance, my foot lands on one of its slick waterlogged parts, which is coated with Gawel's biofilm. My foot skids and slides, and before I realize what is happening I am pitching forward into the lake in a slightly less graceful arc than one of Crisafulli's casts. The water slops over my head, and in that moment of immersion the first thought that comes to me is, *Thank God the* Legionella *and brain-eating amoebas haven't been detected for years.*

My feet find the bottom and I stand, sputtering. The snagged log floats within reach. I find the hook and pry it loose.

"You caught one of the lunkers," Crisafulli calls out from shore, where naturally he has been watching the entire time. "Or it got you."

"I suppose so," I say, wading back to my log.

Crisafulli laughs. "Thanks for not losing my hook," he says.

———

Rainbow trout are one of the most common freshwater game fish in Washington, found in lakes, creeks, streams, or rivers in every county in the state. The Washington Department of Fish and Wildlife plants millions of rainbows in more than five hundred water bodies each year, and those that survive (or are not caught) can live for several years. Full-grown adults average between eleven and eighteen inches from the snout to their tail fork. Their eyes are golden, their backs a rich blue-green that lightens to silver on their sides and belly. Their bodies are heavily speckled, but more so on their backs than their bellies. A swatch of pale red washes down their middle from the gills to the tail, and combined with the other colors gives the trout their most common common name; they are also known as bow, silver trout, and redsides.

Rainbows have a complex and fluid taxonomic history. They were first described in 1792, based on specimens from the Kamchatka Peninsula in Russia. The species was called the Kamchatka trout and given the binomial *Salmo mykiss*, the species name being derived from its Kamchatkan name, *mykizha*. Nearly forty years later, in 1836, a similar-looking fish from the Columbia River was called the rainbow trout and named *S. gairdneri*. Another biologist in California described a population in 1855 that was almost the same as *S. gairdneri*, although not quite. He named it *S. irideus* (*irideus* is Latin for "rainbow"). Names for other populations found elsewhere included *S. stellatus* (1856), *S. truncates* (1859), *S. masoni* (1860), *S. kamloops* (1892), *S. gilberti* (1894), and *S. nelsoni* (1908).

In 1966, Robert Behnke, an American fisheries biologist known widely as Dr. Trout, argued that all of these were actually one species. His observations were reinforced by the genetic work of a Japanese researcher named Toshio Okazaki, and in 1984 *S. mykiss* and *S. gairdneri* were lumped together as *S. mykiss*. Subsequent research then suggested that rainbow trout were more closely related to the genus *Oncorhynchus* than they were to other *Salmo* species, like the brown trout or the Atlantic salmon. In 1989, the year Crisafulli moved to Washington for good, rainbow trout were reclassified *Oncorhynchus mykiss*, and *O. mykiss* they have stayed.

Oncorhynchus is the genus in which all Pacific salmonids are now classified. Where *O. mykiss* differs from the five most famous *Oncorhynchus* species—the chinook, the coho, the sockeye, the pink, and the chum salmons—is that it has several life-history trajectories, of which lake dwelling is just one. Other rainbows spend their lives in rivers or streams. Another version, the steelhead, echoes the Pacific salmon life history if not quite mimicking it, traveling to saltwater and spending years in the ocean before returning to spawn in freshwater.

With rainbow trout present in Spirit Lake, Crisafulli did what he does out of habit: he decided to study them. They might not have arrived on their own, in the way other colonizing organisms might be said to have come to Mount St. Helens naturally (whatever that means); but they were here, they were a part of the ecosystem, and he would treat them as such. Beginning in 2000, he spent—and still spends—a few days in the summer and autumn catching them. He sets gill nets in the middle of the lake or does hook-and-line sampling from the shore. He ranges around the many small streams that feed the lake, looking for evidence of spawning.

The trout Crisafulli and his crews caught in the first years were some of the largest ever recorded for a freshwater lake. Most were well over two feet long. A few weighed up to eleven pounds. Somewhat surprisingly given their massive size, they appeared to be subsisting on tiny prey. When Crisafulli sorted through their gut contents, he found snails among a tangle of aquatic plants; he figured those trout were simply snapping up entire stalks of aquatic vegetation to get at the snails that clung to them by the hundreds. Other trout had pumice stones and even pieces of wood in their stomachs. The scrapes along their lower jaws led Crisafulli to deduce that they were dredging the lake bottom to get at the scads of midge larvae. From late summer to fall, he found trout stomachs filled with caddis fly larvae and adults, as well as terrestrial insects, such as carpenter ants and beetles, which the fish had snatched from the surface.

With the passing years, Crisafulli noticed that the fish were shrinking. He suspected that in the early 1990s, when their numbers were fewer, the trout could gorge and engorge without consequence. But the conditions in Spirit Lake were shifting. The nutrient enrichment brought about by the eruption was starting to wane, reducing the lake's overall productivity. Also, the channels of streams that flowed across the Pumice Plain had stabilized, increasing the amount of available spawning habitat and thus the number of fish. As the population grew, competition became stiffer. The size of the fish he sampled declined by an average of half an inch per year and their weight by three ounces. In

2005, Crisafulli caught a few trout that were under a foot in length for the first time. By 2008, the average rainbow weighed less than three pounds, and the range of sizes was wider. From his gill netting, he knew there were more trout than ever, so pound for pound, the amount of trout in Spirit Lake was unchanged. It was just distributed now among many more smaller fish.

———

That the rainbow trout of Spirit Lake would get smaller was something Lucas and Weinheimer had anticipated as soon as they caught their first lunker. The two had invited some friends out to help them sample in 2001; one described those days on the lake as the best fishing of his life. Word of the enormous trout had spread, as such stories will, and local anglers clamored for access. In meetings with the monument managers from the US Forest Service, state biologists argued on the public's behalf. There was no way those trout were survivors from the eruption, they said. Why not let people take advantage of what was effectively a stocked lake, as they had in the past? Spirit Lake had the chance to be a world-class fishery. The rainbows were big and fat and voracious, tantalizing in their willingness to nip at anything. Even if the Forest Service was reluctant to open the lake to the general public, they should at least consider other options, like a permit system or private, guided trips.

The monument staff said no. How would such a system be structured? How would people get down to the lake? Currently the only way was by a single trail at Harmony Falls. Anglers would want a road to drive down, a ramp from which to launch boats. Where did they propose to put it —through the chronically unstable Pumice Plain? That would mean more infrastructure, more changes, more impacts to a fragile system. The boats would bring invasive weeds or other aquatic organisms to the lake. Also, the log mat posed hazards. Woe betide the angler so focused on wrestling a trout that they did not notice the logs quietly encircling them. The proposition was just far too risky. Besides, the state already stocked Coldwater Lake, and fish from there had reached Castle Lake. Let people fish those lakes with their rainbows aplenty.

The disagreements spilled from interagency meetings over into the state legislature. In 2009, house members proposed a bill to create a raffle-only rainbow trout fishery in Spirit Lake. Anglers would pay a fee, not to exceed $25, to enter the raffle. The winners—ten or so anglers—would be guided out on Saturdays between June and October. Maybe the fishery would be catch and release; the anglers could even provide data on the trout population, recording their measurements.

Scientists were unpersuaded. Roger del Moral and one of his former students wrote a letter opposing the bill. To allow a fishery would mean "the end of the only natural experiment of its kind." Doug Larson sent a predictably scathing op-ed piece to the *Oregonian*. Allow fishing, he wrote, and "future visitors can expect yurt camps, vacation cabins, tacky concession stands and, if the gods are bullish and willing, perhaps even an 18-hole golf course."

The bill passed the house by 95 to 1 before stalling in the state senate. Everyone was left unhappy in their own way. Crisafulli did not like having to fend off recreational interests. He resented the assumption that succession was done after twenty-five or thirty years and so the blast area should be opened for development willy-nilly. Members of regional fly fishers' organizations groused that scientists had had unfettered access to the mountain and the lake for long enough: it was time to let the public in so they could do something other than just walk around and gawk a bit.

Tensions had been simmering in this vein for more than a decade, since the establishment of the national monument. Why turn Mount St. Helens into a museum when it had once been open for the enjoyment of those who lived around it? A highway used to lead directly to Spirit Lake's south shore. That was gone. The woods had been filled with cabins and other small rental properties. They were gone. Lodges and swimming docks used to ring the lake. Those were gone. Now one trail led to the lake, with no plans for any more. None of this sat well with some residents of places like Randle, Toledo, and Cougar. This is not a part of the state where people like being told where they can and cannot go, what they can and cannot do in places they used to call their own. They missed the old ways of knowing the mountain: hiking over it, camping on it, hunting its animals, fishing its lakes.

———

The afternoon lazes by. Blackman catches another trout, but their bitey-ness seems to be waning. Crisafulli enthuses about the fry. Suddenly I feel a tug on the line, which I am inclined to dismiss, but then there is another, this one firmer.

"I think I've got one!" I call out.

"You're sure?" Crisafulli calls back.

A fair question, given the circumstances, so I check, and this time, yes, I can see a trout wriggling on the line.

"It's definitely a fish," I say.

"Congratulations!" Crisafulli says.

I reel in the trout. It pulls and fights, but not unreasonably, I suppose. When it is close, Blackman splashes in with a small dip net and scoops it from the water. She spirits it over to Crisafulli at their ad hoc process-ing station. They and Culhane work quickly, measuring and weighing the fish. I trot over to watch. The trout, a male, is a little over seventeen inches long, and weighs a little less than three pounds—good-sized but hardly one of the monsters from the days of old. Blackman scrapes off some scales so they can estimate his age and inserts a small pink tag through his back just behind his dorsal fin, so that if someone catches him at a later date, they will know he has been caught before.

Through all this the trout lies on the ground, twitching, his mouth agape, his gills flaring uselessly. Watching him, watching everyone labor over him with brusque care, it seems to me that the rainbow trout should perhaps replace the northern pocket gopher and the prairie lupine as the mascot of the new ecology at Mount St. Helens. Those other two were appropriate for their time, being more explicitly ecological, but the rainbow epitomizes the mountain's more complicated contemporary circumstances. Try to untangle this fish from the various hooks and lines that tug at it: it is a species native to the region but was an interloper when humans placed it in Spirit Lake more than one hundred years ago. Then the mountain cast it out, and it disappeared for a time. During its absence, people pledged to leave the lake to its own devices—but not entirely, because that would be civically irresponsible. Hence the pumps and the tunnel. Then a human, perhaps someone working on the tunnel that would help control the lake, snuck a fish back into the lake: the human urge to shape the world to our ends is just as powerful as the world itself. The rainbows lurked unnoticed until they were too big to hide. Their renewed presence now prompts a debate over what the landscape should be, who it is for, where its greatest value lies. To these questions there are no easy answers. Certainly the fish at my feet does not have them. He is just an animal doing the best he can in this compromised space.

"Okay, let's get him back," Crisafulli says. He picks up the trout and wades into the lake. When he is in up to his knees he places the trout in the water and rocks him gently, trying to remind him how to move like a fish. The trout slips from Crisafulli's hands, swimming slowly away until it disappears in the shadows of the logs.

"Good luck, fella," Crisafulli says. He wipes his hands on his pants and then reaches down and touches the water with his fingers, makes a dubious face. "The lake's so warm here that I doubt we're going to get much more," he says. He was hoping for a bounty, but thus far we have caught only fourteen fish. On a good day, when things are really hopping, they might catch seventy. "So this afternoon," he says, "has been kind of a bummer." He brightens. "But still super interesting!" By which he means the abundance of fry and the lack of large rainbows. Then he is off again, splashing back to shore, thinking about what all that might mean. He is at the stage in his career where anything—or in this case, nothing—can be interesting.

So we will give it a few more minutes, and then we will go back to Charlie's Camp, and Crisafulli will make us dinner. I take my place on the shore. Behind me, Crisafulli is talking to Blackman about changes in the age distribution of the rainbows and the stabilization of the streams in the Pumice Plain, and what the implications of that hydrology could be for the trout when it comes to spawning. I cast my line. Crisafulli's voice merges with the *whizzzzzz* of the reel, and the lure traces a parabola through the air before it lands in the water with a gentle *plip*. Ripples radiate from the spot, become the subtlest of waves, lap against the beach.

PART FOUR

CHANGES TO THE LAND

12

DISTURBED ECOLOGIES

VIRGINIA DALE TAKES a collapsible stool from her backpack, sets it down, and tests it to make sure it is stable: the ground may look flat, but under this thin carpet of grass, it is rocky and uneven. Satisfied, she sits. She wears an oversized sun visor over her short blond hair. Tools dangle from her field vest: a magnifying glass, a ruler, what might be a penlight. In her hand are a clipboard and a sharpened pencil that is the Platonic ideal of sharpened pencils. "Okay," she says. "What do we have?"

Spread out around a small meadow, several people start to call out Latin binomials.

"Here's some *Rubus ursinus*," Elsie Denton says. (Common names: Pacific blackberry, Pacific dewberry, Douglas berry, trailing blackberry.)

"There's *Rumex acetosella*," Ginny Dains says. (Sheep sorrel, red sorrel, sour weed, field sorrel.)

"*Cytisus scoparius* in the middle here," Denton says. (Scotch broom.)

"*Lupinus latifolius*," Dains says. (Broadleaf lupine.)

"Several *Alnus rubra* on the edge," Denton says. (Red alder.) She scrutinizes a patch of grass and pulls out a thick guide. "What kind of *Juncus* did you have last time?" she asks. (A genus of rushes.)

"I'll check," Dale says. "But remember, we're just trying to estimate the cover of the top two or three players in a plot. After that it really doesn't matter except for diversity."

"Okay," Denton says. She plucks a blade of the unknown *Juncus* and tucks it in her book. She will identify the species back at camp.

Dale and her crew are on the northern edge of the debris avalanche deposit, fourteen miles or so northwest of Mount St. Helens, near Hoffstadt Creek. They have come to read sixty-three permanent plots that remain from the ones Dale and her colleagues put in over the summers of 1981 and 1982. The plots were last read five years ago, and Dale has not been back since. (She lives in Tennessee, where she is from, and works at the Oak Ridge National Laboratory and the University of Tennessee.)

Of the mountain itself we can see nothing, but pieces of it are everywhere, in the boulders and rocks and sand and dust piled more than one hundred feet deep over the old valley floor. On the hike out, Dale had marveled at the changes to the land, both since the eruption and since her last visit. "Back then it was just gray, gray, gray," she said. "But look at all these alders now. Last time they were nowhere near this big." She stopped to stare up at the living barcode of skinny, swaying, sky-hungry trees, most of which are forty or fifty feet tall. The shadows played across them in such a way that they almost created a moiré effect. Dale swayed with them a little, and then *tsk*-ed and hurried off to catch up with her crew.

———

Dale is an ecologist, although what kind of ecologist has changed a few times over her career. In the spring of 1980, she was a mathematical ecologist who had just finished her PhD at the University of Washington, studying plants at Mount Rainier. Newly graduated, she planned to stay around Seattle and teach a course or two at a local community college. She had given birth to her first child the previous November and thought it would be nice to maybe take it a little slower for a few months.

Unbeknownst to Dale, the day she defended her dissertation—March 20—was the day the first small earthquakes shook Mount St. Helens. When she heard of those stirrings and the plans being made to study the eruption, she was determined to be included. She spent the next weeks making herself, as she said, "indispensable." She assembled a bibliography of as many papers as she could find on the responses of plants to major disturbances. That April, she and A. B. Adams, her close colleague, drove out to the forests around the mountain to set up a series of plots where they predicted the effects of the eruption would manifest themselves, collecting from them some preliminary data. Sometimes she sat in the hall outside the doors of more senior faculty, waiting to talk about possible studies, just so she would be on their minds.

Her persistence paid off. When Mount St. Helens erupted, Dale was asked if she would like to do a project. Like everyone else, she wanted to get out to the blast area as soon as possible; but, also like everyone else, she had to wait until June, when she got a call from Jerry Franklin telling her she had a seat on a helicopter that was due to leave the next morning from Vancouver, a three-hour drive south of Seattle.

Dale had a dilemma. Her daughter was only a few months old and still nursing. Dale needed a way to pump milk for her, but she did not have a pump. Casting about for one, she called the local group of the La Leche League, a breastfeeding support organization. She explained that something had come up and she had to be out of town. Would it be possible for her to rent a pump while she was gone?

The woman said one was available and Dale could pick it up right away.

"Oh, thank heavens!" Dale said. "Now I can go to work!"

There was silence on the other end of the line. After a moment the woman said, "Oh, you work? I'm sorry, but we can't let you use our pump. At La Leche we don't condone working mothers." Dale's sputtered explanations were for naught; the woman had hung up.

Dale managed to find a hand pump and left for Vancouver at 5 a.m. the next morning. She spent the day flying around the blast area, trying to absorb the changes Mount St. Helens had wrought upon the land. Back at home that night, she sat down to organize her thinking. At their barest, she thought, the volcanic processes could be classified in terms of ash, blast, and mountain. The ash had mostly drifted east, and the blast had flayed the land to the north, but the mountain had collapsed to the west. Nearly fifteen miles of the North Fork Toutle River was buried to an average depth of nearly 150 feet, and in some spots more than 600 feet. Mudflows had run across a large, central swath, scouring a flat plain, but closer to the sides of the valley, the debris had formed great piles, like hummocks, some of which were nearly 200 feet tall.

Most people wanted to work in the blast area—the Blowdown and Singe Zones—but Dale wanted to work on the mountain. There would be a lot to explore, and she and her team would have it mostly to themselves. For the rest of the summer, she ranged all over the deposits, searching for surviving plants. She found a few here and there from maybe twenty species, but most were fireweed, thistle, or broadleaf lupine.

The fireweed and thistle were easy enough to understand, but the broadleaf lupine was a surprise. A taller, more richly colored cousin of the prairie lupine, it was sprouting in vigorous clumps around the deposit's flatter areas. When she dug up some of the shoots, she discovered small root fragments at their bases. The plant must have been carried along in the landslide from somewhere higher on the mountain, she deduced. Its leaves and stems had been shredded in the tumult, and the long, woody root had been torn to pieces, but bits of it somehow worked their way upward through the rubble. By the time the deposit settled in the valley, the roots were near the surface and could sprout in soils that had an acidity somewhere between tomato juice and coffee.

Over the next two summers, Dale and Adams put in 104 plots on a pair of transects. (The plots they had placed in April were all destroyed in the eruption.) Their design let them see the effects of the debris avalanche's geological variations, the proximity of survivors on the hills above, and the distance from the crater on plant succession. At first, the work was straightforward, though not easy. Dale would hike out to the plots, and, being careful not to twist her ankles on the rocky ground, scan them and scribble a zero in her notebook. Almost nothing was growing in the first years after the eruption, and certainly no seedlings; the few plants she found were all sprouted from broken roots carried down in the landslide, like the lupines. Unlike the Blowdown Zone with its biological legacies, most species arrived at the debris avalanche deposits from elsewhere. They were classical colonizing species: fireweed, thistle, woodland ragwort. The debris avalanche seemed to adhere to more classical models of succession: an empty space filled by a group of well-adapted incomers.

The years passed with little in the way of community development, although species were slowly accreting. By 1983, Dale was counting a few hundred plants per plot from 10 species, with a total of 76 species on her transects, but average cover was still less than 1 percent. Then conditions started to change. Nine years after the eruption, plant cover had climbed above 10 percent on average, with 11 species per plot, and nearly 90 species total. After fourteen years, plot cover had risen to almost 40 percent, with more than 20 species per plot, and 150 species total. Reading plots started to take longer, as Dale and her crews poked and prodded, and lifted the leaves of one plant to find a new one emerging underneath.

Here, the debris avalanche revealed a quirk. The plant most responsible for its increased greening, Dale saw, was not a flower, but the red alder. For the first three years after the eruption, the trees had been rare, appearing in only a few of her plots, but those that had taken root showed signs of hardiness; one alder was already more than seven and a half feet tall.

At a symposium in 1982, Dale, just to be provocative, had predicted alders would have an outsized influence on plant succession on the debris avalanche deposit. "No one believed me except for one professor who studied alder," she says, but she was insistent. "The largest surge of plant colonization will follow the flowering of *Alnus rubra*," she wrote in 1986. This turned out to be true. Within nine years, red alders were present in more than one-third of the plots. After twenty years, they were the densest plant on the plots, their pale trunks shooting up more than three feet per year, crowding each other and fighting for space.

Here was another species flouting its own natural history. Alders are associated with wet habitats, like riverbanks or floodplains, but here they were thriving on the dry debris avalanche and its acidic soils. Several traits helped them. They had started producing seeds in 1985, and those seeds had been able to germinate. Alder saplings survived at much higher rates than other species, and young trees grew quickly. Other flowering plants benefited from their spread. Like the prairie lupine on the Pumice Plain, alders can take nitrogen from the air and transfer it to the soil through a symbiotic relationship with bacteria in their roots. They provide shade, nutrients, and litter, allowing new species to grow in their shadow without drying out in the hot sun.

"Succession theory emphasizes the steady and unidirectional progression from one state to another," Dale would later write. "Fifteen years of data from permanent plots on the debris avalanche deposit at Mount St. Helens supported the idea of a gradual and linear increase in plant cover and richness over the entire area." However, she noted, that was an incomplete reading. Her results included not just the response of flowers and trees to disturbance, but the complicated response of another organism as well: humans.

———

Between the ash, the blast, and the mountain, the mountain was by far the least settled of the volcanic processes. The debris avalanche had—and continues to have—a unique dynamism. Mudflows were frequent during the first years as continued volcanic activity melted snow and ice in the crater and sent water slicking over the debris. The North Fork Toutle River almost immediately began to eat through the deposit, its channels twisting and multiplying into complicated plaits. Even today, the river's ability to shift its channels in just a few months is astounding. It whips across the land from one side of the valley to the other like a loose fire hose.

"It took the river a while to find itself," Dale likes to say. She would arrive in the summer to read her plots and find in their place a deep gully, a new cliff, or some other impassable topographic feature. By 2000, seventeen of her plots had eroded away, and another eighteen had become isolated and unreachable. She took the change in stride and carried on.

It was something else for which she would have to account when she analyzed her data.

Not everyone shared her equanimity. In the summer of 1980, local, state, and federal officials were already worried about the several thousand tons of sediment the North Fork was eroding from its valley. They feared for the communities along the Cowlitz and Columbia Rivers. The more sediment the North Fork removed from Mount St. Helens, the shallower those downstream rivers became, and the greater the flood risk to the lands they moved through. "There was a sense of 'We've gotta fix this! We've gotta fix it!'" Dale says.

The group asked to fix it was a branch of the Department of Agriculture called the Soil Conservation Service. The SCS had been formed during the Dust Bowl in the Depression years. Its mandates and methodologies were better suited for agricultural settings than scenes of volcanic ruin. No matter. The SCS, now called the Natural Resources Conservation Service, was given $1.7 million to assess the situation, and several teams came out to the blast area to study it. They left troubled. "The ash is massive," one of their biologists wrote. "It has no structure, no organic matter, and is highly erodible."

SCS personnel decided their best option was to use helicopters and artificially seed two hundred square miles of the blast area with legumes and grasses. When Dale heard of the plan, she got in touch to request that they not go through with it. "We have to do something," she was told. She asked what plants they were planning to use. "Whatever we have on hand," was the reply. She was aghast. "Well, why don't you at least use red alder?" she asked. The alder is a native species, and it is a nitrogen fixer and a fast-growing tree. It would hold the soil in place as well as anything the SCS had in mind. "We don't have red alder seed," they said. She protested that dumping tons of nonnative seed could have a profound impact on the plant community that was slowly taking shape on its own. "Don't worry," she was told. "The effects won't be long-term. Anyway, we're just trying to fix the problem."

Dale and other ecologists managed to persuade the SCS to limit the seeding project to the debris avalanche deposit, which was the land deemed most at risk for erosion. In August 1980, helicopters began to fly back and forth, hauling large buckets suspended by heavy cables. They dumped thousands of tons of fertilizer and seeds over thirty-two square miles along the banks of the North Fork Toutle River. The seeds were from the species the SCS planted along roadsides and highways all over the country, like birdsfoot trefoil, clover, Kentucky bluegrass, orchardgrass, ryegrass, hairy cat's ear, and tall fescue.

Dale watched all of this with chagrin. Once, she happened to be working on her plots while the SCS helicopters were overhead. Seeds rained down on her and her crews. When the operation ended in October, eleven of her plots had been seeded with the SCS assortment. Rather than give up on the plots, she followed them to see what would happen. Within a year, half of the seeded area was covered in nonnative species, creating a dense community that was hard for native species to enter. In addition, the nonnative seeds started to spread, carried off in the wind, which also blew away the fertilizer. Deer mice arrived, drawn by the sudden influx of free food and the relative lack of predators, and their population exploded. There were so many they were almost underfoot.

For all that, the seeds did not even do the job they were meant to do. The grasses and clover neither stabilized the inherently unstable ground nor prevented erosion. Their thin, shallow roots might hold together an interstate's narrow verge, but at Mount St. Helens they were no match for the wind, or the wild weaving of a river.

———

Dale's experience with the SCS, along with the timber salvage operations in other areas of the blast area, convinced her, Jerry Franklin, and others that protection was needed for Mount St. Helens's extraordinary ecologies. A coalition of conservation groups, as well as other nonprofit organizations, shared that conviction and had been agitating for the blast area to be preserved in some fashion since the summer of 1980. There was, they argued, nothing at all like this place anywhere else in the world. The volcanic landscape was too unique, too valuable as a scientific laboratory, to turn over to the logging companies to salvage willy-nilly, or to federal agencies to dump dandelions on. To do so was tantamount to pretending that nothing had happened.

Officials with the federal government agreed that the area was worth protecting in some capacity and asked several groups to submit proposals for a national monument. The proposals ranged widely in size and scope. Three ultimately emerged as contenders for consideration. The Mount St. Helens Protective Association, a local group of conservationists, proposed that over two hundred thousand acres be set aside, protecting both the mountain and much of what was left of the forests around it, stretching north well beyond the Green River. The US Forest Service, the agency that oversaw most of the land on which the volcano sat, proposed an eighty-five-thousand-acre monument, with much of the area between Mount St. Helens and Spirit Lake designated as an interpretive zone. Outside the monument, salvage logging and open-pit mining would still be allowed, among other extractive activities. Washington governor John Spellman, after taking office in 1981, put together a proposal of some one hundred thousand acres, bridging the proposals of the Mount St. Helens Protective Association and the Forest Service. It would include most of the mountain and Spirit Lake, along with the Mount Margaret Backcountry and parts of the debris avalanche deposit.

By the spring of 1982, it was still unclear which proposal would prevail. That March, Dale traveled to Washington, DC, as one of several scientists to testify before Congress on the importance of the mountain and the blast area. Representing both herself and the Washington Native Plant Society, she learned a little of what it was like to be a political ecologist. (In her written testimony, she called herself a plant population biologist.) At one meeting, a congressman from eastern Washington asked her what all the fuss over the eruption was about. "The vegetation's going to come back," he said, "so why do we need to set the land aside as a monument?" Dale thought that an excellent question, or so she said. Mount St. Helens, she explained, ought to be preserved not just for its uniqueness, or for its ecology alone, but for what it could show about processes. People needed to learn *how* the plants and animals came back. This was important in many contexts, since land was always changing. Volcanic eruptions might not be common, but large forest fires and hurricanes are. By monitoring the responses to one type of large disturbance, people could learn how better to support recovery from others. They would know what to expect, how to intervene, how perhaps not to.

Later, at a hearing before the Senate Subcommittee on Public Lands and Reserved Water, Howard Metzenbaum, the junior senator from Ohio and a supporter of the monument, asked Dale to expound on how a scene so devastated might be thought attractive to the general public, many of whom might see only desecration. (All the proposals touted the mountain's potential as a tourist attraction.)

"Couldn't you say that it is a beautiful brown?" Metzenbaum asked.

"Actually, sir," Dale said, "it would be more appropriate to call it 'gorgeous gray.'"

At this, Metzenbaum smiled.

On July 19, 1982, a bill for a monument 115,000 acres in size passed the House. Two days later, the Senate also passed a bill, although theirs called for a monument of 105,000 acres. In conference, House and Senate negotiators settled on 110,000 acres, and on August 26, President Ronald Reagan quietly signed the Mount St. Helens National Volcanic Monument Act of 1982.

Without the advocacy of the scientists who worked at the mountain, Dale believed, the monument would not have had a chance. She had been in a Washington US senator's Seattle office when his aides drew what would become the final boundaries, penciling a line on a map of the Gifford Pinchot National Forest. The line they traced ran around the south side of Mount St. Helens, then swung north and blew out over the landscape like the lateral blast cloud, albeit with some sharper angles. A tongue swung out to include the first few miles of the debris avalanche, and then the boundary turned and went up past Coldwater Lake. It continued north, passed over the Green River, encircled Manson's Peak and a little more land to preserve some of the area's last remaining old-growth forests. Then it turned south, going around the Mount Margaret Backcountry with its alpine lakes, around Meta Lake, and down to Smith Creek before swinging west and closing. Dale watched. So easy, and yet so hard. So much had been preserved, and yet it seemed like barely enough.

———

Dale worked at Mount St. Helens for four years before she left to become a research scientist at the Oak Ridge National Laboratory in Tennessee. She returned to the mountain for the Pulses, going out to the debris avalanche deposit for a few days at a time to read whatever plots had not yet washed away. She continued to watch species accrue and compared her unseeded plots with the seeded ones. Given the mixed results from the SCS interventions, she later argued, seeding with native species would have been more beneficial. The Natural Resources Conservation Service, which had replaced the SCS, agreed, and enacted a policy to stock seeds more appropriate to their locales at their twenty-five Plant Materials Centers around the country, so that those plants would be available to help restore sites after a disturbance. That, Dale thought, was a nice legacy to have.

At Oak Ridge, Dale's career shifted from plant ecology to biofuels, sustainable agriculture, and ecosystem management in a changing climate. But even as she saw it less and less, Dale still thought—and thinks—about Mount St. Helens and how it informs larger questions of ecology and disturbance. Now she calls herself a disturbance ecologist—or, if she is giving a talk in public and wants to get a laugh, a disturbed ecologist.

Near the end of the day, as we were walking back to her camp, I asked Dale how she keeps in touch with Mount St. Helens now that she does not see it so often anymore. "Here's what I do," she said. "Every year on May 18, I bake a cake." The cake depicts the mountain's prominence and the first few miles of the debris avalanche. As a cake, it is rich in semiotics. At the bottom, unseen, is a base of strawberry—the magma moving under the Earth's surface. Above that is a layer of chocolate cake—the soil that lies buried under the volcanic material. Over that is a generous helping of chocolate icing, representing the debris avalanche, the lahars, and the pyroclastic flows. Dollops of white vanilla icing atop the cake represent the remaining glaciers. In the crater Dale places a little dry ice, so that it emits steam, just as the mountain still does.

Dale admits to allowing herself some creative license. Although there was not much lava to speak of during the eruption of May 18, she likes strawberries, and so she has dozens tumbling out of the crater like giant red boulders. Pretzel sticks jammed in far-flung edges of the cake are all the downed trees of the Blowdown Zone. Thyme and rosemary leaves are the new vegetation of returning plants. Gummy butterflies pollinate the flowers. Buried within the cake, gummy fish are a tribute to all the animals killed in the blast, while gummy worms crawl among them—the survivors, the biological legacies.

I asked why, given her initial impressions of the landscape, and her gentle riposte with Senator Metzenbaum, she did not try to incorporate some gray element into her cake. Dale laughed. "Well," she said, "gray isn't really a color you want to see in food, don't you think?"

"I guess not," I said. "It sounds like an incredible cake."

"It is," Dale said. "It can feed sixty to eighty people. And now my daughter makes one every year, too, for her friends, so that's nice."

13

FISH IN A FISHLESS RIVER

THE TOUTLE RIVER Fish Collection Facility, or FCF, is about twenty miles up the Spirit Lake Highway from its junction with Interstate 5. The turnoff to it is so profoundly unmarked that it is easy to miss—once, twice, three times—until it at last becomes clear that the small gravel depression on the shoulder actually leads to a road. Quadrupling back, I bounce a short distance down a rutted track to a long chain-link fence that extends over a field of grass down to the river. Six padlocks secure its gate.

The grass is tall, shaggy, and wet from last night's rain. The air smells sweet, as if filtered through the earth and moss. Behind the fence is a ramshackle collection of sheds and the complicated bunker of the FCF. It funnels the North Fork Toutle River through its elevated, concrete-walled chute. The river roars over the chute, frothing brown from silt.

The chute is far too high for even the hardiest steelhead or coho salmon to hurl themselves over as they make their way upstream. The fish are instead directed to a small opening near the base of the FCF, through which some of the Toutle has been diverted. This milder flow ushers them to a sinuous concrete ladder, which they swim up until they arrive at a closed gate near the top. Some seem not to like this, and turn around and exit the way they came, swimming over to the nearby Green River, which joins the North Fork about one hundred yards downstream. But if they want to swim on toward Mount St. Helens to spawn in the streams where they hatched, they have no choice but to wait in the collection pond until someone comes to collect them.

After a few minutes I hear the collectors crunch down the road behind me. The first drives a big flatbed truck with a water tank bolted to it, bearing the emblem of the Washington Department of Fish and Wildlife: the state fish, a steelhead, frozen in mid-leap over some resplendent backcountry lake, encircled with the words "Fish Washington." The truck stops, and out steps a biologist named Keith Keown. A big man with graying hair and an open, friendly face, Keown retired a few years ago from the WDFW, but the agency convinced him to return. He now works part-time at the FCF, coming out two or three times a week during the coho runs in the fall and winter steelhead runs in March and April.

Next to his truck is a Ford SUV with vanity plates that read STLHEDR. It belongs to Hal Mahnke. Shorter than Keown and slimmer, with a thin, neatly trimmed mustache and beard, Mahnke is a retired police captain from Longview, a town about forty-five miles away. He has volunteered at the FCF since 1999; for six months in the early 2000s, he even ran the facility when the WDFW was short-staffed because of budget cuts.

Keown and Mahnke gather gear from one of the sheds: several dip nets of different lengths, vials of alcohol, data sheets, other paraphernalia. These latter items Mahnke arranges precisely on a rickety wooden table while Keown climbs some steps to the mechanism that lowers the water level in the fish ladder, revealing its occupants, if there are any. "Good thing we got a nice rain last night," he says. "That and the warmer temps are good for the fish. Maybe they'll be on the move today."

"Think there's anything in there?" I ask. This is my third or fourth trip down to the FCF since the start of April, but I have yet to see a single steelhead.

"Who knows?" Keown says, shrugging, his eyebrows hopping up his forehead. Last Friday he had twenty steelhead, and Monday he had nine, but Wednesday he got skunked. Today? "Who knows?" he says again. "Maybe we'll get lucky."

———

Steelhead and rainbow trout are genetic twins, but steelhead are the anadromous or oceangoing form of the species, migrating out to the Pacific, while the rainbows stay in lakes and streams. They are bigger than most freshwater rainbow trout, sometimes markedly, and also more streamlined. When fresh from the sea they are silvery; as they move farther up the river, they acquire a darker, more greenish cast. They go by an assortment of regional colloquialisms: sea-run rainbow, coastal rainbow, Columbia River redband trout. Like other anadromous Pacific salmonids, they live in freshwater after they hatch, first as alevin and then fry, before they start to migrate after one to four years, when they are known as parr. During this passage from the North Fork Toutle to the Cowlitz, they transform into smolts through a physiological change called smoltification, becoming sleeker and more silver. By the time they come to the saltwater of the Columbia River estuary sixty or so miles away, they are equal to its demands.

Once steelhead reach the ocean, they diffuse across the northeastern Pacific, hunting for smaller fish, mollusks, and crustaceans. After one to four years they turn again for freshwater, called home in the way all salmon are. As they move back through the estuary and up the river, they stop eating and growing, subsisting only on their reserves of fat. When they get to their spawning grounds, they might wait weeks or even months for conditions to become suitable for breeding. Females then dig nests called redds in the gravel, where they deposit between 1,500 and 4,000 eggs; males fertilize the eggs with their milt. The redds are sometimes so large they can be seen from small planes. Other salmon species die after spawning, but steelhead are iteroparous—they can live to spawn again. Up to 17 percent migrate back out to sea and return a couple of years later. Some spawn three or four times before they are finally spent. These individuals are called kelts.

Steelhead may differ from other *Oncorhynchus* species in life history strategy, but they are in similarly dire straits. The steelhead of the North Fork Toutle winter run are listed as threatened under the Endangered

Species Act, joining twenty-seven other threatened or endangered salmon and steelhead populations across the Western states. In the parlance of salmon recovery, these fish are part of the Lower Columbia River Distinct Population Segment, or DPS. (All the rivers and streams that drain from Mount St. Helens are part of the Lower Columbia River system.) A DPS is the vehicle by which federal managers account for the geographical intricacies of salmonid natural history. Salmon are famously faithful to their natal rivers. In some species, more than 95 percent of adults spawn not only in the same watershed but in almost the exact spot from which they hatched and grew. All of these populations, or stocks, are largely independent, with their own distinctive genetic character and ecology.

Even among Pacific salmon, steelhead have a vaunted reputation. One federal biologist I spoke to said they have perhaps the most complex life history of any of the salmonids: winter runs, summer runs, fish that return to spawn after only a few months at sea, fish that wait years, fish that spawn only once and die, fish that spawn four times or more. The Lower Columbia River DPS alone contains twenty-three stocks, seventeen of which are winter runs. Each of these runs is tied to its own parts of streams and creeks within its watershed. Individuals from winter and summer runs that use the same creeks spawn in distinct spots of it.

The threats to all the stocks, however, are similar: a loss of tributary habitat due to development; the degradation of the remaining habitat from pollution; hydroelectric or flood-control dams that block their migrations; water that is too hot or too dirty; overharvesting at the hands of both recreational and commercial fishers; hatchery practices that have led to a loss of genetic diversity; and so on.

For all this, the steelhead and coho of the North Fork confront exceptionally challenging circumstances. The eruption of Mount St. Helens buried their natal river under hundreds of feet of avalanche deposits and cut it off from its source, Spirit Lake. The fishes' migratory paths were erased, and the river they reach when they return now is much less stable in its channels, apt to change its course suddenly. Where the waters were once clear, they are now the color of café au lait from all the sediments they churn up after winding through the plain of debris.

Historically, the North Fork supported one of the largest steelhead runs of the Lower Columbia River system, with up to fifteen thousand fish per year. These steelhead were one of the core populations of the Lower Columbia DPS, but those old population levels are little more than fantasy now. In 1989, its first year of operation, the FCF caught eighteen fish. The number rose slightly in the years that followed, but the average annual return over the previous decade has been 210 fish. Recovery goals are commensurately modest. For the purposes of the Endangered Species Act, federal biologists will count themselves satisfied when the North Fork can sustain a run of six hundred steelhead.

————

As the water level drops in the FCF, Mahnke and Keown chat while they lean on the fence that overlooks the fish ladder. They have the easy, joshing rapport of two people who have worked together for a long time but perhaps do not know each other terribly well.

"How warm do you guess the water is?" Mahnke asks.

Keown thinks a moment. "Forty-seven," he says.

"Nah," Mahnke says. "Forty-eight."

"Damn," Keown laughs. "I was going to say forty-eight!" The temperature turns out to be 49°F, and when they learn this, both Keown and Mahnke murmur "Ooooooh," in unison; 50°F is optimal for steelhead.

This winter to date the FCF has collected eighty-eight steelhead. Keown guesses the run is about halfway done, so while this year does not look great, it is a lot better than last year, when they had seventy-nine fish total. "We had pretty good runs for a few years," he says. "Now they seem to be going down a bit." He is walking along a railing, stopping periodically to peer into sections of the fish ladder, each of which is defined by a short concrete barrier a few feet tall. The water eddies at the front of each barrier as it rushes through an opening, and he is scrutinizing the eddies.

The swirls all look the same to me, but Keown watches for obscure and slight patterns that mean a fish is present. "Not seeing much," he says, frowning, but just then Mahnke whistles from the first pond and points into it. He gives a thumbs-up and holds his hands a yard apart: a big fish.

"So there's at least one," Keown says. "Good."

By the time the water is low enough, we see the exposed backs of four steelhead in the top collection pond, and three in what Keown calls the J-hook section of the ladder. To catch the first group, Mahnke dons hip waders and climbs down into the pond with a short dip net. The water is knee-deep and wretchedly murky. Mahnke moves gingerly, prodding the invisible bottom with his net, calling out in surprise—"Whoa!"—whenever a large fish brushes against his leg. After a few minutes he has herded the steelhead into a corner and caught them one by one: two males and two females, or, as Mahnke calls them, bucks and hens. Each time he snares one he hands the net up to me, and I lift it over to an enormous tub of cool water next to the processing table, dropping the fish in and closing a lid to keep it from jumping out onto the pavement.

Keown, meanwhile, is trying to catch the steelhead swimming in the J-hook. Since he is not allowed to climb down into the fish trap for safety reasons, he must coax the steelhead into a heavy, long-handled dip net from a wall ten feet or so above. His jaw grinds in concentration as he drags the net around. Sweat drips from the tip of his nose. The fish are quick and the net slow to respond to his maneuvers. The muscles in his arms twitch and jump. "C'mon, you, get in there," he mutters when another fish evades his swipes. Finally he has caught two of them, but the last one is proving to be a real challenge.

"An old-timer, I bet," Keown says, leaning against the pole and breathing hard. The steelhead appears at the surface. A large gash mars his back and right flank, about three-quarters of the way down his length, just in front of the small adipose fin near his tail.

"He's got a chunk taken out of him," I say.

"Doesn't seem to be bothering him much," Keown says, while the fish noses languidly along the concrete wall as if testing it for weakness.

Keown laughs. "Look at him down there, just swimming around," he says. "He's as big and obvious as an American flag."

—————

Before 1980, the upper reaches of the North Fork Toutle River had some of the most productive waters in the river's drainage. This meant it had some of the most productive waters in southwest Washington. Tens of thousands of anadromous fish spawned throughout more than five hundred square miles of watershed. In addition to winter and summer steelhead and fall coho, there were runs of chum, and spring and fall chinook. There were also white and green sturgeon, eulachon, minnows and suckers moving up or down the river.

This is not to say the North Fork was a fish paradise. Overharvest and a sustained loss of habitat downstream from logging and urban development led to predictable declines of salmon and steelhead from the 1960s on. By the late 1970s, most of the fish in the river came from hatcheries downstream, but the river itself remained for the most part clear and true, until Mount St. Helens collapsed and buried it. Between the debris avalanche on the North Fork and lahars on the South Fork, more than three-quarters of the salmon and steelhead habitat was destroyed.

The fish at sea in the summer of 1980 knew none of this. A few months later, first the coho and then the steelhead started to return, as they did every year. All salmon navigate in freshwater mostly by using olfactory cues, drawn to their home streams by the ever-stronger smells, but the rivers these fish found were so altered as to be unrecognizable. The Toutle, the Cowlitz, and the Columbia were filled with ash and silt— the wrack of the fallen mountain. Most coho and steelhead did not bother trying to move up them but strayed instead to other tributaries along the Columbia. (It is this penchant to stray that allows runs to endure in the face of unpredictable environmental conditions.) But salmonids are genetically predisposed to doggedness, and not all the fish turned away. Hundreds of steelhead pushed through the brown waters of the Cowlitz and the Toutle, navigated through silt and rocks and slaughtered trees, tried to draw breath from the hot slurry. Almost all of them died, but a few managed to reach their home streams and spawn. "Darwin could not have devised a more ingenious test for 'the survival of the fittest,'" one biologist would write of their feat.

Those doomed stalwarts aside, biologists believed it would take years, if not decades, for fish to return in any number. Once again they were surprised. Winter floods started to flush away much of the sediment that clogged the South Fork Toutle and the Green River, which were flowing along their original beds within a year or so. The number of steelhead redds on the South Fork Toutle River rose from zero in 1980 to fourteen per mile in 1984 and nearly forty per mile in 1987. "Most of us have witnessed nature's awesome destructive forces," a fisheries biologist wrote in a report in 1985. "These remind us that instead of ruling the land, we are temporary, and often powerless, tenants. Perhaps even more dramatic, however, is the chance to watch nature heal herself."

The steelhead of the North Fork are not yet part of this healing. What will help make the Toutle a viable, fish-bearing river in the way it used to be is the regrowth of vegetation, the dynamics of which Virginia Dale is documenting a few miles upstream of the FCF. Grasses and shrubs and alders will help hold the ground in place, and with it, the river. They will keep the water cool, add coarse woody debris to it, slow it down. Until then, the counts at the FCF will likely stay meager. But it is not the steelheads' first such test, nor will it be their last. Mount St. Helens has a long history of activity. Most of the fish populations here have gone through periods of extirpation at one point or another, their streams and creeks wrecked by the mountain, only to return again, the sense of home saturated so deep in their bones that only extinction will drive them from this place for good.

———

After all the steelhead are captured and secured in the big tub, Keown measures and processes the first two with a practiced ease, but before retrieving the third, he turns to me. "Do you want to do this one?" he asks.

"Sure," I say. I net the steelhead from the tub and heft him to the table. When I place him on his side atop the ruler, I see it is the wounded male. He flops and wriggles until he has worked his way upright, as if he would swim away. I almost lose my hold, but Keown reaches out and restrains the fish with his big hand. "Put your whole arm on him, just to keep a little pressure," he says. "Once they feel pressure, it's like they know the jig is up."

I rest my forearm along the length of the fish, and as Keown predicts, he stills. His flesh is cold and slick and firm with muscle. I am not a fisherman and so am not versed in angling mythologies, but this steelhead is a beautiful animal. Now that he has left the sea and is on his way up the river, his polished back is no longer bright silver but has turned a more muted gray-green under patterned lines of black matte flecks. His gills are bright red, as if he is out of breath, which I suppose he is. The red patches extend down his sides almost to his tail, lightening as they go. Scored across his body are faint rake marks as if from claws, in addition to the wound on his back.

"Mammal damage," Keown says, and Mahnke makes a note on the datasheet. "Between the scratches and the bite, this guy got it pretty good." Keown examines the wound. It is deep and ugly, the exposed flesh purple, swollen. Loose skin flaps at its edges. "Looks like it goes almost to his spine," Keown says. "Ouch."

"What did this?" I ask.

"Sea lion, probably," Keown says. The closest sea lions are far down on the Columbia River, so this fish has swum at least forty miles upstream with this gaping hole in him.

"Will he survive to spawn?" I ask.

"He made it this far," Keown says. "Steelhead are tough."

Now I measure him, wedging his nose against the front of the ruler and noting the center of his caudal fin, or tail. He is about twenty-nine inches long. The largest specimens might be nearly four feet long and weigh more than fifty pounds, but on average they are much smaller, like this one: about two or two and a half feet long, and ten or eleven pounds.

I use a hole punch to take a snippet from his tail, which Mahnke collects and slips into the vial of alcohol. They will use it to test the steelhead's DNA. I next mark him with a bright pink tag about one inch long. This entails jabbing a needle gun through his back just below his dorsal fin and depressing a trigger to shoot a little plastic anchor through to the other side, like a price tag. Getting the needle from one side of the other is hard—I need to jab twice—and the tag gun misfires, also twice, but with Keown's help, I soon have the tag dangling from the steelhead's back.

"How long has he been out?" I ask.

"About thirty seconds," Keown says. "He's okay. He can handle it for about a minute and a half or so. That's when I start to get worried."

Now I need six of the steelhead's scales. The best way to get them is to use forceps, wedging the tips under individual scales and plucking them out, but the first three times I try I get nothing. "It's just like pulling out a hair from your head," Keown says. "The same tug, the same resistance." As an image this is not the most attractive, but it is facultative. I start removing scales more adeptly and stick them to the card.

To work with a fish out of water that one intends to keep alive is to feel the true meaning of a hard deadline. While I am collecting his scales, the steelhead snorts into the net. More than his twitches and shudders, it is his sound that catches me. I know some fish can make noise underwater with their swim bladder, but a snort through the mouth is too terrestrial, too much the sound of an animal that breathes air to live. Such as myself. Later, in the controlled environment of my basement, I lie on the floor and time myself holding my breath for as long as I can. I can go about a minute and fifteen seconds before my lungs scream. I next imagine fasting for two months and then being forced not to breathe while someone pins me to a table and jabs me twice in the back with a needle and yanks out six of my hairs one by one. A terrible thought, but also, I see, a testament to Keown's skill as a teacher. He gave instruction calmly and did not get irritated when I made the same mistake two or three times, and because of this I did not dwell overmuch, at least in the moment, on the fact that for every second I was fumbling around, the steelhead was that much closer to dying.

———

The US Army Corps of Engineers built the FCF in 1989. It is paired with a large embankment dam constructed in the same year a little more than a mile upstream. The official name of that dam is the Sediment Retention Structure, but most people know it as the SRS, or the Sediment Dam. It is the last in a series of dams built in response to the eruption. An earlier dam, built higher upstream in 1980, was less than forty-five feet tall. Sediment quickly piled up behind it, and floods breached it within the year. The Corps rebuilt the dam in the spring of 1981, but a lahar breached it in 1982. The Corps built this one farther downstream and has steadily added to its height as sediments have piled up behind it. It now stands 125 feet tall and stretches 1,800 feet across the Toutle River valley.

The SRS's stated purpose, as its name indicates, is to retain what remains of the nearly four billion cubic yards of silt, sand, and gravels that the 1980 eruption sent into the valley. All that material would otherwise be in constant motion. It was on the move almost as soon as it was deposited, first in mudflows that sloughed down the Toutle River during the eruption and for a few years afterward, and later after a winter's heavy rains, or during the spring melt. As many as six million tons of silt are still flowing out every year, and that is just a small fraction of what is left. Were the rest to flush in a single gout—if, for instance, the debris dam failed at Spirit Lake—it would overwhelm the Toutle River, the Cowlitz, and, eventually, the Columbia in a terrible recall of the 1980 eruption.

By retaining sediment, the SRS lessens the flood risk to the small towns that occupy those more heavily developed floodplains, but it does more than just trap sediment. Fish can pass the SRS when they are heading downriver as juveniles; or, rather, they can tumble down its 2,200-foot spillway, with its rough rocky channel at a 7 percent grade, often injuring themselves in the process. But it is almost impossible for them to swim up past the dam when they come back as adults to spawn.

In this blockage of what Corps engineers call "volitional upstream passage," the SRS prevents steelhead and coho from reaching as much as fifty miles of upstream habitat, including what remains of their traditional spawning grounds in Hoffstadt and Alder Creeks, on the north and south sides, respectively, of the North Fork Toutle's valley. The only way for fish to get to those places is to be rounded up at the FCF and then trucked past the SRS. The smaller fish that would join them—the minnows and suckers of the more complete food web—must find their own way.

Once, after one of my earlier, fishless visits to the FCF, I had some time to spare, so I drove across the road to visit the SRS and see the dam up close. It is concealed from the Spirit Lake Highway, in part by some woods and in part by the river's own bends. The day was sunny, the clouds thin and wind-spun. I parked in the small lot in front of a small kiosk. On the kiosk hung some faded informational brochures and a story the Corps press office had produced about the SRS in 2010, which I perused before hiking off through some second-growth conifer and hardwood forest. The sun filtered through skinny firs and tall, swooping alders; clusters of sword ferns burst from the soil. The trail emerged half a mile or so later onto an open hillside, and I realized I was standing on the SRS itself.

For a dam, it was subtly embedded within the landscape. The top of it doubled as a grassy service road to an unseen official entrance. Squat concrete traffic barriers bracketed the road, and a tall chain-link fence ran the length of its west side, with barbed wire atop it; a few sparrows perched among the barbs. I walked out into the middle of the road. Swallows whipped around me like little fighter jets. Just beyond the base of the SRS, I could see that enough sediment had built up, or been retained, to become a kind of barrier beach. Some spindly marsh plants were growing there. Behind them was a featureless plain of beige muck, stretching back several miles. Shallow water slugged across it, the once wild and mighty Toutle brought to heel. I watched some quantum of the river float along until it arrived at the base of the SRS. There it eddied lazily, as if testing the structure, always testing it, the way water does.

I walked farther to where the road ended in a chain-link gate with "No Unauthorized Entry" signs. Past them, near the far bank, was the notch that marked the top of the steep spillway. If the river was lazy at the dam, here it rediscovered its older energy, sluiced over, and raced away. I could not imagine a fish swimming up such an incline against such a force of water, but apparently a few can and do. One study in 2013 found that while coho were unable to pass the SRS at all, 13 percent of steelhead swam all the way up the spillway and into the Toutle unaided. They kept on swimming, passing up the impassable river, until they reached the clearer waters of their home creeks, where they spawned. (When I asked the USGS biologist who headed the study if I had understood this correctly, she laughed. "Steelhead are a capable, jumping fish," she said. "They're tough.")

Below me, I saw that the upstream-facing bank of the dam was terraced, with hundreds of small pipes sticking out of the ground at regular intervals. I assumed they performed some sort of drainage function, but in their perfect orderliness, they looked like cannons set against the mountain and its unruly inclinations. More than the official monument boundaries, it was these cannon pipes, the SRS, and the FCF as a kind of junior colleague that drew the starkest and most human line around the effects of the eruption, or so it seemed to me. They are substantial, and they impede: passage, both in (by fish) and out (by the rest of the mountain's oozings).

Walking back to the trail that led into the trees, I thought of the story tacked to the kiosk in the parking lot. Buried among the paragraphs of PR fluff had been what struck me as a remarkable admission by a Corps employee named James Stengle. "Environmental awareness and regulations have evolved immensely over the past thirty years," he had said. "Many of the actions and responses that occurred in the 1980s would likely not be permitted today." Was Stengle talking about the

SRS? Maybe, maybe not. The question was moot, whatever the case. I walked into the alders. The afternoon was quiet save for their swishing, the buzzing of insects, the chittering of swallows, and the faint trickle of a river and its fish still trying to find their old paths.

———

When Keown and Mahnke have measured and loaded all the steelhead into the Fish Washington water tank, it is time to let them go, either within the Hoffstadt Creek watershed or in Alder Creek. Today, Mahnke says, we will deposit our fish in Bear Creek, which is a tributary of Hoffstadt Creek. "We like to alternate," he says. "Keep things as even as we can."

The Bear Creek drop site is seven miles up the Spirit Lake Highway from the FCF. Mahnke and I hop into the fish truck; Keown will stay behind to let the ladder refill with river water and put everything away. The sky has cleared some, and the sun peeps through, but up ahead Mount St. Helens is still wreathed in clouds. Mahnke tells me about his history with steelhead as the truck rattles along. He says he came back to Longview after serving in Vietnam, and became a police officer. This was also about when he started fishing. He used to fish all the time, and steelhead were his favorite.

Among anglers, he says, steelhead might be the ultimate game fish. They are strong and crafty and can put up a fight, but they are also subtle and finicky. To catch them with something more than luck demands a feeling for the organism, for its place. You have to know the river well, its banks and pools and contours. Mahnke fished for steelhead for decades, and the Toutle River was the best place to do it. Once on the South Fork he caught more than twenty on a three-day trip. "One of the best times of my life," he says. Then something happened, or did not happen. Out in the South Fork, he hooked a summer steelhead, but when he reeled it in and beheld it, he felt nothing.

"You know Patsy Cline's music?" he asks.

"Not real well."

"She's got a song, 'Is That All There Is?,' and that went right through my mind with that steelhead." Mahnke shakes his head. "The thrill was just gone. I don't know why. I went home and hung up my gear and haven't fished since."

"But now you volunteer with the fish," I say. Fridays he comes to the Toutle FCF; Mondays, he's down at the Kalama Falls Hatchery, closer to his home. He also helps out on special salmon projects when he can. He has done this for thirty years. He devotes so much time to salmon, in fact, that he has a WDFW volunteer belt buckle, worn so often it is burnished to a shine; and in 2012 he was named a WDFW Volunteer of the Year.

"Yes, I did, and I do, and I love it," Mahnke says. "It's fun to rub shoulders with biologists. You learn a lot. Plus I feel like I'm giving back to the fish." He gazes out the windshield for a moment. "I guess I went from just a plain old Man versus Fish story to trying to see the wider world where the fish lives."

"That's a nice way of putting it," I say.

We arrive at the pull-off for Bear Creek and trundle down a mile or so of twisting, unkempt logging road—like many around here—to the WDFW's Mount St. Helens Wildlife Area. Mahnke tells me this part is officially closed to the public right now because it is a winter reserve for the area elk herds. "This is their winter foraging range," he says.

We pull around on the grass to get as close to Bear Creek as we can. To the east, I can just see the white fringe of Mount St. Helens peeping at us over the hills. What I know to be the crater rim looks as airy and insubstantial as a cloud.

Mahnke hauls himself up onto the truck's bed and opens the tank lid. He says he will get the fish out one by one, and I can take them down to the creek. He nods to a large green gas cylinder connected to the tank. "We keep the water good and oxygenated, so they'll come out feeling pretty pumped up," he says. "Just so you're warned." He works the dip net into a corner and catches the first fish, the second, the third, the fourth, and the fifth, each of which I ferry to the creek.

Now there is just one left. The last is always the toughest; it has the most space in which to evade capture. "Ah! Got him!" Mahnke says, and withdraws the net. In it is the bitten buck. He jolts and thrashes as Mahnke hands the net down to me, and I hustle over to the creek with him. The creek here is shallow and quick and chatty. Along this fringe of the debris avalanche, the alders are tall and thin. They lean out over the creek, casting their shadows upon it. I prop myself against one so I will not slip and fall in, as I almost did with the third fish, and use a branch to lever the net out. The buck hangs in the air. He lies still, maybe exhausted or relieved or both; or maybe he is just a fish near his home water, perhaps within a drainage or two of where he hatched.

After all the stress we have subjected him to, what with handling him and piercing his skin with the tag and yanking out his scales, it will feel good, Mahnke had told me, to release the steelhead into the creek. He is right. It feels very good to lower the net into the cool water and watch the steelhead taste it, feel it, use its continuous motion to maneuver himself out of the mesh and into the current. I pull the net out from under him, and he settles in the shade of the bank, flicking his tail.

Mahnke has come over to watch. "Look at him," he says. "He's darkening, so he matches the bottom." Mahnke calls this the "chameleon effect." I do not know if it is a trick of light or if the steelhead actually is somehow altering his scales and hue, but he does seem to blend in better with the creek, his body a rich slate except for his angry purple injury and the fluorescent pink tag that waggles in the current like a lure.

No doubt he senses the intrusion of my form. He moves out from under the bank into the middle of the creek and holds there above the gray stones. Light plays off him, the sun flashing in the riffle. The creek runs around his body. He lets it carry him, appears for a moment weightless, and then, like the other fish before him, whirls and turns downstream, bursting away in a surge of strength and spray.

14

THE ELK IN THE CARDBOARD BOX

THE UNIVERSITY OF Washington's Burke Museum of Natural
History and Culture stores its surplus wonders in a large building
at an undisclosed location in Seattle. "Please don't share the address,"
Jeff Bradley, the mammalogy collection manager, had requested, and so
when I pull in one morning at the appointed hour, I half expect him to be
crouched behind a bush or in disguise, or at the very least wearing a hat
to hide his curly reddish hair. Instead, he drives up a couple of minutes
later in a bright white university minivan and hops out.

"You found it!" he says as we walk across a loading dock to a nondescript outer door. "Great!" Inside, a second door reveals the interior
of a cavernous warehouse, full to bursting. A great Salish oceangoing
canoe sits on the floor, and skins and bones are draped across tables or
arranged on the bottoms of shelves. Above them are stacked all manner
of containers—cardboard boxes and plastic tubs in different shapes and
sizes, aisle after aisle of them, shelf upon shelf, reaching up to a ceil-
ing that must be twenty or twenty-five feet high. "It's like *Raiders of the
Lost Ark*," I blurt. "That scene at the end when the warehouse guy puts
the Ark—" I realize what I am doing and trail off. "I bet everyone says
that to you."

"Nope," Bradley says, his face perfectly expressionless. "You're the first."

We head to the rear of the room to a shelf on which over forty medium-
sized boxes are neatly organized. Stuck to the shelf is a yellowing sticker
that is perhaps two weeks away from fluttering to the floor and vanishing

Stacks of boxes filled with elk remains collected at Mount St. Helens, held in the Burke Museum's offsite storage facility. Photograph by the author.

forever. "*Cervus elaphus* skeletons from Mount St. Helens blast zone" is written on it in fading blue ink.

"So this is our elk herd," Bradley says. He hauls down a few boxes, pries one open to peer inside, and removes a large plastic bag that clunks with bones. Storage of the Mount St. Helens elk collection would best be described as casual, and Bradley, even though he was not responsible for this state of affairs, is generally apologetic. "Back in the day there was a scramble to, you know, just get everything into boxes, and when that was done they put 'em on the shelf, and they became a long-term museum problem," he explains. "And you know what happens to long-term museum problems." He gives me a look over the top of his glasses. "Let's just say I've got a list full of 'em."

He goes back to rooting through the plastic bag and pulls out an elk skull. He considers it. "A good chunk of the St. Helens herd was zapped in a second," he says. "You can imagine it from their point of view. They're just lying there on a morning like any other, and then, BOOM! And it's like, 'Oh yeah, my world sucks now.' And to not even understand what's going on." He shakes his head and lays this cervid Yorick on the

THOMAS BURKE MEMORIAL ♀ ~3yrs
WASHINGTON STATE MUSEUM *Killed by volcanic blast effects.*
University of Washington

Name *Cervus elaphus*
ELK (Wapiti)
Locality *WA, Skamania Co.;* Mt. St. Helens Volcanic Eruption *(18 May 1980) Blast Impact Zone.*
Gifford Pinchot National Forest. Site 12: Clearwater River Drainage
T9N, R6E, SW 1/4 of SE 1/4, Section 11. Elev. 2400 feet.
Collector *R.D. Taber 1201 / K. Raedeke*
Date *22 October 1981* No. *33442*

"Killed by volcanic blast effects": label on a box of elk remains. Photograph by the author.

floor. "That must have been rough," he says, and laughs ruefully. "But at least it was over quickly, I guess."

He next pulls out a jawbone and some ribs. While he arranges the bones, I look at the small label on the box. It is conventional as museum labels go, but packed with tight, neat handwriting.

All the crammed details read like a remonstrance to the designer of the card, its subtext a question: how could anyone conceive of a circumstance when it might *not* be necessary to scribble so much about an animal that so well captures the current complexities at Mount St. Helens—killed by the mountain it called home, its remains now stored on a shelf far from it?

———

Elk were until recently thought to be the same species as the red deer, *Cervus elaphus*, which ranges over much of Europe, parts of Asia, and around the Mediterranean Sea into northern Africa. Only within the past twenty years did genetic tests show that the two animals were distinct. Elk, now *C. canadensis*, have since been divided into fourteen subspecies, twelve of which are still extant. The elk of Mount St. Helens are from the Roosevelt subspecies, one of four to survive in North America. The largest of the subspecies, it is also the only one native to this part of the Pacific Northwest. Bulls can grow to be up to ten feet in length, stand nearly six feet at the withers, and weigh more than one thousand pounds. Cows are smaller, but only by elk standards; they still can weigh up to six hundred pounds.

Historically, Roosevelt elk were widespread throughout the lands now called Oregon and Washington. Nonindigenous settlement in the 1800s and consequent overhunting led to sharp declines in the Washington population. In the early 1900s, dozens of the Rocky Mountain subspecies were translocated from Yellowstone National Park and Montana to bolster the shrunken herds. Hunting did more than drastically reduce the number of elk: it also drove those that remained into habitats they were not previously known to have occupied. Small herds were first recorded in the vicinity of Mount St. Helens and Spirit Lake in 1931. By 1939, roughly 450 elk were estimated to dwell near the headwaters of the Toutle on the slopes of Mount St. Helens, as well as on the Green River and in the Mount Margaret Backcountry.

The greater herd of which these elk were all a part—the Mount St. Helens herd—is one of ten herds recognized in Washington. Most of its constituents are Roosevelt elk, but not all. Genetic analysis found that some Rocky Mountain elk keep to the east side of the mountain, while Roosevelts occupy the central and western slopes, although the two subspecies hybridize.

More than fifteen hundred elk are thought to have died in the 1980 eruption, along with five thousand deer, two hundred black bears, fifteen mountain goats, and an unknown number of cougars and bobcats. These animals, referred to in official reports as "surface-dwelling wildlife" or "above-ground fauna," were much more vulnerable than smaller, burrow-dwelling mammals, and none were spared: "Volcanic-related mortality agents were non-selective to age, sex, and taxon," one scientist wrote. Most died when the lateral blast cloud swept over, crushing them under the falling forest, striking them with flying stones, or picking them up and hurling them bodily through the air. Others succumbed in the hours that followed, their pelage burned and their lungs seared by hot volcanic gases, or they suffocated in the thick ashfall and were buried under nearly three feet of tephra.

Although the event was, as Bradley says, tragic, one benefit of all those elk being killed so quickly, for ecologists at least, was that the locations of their bodies provided valuable information on their habitat choices. A year after the eruption, Dick Taber, a wildlife biologist from the University of Washington, and two archaeologists, Lee Lyman and Stephanie Livingston, began what they would call their "crispy elk project." Over the next couple of summers, the three searched in the hills above the North Fork Toutle River and in the Clearwater Valley to the east. They found the remains of about one hundred elk. Although a few had clearly been carried and flung down by the lateral blast cloud, their bones scattered among mangled vegetation, many appeared to have died where they stood, and so the skeletons were relatively intact. If the grass had been deep enough, the searchers might even find an elk-shaped depression around the bones, where the animal had been lying when it died.

Sometimes Taber, Lyman, and Livingston found well over one hundred bones from a single animal, other times two or three. Only a fraction showed signs of having been chewed; the eruption had done away with larger scavenging animals, too. From bones and teeth, the researchers could determine an elk's age and sex. Most of the bodies were grouped together, but some were alone. Sorting through the bones from isolated animals yielded a surprising discovery. Mingled within the larger skeletons, or lying a short distance from them, were smaller ones. Of those paired bones, they saw, the big ones were adult females; the little ones were the fetuses they had carried almost to term.

On the western slopes of the Cascade Range, elk cows usually give birth around the beginning of June, so in mid-May, most were in the late stages of pregnancy. Elk are highly social and travel in herds for most of the year, but when it is time for them to give birth, the cows leave their herd. They do this to evade predators; they may not rejoin their herd for several weeks, waiting until the calf is large enough to run from predators on its own.

State biologists had wanted to know where the calving sites were, but they had been unable to find them. In the late 1970s, the only way to follow an elk remotely was to fit a bulky radio collar around its neck. A field tech was then sent up to some exposed point with an antenna. They would hold it aloft, wave it around, listen for a beeping sound, and from this attempt to pinpoint the elk's location. It was an imperfect method, with success contingent on luck and atmospheric variables. But the eruption showed exactly where the cows had gone to give birth.

"Now we have GPS radio tags and can watch elk from space," Bradley says as he puts the bones back in their bags. "So technology saves the day once again." Humans and elk alike, I am sure, must be relieved to know that it no longer requires an erupting volcano to reveal the filigrees of their natural history.

———

Not all the elk within sight of Mount St. Helens perished. Some were only a short distance beyond the fringe of scorched trees, and these survived. They were probably the first large animals to return to the mountain. More than any creature except a bird, elk can move long distances quickly. Within days they started to make tentative forays into the devastated area, nosing at its margins. On his reconnaissance flights a couple of weeks later, Jerry Franklin saw their hoofprints, the light stitching of which rejoined the radically new terrain to its older, less altered surroundings, like a patch in an enormous quilt.

Following after the living elk came a biologist named Evelyn Merrill, a graduate student of Taber's. Like so many of the young scientists who ended up working in the blast area, she had been doing PhD research on a related topic elsewhere— in her case elk distribution around Mount Rainier—when Mount St. Helens erupted, prompting her to move her project south fifty miles.

During her first full season, in 1981, most of the elk Merrill saw venturing into the blast area were cows. They would go in a few hundred yards and then leave. Even with the biological legacies Franklin and others were studying in the Blowdown Zone that first summer, the landscape held little food, so the elk never stayed long. But Merrill suspected they might have had home ranges there prior to the eruption; a typical range for elk in this region is between 1,500 and 4,000 acres.

In spite of losing more than 10 percent of its members in an instant, the Mount St. Helens herd as a whole, Merrill saw, was quite resilient. Their incursions grew longer, until elk were consistently wandering more than two miles into the blast area from its greener edges. The newly open habitat suited them. When plants started to grow again, it suited them still more, and their numbers surged. In 1981, Merrill had counted 203 elk making use of the blast area. By 1985, their population had more than tripled, to 634. Calving rates rose as well, until within five years they were indistinguishable from those of other herds around the state. But when Merrill calculated the herd's rate of increase, she found it was more than could be accounted for by calving alone. Other elk had to be moving in, encouraged by a string of mild winters.

Merrill documented an emerging symbiosis: new vegetation attracted the elk; the elk in turn brought new vegetation. They were dispersal vectors for plants, gorging themselves outside the blast area, wandering back into it, and defecating seeds, along with a helpful prill of nitrogen fertilizer. Piles of their droppings could persist for over a year, slowly leaching nutrients into the ground. Sometimes, the elk themselves were the vessels of dispersal. As she hiked in the debris avalanche or the Blowdown Zone, Merrill sometimes saw a green patch in the midst of otherwise bare space. When she dug around the plants, she would find a dead elk decomposing at their roots. Its body had become a nursery for the undigested seeds in its gut.

Elk took advantage of larger human interventions as well. The SCS's early seedings of the debris avalanche deposits, which had so bedeviled Virginia Dale, were for elk a boon. What had been little more than loose rubble was transformed into acres of what Merrill calls "elk ice cream": clover, rye grass, other plants perfect both for municipal uses and for a ruminant's chambered stomach. The seeding may not have done much to stop the North Fork Toutle from eroding its banks, but it did create wonderful elk habitat, especially during the winter.

So common did the elk become on the debris avalanche deposits, and so quickly, that state wildlife managers decided action was needed. In 1982, the Washington Department of Game opened a brief elk hunt in the hope of thinning the herd. A second hunt was held the following year. Merrill considered that year, 1983, to be a watershed for elk and their relationship with the blast area. Rather than retreat to higher elevations or into the forests to avoid people, as they might have done before, elk moved to another swath of land where they would be safe: the 110,000 acres of the newly created national monument, where no hunting was allowed.

Once elk moved into the monument and onto the Pumice Plain, the full extent of their successional capacity was on display. Like the northern pocket gopher in the Blowdown Zone (mixing the ash with the soil it had buried) and the prairie lupine in the Pumice Plain (facilitating its own growth and that of other plants), elk were effective agents of those critical secondary-disturbance processes that made the pyroclastic flow deposits more hospitable for plants. As they trotted around, the steady beat of their hard hooves broke through the crust of ash, creating small depressions or cracks that acted as seed traps. "Consider a perfectly uniform pumice slope," Jerry Franklin would write. "The pattern and rate of recovery on that slope can be forecast with some accuracy, but passage of one elk may produce sharp contrasts between sites a few centimeters apart by subsequent influences of rill erosion and plant survivorship."

It was a funny turn of events, Merrill thought, showing the odd and knotty way human management actions can bring about unexpected results. Without the hunt to drive them in, how long might it have taken the elk to move into the heart of the blast area? But they had come far since the first days when she had watched them gazing out at the supposedly lifeless land from the safe distance of a ridge, when something about their silhouettes had seemed slightly off, and it had taken her a moment to realize that the twitching nubs on their heads were all that was left of their ears, burned off by the blast.

———

Currently the Mount St. Helens elk herd is the state's largest, with somewhere between eleven thousand and thirteen thousand individuals, according to the most recent estimates. The herd's home range spans five counties in the southwestern corner of the state, all east of Interstate 5. Its resurgence following the eruption was generally celebrated. Elk were always creatures in the public eye, and especially after 1980. "Because of the herd's history," state biologists observed, "because of the tourist appeal of the volcano, and because the herd area is bordered by developed corridors with sizable metropolitan populations, the Mount St. Helens elk herd is a high profile herd, featured often in local news media." (The elk also contributed an estimated $30 million to the local economy during the hunting season.) But the elk's story would take a darker turn. As plants and shrubs returned to the blast area, the elk thrived. When trees appeared and grew tall, especially on the private timberland plantations that surrounded the monument, and the forest canopy began to close over their heads, they did not.

Elk need great quantities of forage, especially in the fall, so they can fatten up sufficiently to survive the winter. Years of steady population growth around Mount St. Helens left the herd struggling to find enough to eat in a contracted territory. So worrisome did their predicament become that in 1999 the WDFW began to survey for winter-killed elk around the North Fork Toutle River. They counted seventy-nine dead elk the first year, but the next year they found just one, and the year after that, zero. But then they counted sixty-three. Two years later, 158 elk starved to death, some in distressingly public ways. Grainy videos spread of emaciated animals, some too weak to stand. They thrashed in the mud, their hides stretched taut over their bones. One person who lived on the North Fork put hay out for eighty famished elk that were lingering on his property. "What I'm trying to do is what I believe is the right thing," he said. "I don't think they need to be any more abused than they already have been."

Responding to the public outcry, the WDFW decided to provide feed to the hundreds of elk that spent the winter on the debris avalanche. ("We are a public agency," the head of the wildlife division said. "We have an obligation to do what the public asks us to do.") Hay trucks drove out to the winter range, heavy with bales of alfalfa from eastern Oregon. More than one hundred tons of hay were distributed. Elk gathered by the hundreds to eat it. These were risky congregations. The elk were thin and weakened, and illnesses spread through the herd, including hoof disease. Local reporters likened the elk to cattle in a feedlot. People questioned whether this was the way wild animals should really be treated, whether it might not be better to let nature take its course. No one was sure that the elk would even be able to digest this novel food. Some starved anyway, with their bellies full. State biologists later conceded they could not say whether the artificial feeding had done more good than harm.

Whether the land can support as many elk as are here remains an open question. Surveys show the herd is getting smaller. Seventy-one died in the most recent available winter-kill count. This was markedly more than the previous year (forty-six), and the one before that (twenty-nine), but the numbers rise and fall with the severity of the winters. Maybe things will get better in future winters, or maybe they will not.

These days, elk become most conspicuous at Mount St. Helens in late September, when hundreds gather in the blast area for the annual rut. During the rest of the year, they roam as herds made up either of cows and calves and perhaps younger bulls, which are often led by an older female, or herds made up of older bulls. Come fall, they start to mix, as the bulls compete to gather cows into their harems. A large bull elk can have a harem of more than twenty cows. Bulls spar for them with their antlers, but the biggest bulls sometimes just have to give a small bull a stern look to make the latter high-tail it away.

Internal squabbles aside, elk like to keep their distance from humans. Their buff coats blend well with the light brown of withering grass, but the Pumice Plain is so wide and open that the movement of their lighter flanks can draw the eye from more than a mile away. What until moments ago looked like a series of odd lumps down by Spirit Lake proves to be a group of large and majestic animals, fifty or sixty or sometimes more, all of them standing or resting on the ground or idly milling about, relaxed, appearing for all the world to be enjoying themselves.

———

Late fall is also the time of year when Charlie Crisafulli begins to gather the monitors and sensors he spread throughout the blast area at the beginning of his field season. Small temperature loggers called HOBOs that he has placed at dozens of sites across the Pumice Plain, others tethered to buoys in Spirit Lake, remote cameras bolted to trees in the Blowdown Zone—all of these have to come down so that their data can be downloaded and analyzed over the winter. Today Crisafulli is in high spirits, though also ambivalent. Another summer gone. Who knows what next year will bring?

We are walking up the Windy Trail (#216E) to one of the four springs in the bedrock at the top of the Pumice Plain, where it melds with the mountain. The day is crisp and bright, but a haze lingers after a summer of intense forest fires. "It was pretty awful here all through August," Crisafulli says. "Some days the smoke was so thick you could barely see the mountain."

At the stream's source, water rollicks past with such force that it seems like a small scree waterfall. While Crisafulli splashes down to cut his

HOBO from a rebar stake—"Whew, this is cold," he calls out as his fingers go red and numb—I fill my water bottle. Mere yards from the point where the stream emerges from the rocks, I do not have to worry about it being rife with bacteria, Crisafulli has assured me. "This water is so sweet, and mountain-filtered," he had yelled over its mild roar. "It tastes like Earth's nectar." He stuffs the HOBO in his backpack, and we follow the stream down into the Pumice Plain, where he has lashed another HOBO a third of a mile away.

As we walk, I keep an eye out for elk. Recognizing the hints of their presence is a skill I am still acquiring. "Are they often around here?" I once asked Crisafulli as we walked along the Hummocks Trail on the west side of Mount St. Helens, in the debris avalanche. "They don't seem to be having much of an impact."

Crisafulli had goggled. "Are you kidding?"

I nodded to a small fir we were passing. It was maybe three feet tall, green, reasonably lush. "That tree doesn't look like it's been too heavily browsed," I said.

Crisafulli gazed at me with a look that was somewhere between amusement and deep pity. "No, they've been chowing down on this one." He pointed to its odd, inverted shape: narrow on the bottom, widening at the top—a sign of thorough cervid pruning. "Maybe you're thinking of porcupines," he said kindly.

"Yeah, maybe," I mumbled, but I was not. Porcupines strip the bark rather than nibble off the new growth, and no bark was missing from this one.

Crisafulli chuckled. "I'd hate to see your Christmas tree if you think this is what a normal tree looks like," he said, and we walked on.

On the Pumice Plain, elk and their sign are more obvious to me. Their rough game trails crisscross the bluffs made of the pyroclastic flow deposits, wend a little, and then veer off down impossible slopes. "It's amazing to watch them run up and down those things," Crisafulli says. Depressions in the grass, often fringed by piles of droppings, show where elk have bedded down for the night.

"The elk treat the Pumice Plain like a de facto refuge," Crisafulli says. Also, like the northern pocket gopher, they have outgrown their old role of savior and become a creature of more complex influence. A few years ago, Michael Fleming, one of Roger del Moral's graduate students, came here to study the effects elk were having on plants. "Although elk have been labeled a keystone species in the Pacific Northwest and elsewhere," he wrote, "the effect of elk activity on Mount St. Helens vegetation has scarcely been touched upon by researchers there." Biologists had generally been so concerned with the elk in their own right that no one had studied the ways they were changing the landscape.

Their effects could be significant, Fleming showed. When they browsed, they suppressed woody plants while promoting grasses. In sites of heavy elk activity, exotic species were increasingly becoming established. Elk hooves were no longer trampling pumice and ash, breaking it up and opening space for plants, but trampling and damaging the plants themselves. The question was how meaningful these effects were in the grand successional scheme of the Pumice Plain. Fleming thought some qualification was in order. "Elk contribute to patchiness of vegetation on Mount St. Helens, but they constitute only a moderate to weak influence on overall successional dynamics during early succession when compared to annual fluctuations attributable to extreme weather events, pathogen outbreaks, or insect herbivory," he wrote. "Only by keeping elk out of large portions of the landscape for many years would we be able to determine confidently if, how, and to what degree their activity significantly alters succession of this recovering vegetation."

To Crisafulli, such caution was unnecessary, even counterproductive. "Look around you," he says. "The elk are knocking the shit out of the vegetation." They have nibbled off the new growth from most of the young conifers we have passed, leaving them twisted like strange bonsai trees. They nibble the shoots of cottonwoods and willows, forcing trees that would otherwise have grown to between twenty and thirty feet tall to direct their resources laterally, so that they spread out over the ground like heather. "The elk just keep coming and coming and coming,"

Crisafulli says. In just an hour, a herd of elk feasting on a patch of land can set succession back a decade. Given the distances they can cover, that is a lot of patches whose successional trajectories are set back.

What the ecosystem needs in order to be complete, Crisafulli feels, is that one last, infamous player, the wolf. Mount St. Helens cries out for wolves, with its hundreds of thousands of acres of relatively undisturbed forest and great numbers of elk so untroubled by anything other than the occasional cougar that some starve to death from their own excess. But the possibility of their return is a complex matter. After a seventy-year absence, wolves have been breeding in Washington since 2008, but most packs are in northeastern Washington, where their presence is, to put it extremely mildly, contentious. The nearest wolves are the Teanaway pack near Cle Elum, almost ninety miles away. State politicians from the northeast often grouse that if people west of the Cascade Crest want wolves in their backyard so bad, they are welcome to them, but Crisafulli would never dream of trying to translocate any to the monument, as people did with elk a century ago. "*Wolf* isn't something you really want to say out loud around here, especially when you're talking about federal lands," he says. "They'll get here eventually, probably within twenty years, but we're just going to have to wait for them."

In the absence of the wolf, Crisafulli agitated to let in a surrogate predator. People had hunted elk on state and federal lands around Mount St. Helens for decades, but in 2005, he proposed that the Pumice Plain— the core of the monument—be opened to hunting. The way he conceived it, a few hunters would pay a premium for an elk tag (and maybe the money could be put toward research), they would have, in his words, "a blast!," and the elk would scatter to other parts of the monument, where their impact would not be so concentrated.

The hunt did not go as he hoped. Several areas around the monument were opened to hunting, not just the Pumice Plain. The hunt was not the one-off event he envisioned, either; more than a decade later, hunters still anticipate the annual Mount St. Helens elk hunt. "Once you open that door, it's really hard to close it," Crisafulli says. It was a management decision that he lost by winning. "I was so naïve," he sighs. "Or worse, ignorant."

I ask what it was about the elk that made him choose such a route. From the sound of things, it is almost as though they offended him.

"I don't know," he says. "I guess I was frustrated. They were absolutely hammering the trees. But there are other factors." With their large home ranges, elk easily cross jurisdictional boundaries—monument land, more generic Forest Service land, state land, private timberland. All those landowners have different management objectives. Some of those objectives are good for elk; others less so. The elk therefore choose, or are forced onto, the land that best meets their needs.

So hundreds of elk are still in the Pumice Plain, and they show no signs of leaving. At Charlie's Camp later that night, as the temperature plunges to freezing and I burrow into my sleeping bag and cinch it tight around my face, I try to square Crisafulli's arguments about elk with the mandate he has spent so much of his life and energy embracing, justifying, operating under, and fighting for: "Ecological succession to continue substantially unimpeded." Elk at Mount St. Helens were a natural component of its landscape until the eruption destroyed them. Almost immediately they came back on their own. Surely their presence in the monument is as much a part of succession as that of the fireweed, the prairie lupine, the fir tree? Why is it so terrible if they eat all the trees or stomp on the wildflowers? They did it before, so why stop them now?

Perhaps the issue is that the elk are not bound to the mountain in the way the rest of the organisms are. Aside from people, they are the most numerous large animal in the blast area, and in the weave of Mount St. Helens, they have often provided the tug that pulled its various threads together, connecting the idealized world inside the monument boundaries with the more obvious messiness of the world outside. In so doing, they make plain some of the pretensions and more obstinate contradictions of this place, namely that anything anywhere could be said to be substantially unimpeded by the human hand. That may be reason enough to try to lessen the influence of the elk. But as the number of interventions with them in mind has increased, they also pose a threat to the monument's original purpose. More than Franklin, more than del Moral, more than Dale, more than almost any other researcher who has come here over the years, Crisafulli really and truly wants to know: What happens when every single living thing, big or small, plant or animal, is burned away or buried, and nothing is left but rock and ash for hundreds of square miles? What does succession look like when it is left to run unhindered? What can the land be if it is left alone? Is that even possible? This recitation seems as appropriate a conclusion as any to come from Mount St. Helens, in that it is not a conclusion at all. Only more questions.

———

A couple of weeks later, in mid-October, I come back for a day hike in the Mount Margaret Backcountry. By now Crisafulli has largely closed up Charlie's Camp for the season; I drove over to see it before coming to the trailhead. The big canvas wall tent had been taken down. Inside a smaller tent, all the field equipment—the dip nets and crates, the boots and the buckets—was crammed inside, in mostly neat piles and bundles. (Jim Gawel was going to bring up some of his students from Tacoma to help load everything onto a flatbed truck.) The field crew's tents were all gone, except for Crisafulli's, over in its alcove. He is away on the Pumice Plain, but I have no idea where, or what he is up to.

From the parking lot at Norway Pass, the trail climbs steadily. After a couple of miles on the lee side of a hill, where a few trees were sheltered from the lateral blast, I come to the pass, and catch my first sight of Mount St. Helens. It is perfectly framed here by two descending slopes that converge below its rim in almost perfect symmetry, so that, with Spirit Lake mirroring it in form rather than reflecting it, the scene is like a negative: the dark mountain over the clear water, the wan sky above the verdant earth, each positioned with its opposite.

I stop to catch my breath. A couple of summers ago Crisafulli brought me here. He was one of the people involved in drafting the Mount Margaret Backcountry Management Plan. That day he spoke of the prospect of retirement and all the things he planned to do (travel, watch birds, cook even more). As he was talking—moments after he had finished saying, "Mount St. Helens gives you a lot, but she takes a lot from you, too"—he raised his camera and took a picture of the mountain. "Lookin' good today," he said, maybe to me. I thought, *Charlie's never gonna leave.*

I continue beyond the pass and up to the junction with the Lakes Trail, which goes around the hill and drops into a basin to reach first Grizzly Lake, and then Obscurity Lake, Panhandle, and others with similarly wonderful names. I go the other way, taking the Boundary Trail toward Mount Margaret, keeping Mount St. Helens in sight. Snow has started to accumulate on the upper half of the prominence, making the mountain look hoary, austere, sleepy.

The trail keeps ascending, crosses a wind-swept ridge, goes up some more, and then follows a contour for a spell. There is a curve and a corner, and I am walking along thinking of nothing, just smelling the air and feeling the wind, when I hear two loud calls: *Skweeeeeeeeee-ump! Skweeeeeeeeeeee-ump!*

The calls are much closer than I am prepared for. I take a few more steps and a bull elk appears from behind a fir that was perfectly positioned to conceal him. He is enormous, an exemplary specimen, with a rack that adds several feet to his already considerable height. His thick brown neck was lowered and extended somewhat for his bugle, but now he straightens and turns his head—I can almost feel the weight of his antlers—and stares at me. He is tense and still, but regal in his stillness.

The elk and I look at each other. In the past I have sometimes wondered why the call of a bull elk is called a bugle. To me it sounds nothing at all like the small brass instrument used to rouse Boy Scouts at dawn, and as I stand frozen on the trail, I realize this assessment is born of the fact that I have always been too far from the source. At this proximity—too close—a bugling elk becomes something old, otherworldly, majestic, powerful. His voice makes my blood run cold. It is a summons for ghosts, of which this land has so many.

The bull regards me out of one eye; with his other, he scans his lines of flight. I wait for him to decide what he will do, since it is he who will determine the outcome of this encounter. I could not move if I wanted to. He breathes out in low, deep, controlled snorts, punctuated by bursts of cloud from the black pits of his nostrils. He is wary but does not seem overly troubled, and after a few seconds he turns and canters down the hill, unhurried, his head held high.

EPILOGUE

VOLCÁN CALBUCO

A T 6:05 P.M. on April 22, 2015, a mountain in southern Chile named Volcán Calbuco erupted with almost no warning. Chilean geologists with the Southern Andean Volcano Observatory, or OVDAS, detected a surge of seismic activity in the early evening and rushed to change Calbuco's alert status from level 1/green to level 4/red. This prompted an evacuation alert to be sent to every town within a twelve-mile radius of the mountain. Fifteen minutes after the alert, as thousands of people were rushing to their cars, the mountain gave a sudden jolt, there was a loud boom, and ash began to fill the sky.

The eruption lasted ninety minutes, but the ash column rose almost ten miles in that short time. Around 1 a.m. on April 23, Calbuco erupted again. This eruption lasted six hours and was much more powerful. The ash column rose even higher and was laced with blue and purple lightning bolts. The sky looked like it had been set afire by the mountain. Almost a week later, on April 30, Calbuco erupted a third time, although briefly and much less forcefully.

Calbuco had been still for more than forty years until then, but it had a lively history. An eruption that began in 1893 and lasted two years was one of the largest ever in southern Chile. Part of the mountain collapsed, and huge lahars swept down the Rio Blanco valley into nearby Lago Llanquihue, the country's second largest lake. In the twentieth century alone, Calbuco had major eruptions in 1906, 1907, 1909, 1911, 1917,

1929, 1932, 1945, and 1961. Its most recent activity—a small explosion of gas and smoke—was in 1972.

Set within that history, the 2015 eruption was mild. No one was injured or killed. There were no devastating pyroclastic flows or lahars, and although a hydropower facility was destroyed, the damage in the closest cities was minor. The ash plume spread nearly three hundred miles to the north and northeast. Air traffic in Brazil was disrupted, but the most pronounced effects were confined to within a few miles of the mountain—a little more than a foot of tephra, a few broken windows, and some damaged roofs.

After the April 30 event, Calbuco went quiet again. OVDAS geologists watched it for a couple of weeks, and its status remained red, but by May 18, 2015, they were satisfied that the eruption was finished. The next day they downgraded Calbuco to alert level 3/orange, and the travel restrictions were removed.

———

In late January 2016, during the austral summer, I am driving a rental car away from the airport in Puerto Montt, which is more than six hundred miles south of Santiago. Forty miles northeast of here is my destination, the small town of Ensenada. The highway traces the southern shore of Lago Llanquihue, its sparkling waters a postcard shade of aquamarine. Southern snowpeaks frame the scene. To the east is Volcán Osorno, 8,700 feet high, its cone perfect but for the slightest off-centeredness. Peeping out behind it is the sharp, hooked peak of Volcán Puntiagudo, which is only a few hundred feet shorter. Calbuco is on the other side of the road, appearing from time to time in the southeast, but mostly it crouches behind the hills, as if reluctant to be compared with its more picturesque neighbors.

The road passes through Ensenada, and I turn in at a little resort near the outskirts of town. I have come all this way to meet Charlie Crisafulli and Fred Swanson, who have both been in Chile for almost a month. As they are out in the field right now, the proprietor points me to the little *cabaña* they have rented for the week.

Spectacular though its eruption was, Calbuco's was merely the latest of three in Chile in the past eight years. The first was at Chaitén, a small mountain a little less than 3,700 feet high that is 150 miles or so to the south. It erupted at 2:40 a.m. on May 2, 2008, sending up a plume of ash and steam at least thirty-five thousand feet high. Four thousand people in the town of Chaitén, six miles away, were immediately evacuated, and one person died in the process. Over the next few weeks, the mountain erupted several times with greater strength and vigor. Devastating lahars flooded the town, and a subsequent ash column rose nearly one hundred thousand feet high. Ash drifted over to Argentina, where it closed roads, schools, and an airport. A new lava dome started to grow, before long surpassing the height of the old one, before it partially collapsed in February 2009, causing pyroclastic flows. Then the mountain went still, as it had been since at least the seventeenth century.

Three years later, 160 miles northeast, a massif named Puyehue–Cordón Caulle erupted at 3:15 p.m. on June 4, 2011. English-speaking geologists refer to this as the Puyehue–Cordón Caulle Volcanic Complex, or PCCVC. In addition to its eponymous features—a stratovolcano more than seven thousand feet high (Puyehue) and a rift zone (Cordón Caulle)—the PCCVC also includes the Cordillera Nevada caldera and the Mencheca volcano. A fissure in the Cordón Caulle zone erupted, sending an ash column more than forty-five thousand feet high and spilling lava down its sides. The plume blew east to Argentina. Pumice rocks the size of golf balls were found near the Chile-Argentina border almost fifteen miles away, but no one was injured.

When Crisafulli and Swanson heard of the Chaitén eruption, they thought it would be a wonderful chance to take everything they had learned at Mount St. Helens and apply it somewhere else. They first visited it in September 2009 with some Chilean scientists and set up transects to monitor the vegetation and arthropod response. After Cordón Caulle erupted, they traveled there in 2012 and established similar transects. When Calbuco erupted, they were likewise eager to add it to their study sites, and as soon as possible. "Mount St. Helens showed us that being there for the first growing season is really important," Crisafulli told me before he left.

Now I drive over and park next to the *cabaña*, go inside—the door is unlocked—and stow my luggage as best I can in the little space left among jumbled piles of knapsacks, sleeping bags, and cartons of equipment. Having nothing to do but wait, I go for a short stroll around the grounds. A gate leads out to the lakeside beach. The sand is warm, and if I position myself just so, I can see both Calbuco and Osorno, the latter resplendent across Llanquihue with its smooth white slopes, and the former lurking on the other side of the *cabaña*, its summit so broad and rumpled it seems more like an ambitious foothill than a mountain. I sit down on the sand, and in the sleepy daze of the afternoon imagine a dialogue between these two peaks, Calbuco gazing at Osorno and warning, *Preen now because you can, but your time will come.*

———

The next morning I head out with Crisafulli and the team. In addition to Swanson and Julia Jones, Tara Blackman and Elsie Denton are here from the US; joining them are a pair of Chilean ecologists who have driven down from Austral University, in Valdivia, with five of their own students.

Crisafulli wants to focus on just a few spots of Calbuco's northern flank. This part of the mountain is on private land—a group of Chileans bought it and are trying to turn it into a bioreserve—but Crisafulli has befriended them. ("I'm bringing them out to St. Helens next year," he says.) We drive through Ensenada and turn up a dirt road not far from the middle of town. The road climbs into the foothills and becomes progressively bumpier. The pickup rocks and sways like a boat on high seas, and then we reach an open plain and Crisafulli stops. We will hike the rest of the way.

The air is cool and sweet, except for the occasional pungent whiff of sulfurous fumes. Out of the trees come the loud, eerie calls of the chucao tapaculo, a small songbird. Crisafulli divvies gear among the young people, whom he calls "my pack animals," and we all crunch into the forest.

The terrain here is nothing like Mount St. Helens. Every eruption is different. This one was smaller, with a rating of 4 (large) on the Volcanic Explosivity Index, which classifies eruptions based on the volume of their output and the height of the eruptive column. (Mount St. Helens was a 5, very large.) The main contribution to this landscape was small rocks impressively uniform in size, an inch or so in diameter. The rocks are a dark gray, cindery basaltic andesite called scoria. A thick layer covers the ground so completely that what was once meadow and forest now looks like a gravel parking lot, with big shrubs and trees jutting out here and there.

While we walk, Crisafulli explains his plans. He wants to "lift the sampling design of Mount St. Helens and superimpose it over Calbuco," as he has at Chaitén and Cordón Caulle. He intends to have at least two transects—ideally three—at different elevations. Each will be just shy of 60 meters long, with three 250-square-meter macroplots along it, and twelve microplots in each of those. Within the macroplots, every single overstory tree, living or dead, will get a little metal tag, and all the shrubs and grasses will be identified and their abundance estimated; within the microplots, every single seedling, living or dead, will be tagged and measured; and old soil will be collected and compared to the scoria by physical and chemical assay. There are a number of other things he wants to look at if time allows.

We reach the desired elevation, and people spread out in small groups, laying out long measuring tapes and hammering rebar stakes into the ground. As they work, Crisafulli, Blackman, Denton, and the Chilean professors, Mauro Gonzalez and Antonio Lara, start identifying and tagging the biggest trees. "This is the first posteruption growth assessment," Crisafulli says. "Survival and sprouting, resistance and resilience—that's what we're looking at."

The predominant trees are *Laureliopsis philippiana*, a species endemic to Argentina and Chile that is known colloquially as tepa. These are broadleaf evergreens that can grow up to one hundred feet tall and live for several hundred years. They are found in humid areas with deep soil, at elevations between approximately two thousand and three thousand feet. Normally they are green almost from crown to base, covered not only with their own foliage but also with the leaves of the many epiphytes that twine around their thick trunks, but the tepa at Calbuco now range in color from a stark white to a sickly gray. They have been battered and scoured by what Crisafulli calls the "scoria rain" during each of Calbuco's eruptions. The rain pocked the bark and tore chunks from it while pruning all but the sturdiest canopy branches and tearing off almost all their leaves. Yet small leaves have already begun to sprout from many of the trees, almost with an air of defiance.

Documenting this arboreal defiance is what Crisafulli and the four others are doing now. Crisafulli wants to assess the sprouting of each tree on a four-point scale, from zero to high, on three parts (the bole, the axils, and the branches). As with any initial effort in the field, the five of them must calibrate their measuring techniques so that they all make consistent assessments. This means they spend a lot of time squinting into the treetops and debating rough percentages.

"How's it going?" Crisafulli asks Blackman at one point, as she and Denton discuss where the cutoff between "low" and "mid" should be.

"Okay," Blackman says. "I'm feeling confused about the axil." This is the junction between a leaf stalk or branch and the bole (that is, the trunk) from which it grows.

"Feelings are for Barry Manilow," Crisafulli says. He peers up at the highest branches, which twist and turn like fractals. "I do agree this would be a lot easier if all the trees were dead."

"Yeah," Blackman says.

Crisafulli walks over to Gonzalez, who is staring up at the top of the tree. "Tomorrow I'll bring binoculars," Gonzalez says. "But this is really something, all the growth."

"The epiphytes, you can see they're doing great, snaking up the bole like that," Crisafulli says. "But the trees aren't looking so hot. They're wimps. I bet many of them will be dead within a year or two."

Gonzalez turns to stare at him. He is a jovial man, given to laughter, and he laughs now. "What are you talking about?" he says. "These trees are three hundred years old! Calbuco has erupted many times, and they've survived them all."

Crisafulli shakes his head. "Not like this time," he says. "They've never had to come back from an eruption that had output like this, with all the damage to their boles."

Gonzalez laughs again and goes back to staring at the heavens. "Well, we shall see, my friend," he says. "I think the tepa will survive. They will fight to their *último suspiro*."

I do not know much Spanish, but I can figure out what *último suspiro* means: their last breath.

———

Since I am worthless at recognizing Chilean montane flora, Crisafulli asks if I would like to help out by being the "tephra removal specialist." This is his polite way of asking if I would mind digging pits to establish a set of plus-or-minus tephra plots. The design he borrowed from Don Zobel and Joe Antos, but I will not need a vacuum or a toothbrush to remove this tephra with near-surgical delicacy. A shovel will do. Crisafulli points me to a pair of them, and heavy leather gloves. "Two meters by two meters would be great," he says.

I start digging. The scoria is large and coarse, but also densely packed. It rebuffs my shovel's attacks and has a way of efficiently and disdainfully refilling my progress. Digging is frustrating, the labor of prisoners and scientists, but after forty-five minutes or so I reach the old soil, brown and rich and stitched with the abraded roots of plants. Most are either dead or close to it, but some have new sprouts pushing up through the scoria. I find a squirming earthworm and some sort of insect larvae that survived even after they were pummeled. I set them gently to the side and wish them luck.

Swanson and Jones and Jorge Romero come by to see how things are going. They have been more loosely attached to the project, coming and going as they please so they can, as Swanson says, "get a read on the geological tableau." Romero is one of the Chilean students, a slight young man who dresses very neatly for fieldwork and somehow manages to keep his clothes clean. The others are ecologists; he is studying to be a geologist. Although he is in his early twenties and has not yet graduated from college, in a few months he will be the lead author of the scientific paper that describes Calbuco's 2015 eruption.

"Mount St. Helens is a piece of art," he says to me. "You know there is a volcano in Chile that is just like it."

"Oh?" I say, glad for the excuse not to dig for a moment. "When did it erupt?"

"Ten thousand years ago," Romero says. "But it has almost the exact same structure: the crater, the dome rebuilding. It's almost complete now. You can see the dome has grown to the crater rim."

"So Mount St. Helens might look like that in time?" I ask.

Romero nods. "Assuming it doesn't erupt again, yes," he says. "But that is the life of a volcano, right? To get big, to get small, to get big, and if we are very lucky we get to watch a little of it." He leans over and admires the pit—"You've dug a lot!"—and then excuses himself to find Swanson and Jones.

I watch him leave and resume my digging. Late morning turns to afternoon. My arms start to ache, and I can feel blisters forming on my thumbs and palms despite the leather gloves, but none of this bothers me because I have stayed lost in that image: a time-lapse progression of a mountain rising and falling to its own rhythms, rising and falling as the millennia fly by, rising and falling like the chest of a person breathing.

———

After a couple of days of digging pits in the scoria, I wake up one morning and decide, somewhat on a whim, that I want to climb Calbuco. Blackman had told me that Crisafulli tries to climb the mountains he works on, but he is not sure he will have time for Calbuco this trip; getting the transects in is taking longer than he thought it would.

I nurture this thought all through breakfast, all through my discreet packing of a larger lunch than usual, all through the drive out to the site, all through the short hike up to the unfinished transect, until the moment Crisafulli says to me, "Well, all the pits are dug that need to be dug, so what do you feel like doing today?"

"I was thinking of climbing Calbuco," I say. "If that's okay."

"Oh," Crisafulli says. "Okay." He looks surprised but nods slowly. "Yeeaah, sure, that would be fine." He looks up at the thickly clouded sky. Calbuco is invisible even though we are standing on it. He grins. "You picked a great day to go."

"Yeah."

"When should I expect you back?"

"Say, late afternoon?" I say. "Don't worry—I'm a big chicken. I won't do anything stupid."

Crisafulli chuckles. "Oh, I'm not worried about that," he says. Then he has a thought. "Hey, since you're headed that way, maybe you can do me a favor and carry this rebar up to treeline—we're going to start putting a transect around there when we're done here."

This is how I end up hauling more than thirty pounds of three-foot-long rebar stakes by hand for what feels like miles to the last stands of stripped trees. My shirt is soaked through with sweat and my arms feel like rubber. I worry that I will have spent all my energy before I even leave the treeline. I lean the rebar against a tall snag, mutter imprecations at Crisafulli, and continue. I pass through the remains of a bamboo forest, whose stalks stick from the ground like thousands of white straws, some of them well over eight or ten feet tall. So far as I can tell, every single stalk is dead, and it would be tempting to think the eruption is responsible. But it is not. Bamboo, Gonzalez explained to me yesterday, grows for about sixty or seventy years, and then the stalks flower, drop all their seeds, and die all at once. These bamboo stalks were dead well before Calbuco sent its scoria rains down on them. Under normal conditions the seeds would grow and the forest return, but they are now under a foot of abrasive rock, so who can say what will happen? "You have to know the natural history of the place," Gonzalez said. "If you don't, you make mistakes."

At around three thousand feet in elevation, the last vestiges of vegetation disappear. Now the mountain is just a towering heap of small, gray rocks wrapped in heavy gray clouds. The climb is not technical, but the slopes are steep, almost absurdly so in places, or narrow and bouldered, the sides plunging away to drops of unknowable distance. The wind is subtle but persistent, clammy. Not many people have gone up the mountain since it erupted, so there are no footprints for me to follow, at least none I can see. In some ways this is a gift. I can focus on my breath, my steps, the rough rocks I walk over. But more than once it occurs to me that I am climbing an unfamiliar mountain all by myself, I cannot see more than a few feet in front of my face, and I have not even looked at a map, much less brought one. But what good would a map do? All the landmarks it might show—the valleys and meadows and such—are buried under at least a foot of scoria, because, lest I forget, Calbuco is an active volcano that can erupt at any time with little or no warning.

Sometimes I am nervous. The rest of the time, it feels incredible to climb this living mountain. As I near what I think is the top, the wind picks up and I start to shiver, but after I reach the lip of the last slope I seem to have crossed some sort of threshold, for suddenly the air around me is warm. Steam rises from fumaroles all around. Everything smells of sulfur, and some of the rocks are coated with its thin yellow film. I walk around large circular fissures where the force of the eruption may have inflated the ground like a bubble before it sagged back on itself, or maybe ice entrained within the rock melted abruptly. This is a terrain I do not know how to read.

Calbuco is a little more than 6,700 feet in elevation, but as with Mount St. Helens, identifying its exact highest point is academic, owing to the serrated topography of its summit. Once at the top, I have a choice of turning right or left. The clouds make it hard to tell whether either direction leads anywhere significantly higher, so instead I walk across a rise toward the south, where I can see sky. I have never been in a landscape like this, with these spires of stone and snow, and I am at a loss for words, have access only to the most basic of descriptors: red, black, rock, snow, cloud, heat, fear, awe. Everything is silent, and it is amazing to know, as much as I know anything in this world, that I am the only person on the mountain.

I walk until I reach a place where the land's general trend seems to tip from up to down. Here I stay for maybe an hour and a half, taking in the silence, climbing around the boulders and fissures, or sitting on the warm rocks in the warm air and letting the volcano's deep warm breath drive the cold from my bones. Then I happen to turn and see an even thicker, more massive wall of cloud rolling up the north slope, piling higher and higher, smothering the sky. It seems a good time to leave. I scramble back to the slope and start to step-slide down the rocks, almost as if I am skating, and in a disappointingly short time I have descended below the clouds and see Lago Llanquihue and Osorno gleaming in the distance.

When I make it down to the snag, the rebar is where I left it. After a pitched internal debate, responsibility wins, and I pick up the bars and haul them down a quarter mile or so to where Crisafulli and the rest of the crew are at work. He spies me coming and waves. "You're back!" he says. "And you've got my rebar! We were wondering where you left it."

"I put it up at treeline!" I gasp in a state of high dudgeon. "Just like you asked!"

Crisafulli laughs. "I didn't mean haul it up to the very last tree. But that's fine that you did. I bet it was good for you."

———

The work carries on. The next day, all the transects are staked out, the trees and seedlings tagged and identified, the tephra pits dug. That night we have a farewell dinner—the Chileans are leaving tomorrow, along with Swanson and Jones. The festivities extend from the small restaurant in Ensenada back to the Chileans' *cabaña* across from Crisafulli's, where a rowdy party for the younger people promises to stretch late into the night.

Over in Crisafulli's *cabaña*, Swanson and Jones are trying to sleep, but Crisafulli and Jorge Romero are talking in the sitting room. Romero wants to know more about Mount St. Helens, about Crisafulli's work in Chile, about what brought him here. He sits before Crisafulli like a disciple. Music from across the lawn pounds through the walls. It is oddly meditative.

"No one was really doing this sort of ecological work in Chile," Crisafulli is saying. "Most ecologists don't take the time to understand disturbances. They just want to know what's there, what's not. But when you have forests that take two or three hundred years to develop, you have no choice but to be in it for the long haul." He is holding a glass of red wine and feeling expansive. "One thing that makes me happy," he says, "is knowing that, whether it be in Chile at Chaitén or Calbuco, or at Mount St. Helens, I, whether as a young man or old, drove a piece of PVC into the ground when the ground was still hot, and I can pass that on to someone, and they can pass it on to someone, and we can understand the birth and development of a forest. It makes me giddy to think of the possibilities of that happening."

Romero nods. "I would like to do work like that here," he says. "Get something going like what you have with Mount St. Helens."

"There's nothing like it," Crisafulli says. "It's shaped my view of the world, it shaped my identity. It's hard to separate who I am from Mount St. Helens, because I've dedicated my life to Mount St. Helens. It's a connection, I've spent my life working there—more than thirty-five years. I spend eighty, one hundred days a year up on the mountain. Few people have done that." He pauses. "All of the friendships that have formed, all the young people I've helped train. My family. For my daughters, my friends, my former spouse, it's going to Mount St. Helens to pick huckleberries, to hunt elk, to trout fish, to go skiing. My daughters learned to ski on Mount St. Helens. We used to cut our Christmas tree up there and ski out. It's where they learned to camp. It has shaped my essence."

He slips into a ruminative silence, swills the wine in his glass. Romero waits a moment, and then asks why he has come to Chile, what he hopes to get out of it.

Crisafulli nods, brought back to the moment. "It's good to get away from Mount St. Helens, to come here," he says. "*Great* to come down here. It makes me a little sad, actually. On the one hand, I love ecology, I love plants, I love animals." He pauses again. "You kind of long for the old days, when the physical environment was in charge, when it was steering the ship, and not, you know, all the other things that often end up dictating what happens in a place. Like people." He chuckles. "That's why Chile is so attractive for me. The plants are just beaten into the ground. The physical environment has overwhelmed them. There's a simple beauty to that." He brightens. He has hit on something. "Coming to Chile is a renewal. I was so young and so naïve when I first started working at Mount St. Helens, but now I can come with a speck of wisdom and understanding and look at the environment objectively, and now I know what to look for. This is what I'm looking for."

———

The next morning, the Chileans depart for Valdivia, and Swanson and Jones head back to Puerto Montt. Crisafulli, Blackman, Denton, and Pilita Carrera, a Chilean who spent a season at Mount St. Helens, leave to go climb Calbuco. (It turns out there is time after all.) Crisafulli had asked if I wanted to join them, but I begged off. In part I was still tired from my own climb, and in part I had a plane to catch and was reluctant to risk a delay; but in part, too, my own experience had been so singular that I did not want to dilute it with a second ascent.

"Okay, buddy," Crisafulli said. We hugged goodbye and he patted me on the back. "Have a safe trip home." Then the four of them hopped in the truck and drove off. Unspoken in their wake was Crisafulli's assessment of my decision: *Your loss.*

I go back inside the *cabaña*, then out to the beach for one last look at Osorno over Lago Llanquihue before the drive to the airport in Puerto Montt. Standing in the sand, dazzled by the sparkling lake, I know Crisafulli is right. It will be my loss. The sky is clear, the sun already high and bright. Everything I could not see when I was climbing Calbuco, he will see. He will pass among the enormous, scarred tepa that may or may not be doomed, the bamboo forest dead to its own natural rhythms, and the electric green ferns bursting from the ground. He will reach treeline and see the route to the broken top of Calbuco laid out for him, and the whole of the mountain—its ridges, its flanks, its cathedrals of rock. He will climb quickly, because that is how he climbs, and the others will have trouble keeping up with him, because everyone does.

A couple of hours later, he will come to the point where the air turns warm, and he will turn left, because he knows that is the way to the crater. He will haul himself a hundred feet or so up one last slope, and the ground will get hotter and hotter, and he will wonder if the soles of his boots are going to melt. The higher he goes, the more the air will reek of sulfur. Finally, he will reach the rim and look over into a crater that is more than six hundred feet deep and a thousand feet wide, venting steam from hissing fumaroles. Everything about it will blow his mind, and he will turn and see Blackman making her last push up the hill, with Denton and Carrera behind her, and he will call out, "Tara! Tara, get up here! Tara, you've got to see this!"

ACKNOWLEDGMENTS

From a distance, the stratovolcanoes of the Pacific Northwest look like great, singular entities; up close, you realize each one is just an enormous pile made up of many, many rocks. Likewise a book: from a distance, it is something written by a single person; up close, it is something many, many people had a hand in. That is especially true with this book.

My biggest acknowledgment and deepest gratitude must go to Charlie Crisafulli. I met Charlie at the 2015 Pulse, and for the first few days I watched him whirl about as master of ceremonies. On the next-to-last day, somewhat to my surprise, he made time for us to take a long hike into the Mount Margaret Backcountry—an experience that to this day remains one of my favorites. On various occasions for the next several years, Charlie let me tag along with him and his crew, welcoming me and treating me like one of his own. He later read almost all of the manuscript and was a deft enough editor not only to correct whatever staggering inaccuracies he found with kindness, but also to make clear that he was fine with whatever direction I chose to take the book, even if he did not necessarily agree with it—a rare quality for a scientist who has been working at a place for as long as he has. Getting to know Charlie was one of the real pleasures of this project.

An equally great pleasure was spending time with Fred Swanson and Julia Jones. I also met Fred at the 2015 Pulse, where he fraternized with the artists and writers. He later kindly invited me to his and Julia's home in Corvallis so I could talk to him at greater length about the early days after the 1980 eruption, and what it was like to be a character in Gary Snyder's poem cycle about Mount St. Helens. ("It made me a little uncomfortable," he said.) I have been down several times since for a number of reasons, and will be sorry to lose my annual excuse to make the five-hour drive from Seattle to Corvallis.

As this project stretched on, I came to think of Charlie and Fred as the spiritual poles of Mount St. Helens, in a way. They both cared about it deeply, Charlie from up close, Fred from a bit farther away. Their complementary approaches were best exemplified for me at the start of that wonderful hike with Charlie. We ran into Fred fairly early along the trail as he was returning from his own hike with a small group. "Hey, Fred," Charlie called out. "How's the storytelling going?" Fred laughed and did a funny little dance and said, "Oooooh! The data monster!"

Beyond Charlie and Fred, I was lucky to get to interview many people, over the phone, in their offices, or out in the field. Their names are too many to list, but I will try, and roughly in the order they appear in this book: thanks very much to Jerry Franklin, Mark Swanson, Jim MacMahon, Roger del Moral, Cynthia Chang, Don Zobel, Joe Antos, Abir Biswas, Dylan Fischer, Cliff Dahm, Doug Larson, Jim Gawel, Bob Lucas, Virginia Dale, Keith Keown, Hal Mahnke, Jeff Bradley, and Evelyn Merrill. Fred, Cynthia, Roger, Don, Joe, Doug, Jim, and Virginia also read relevant chapters and passages and provided much helpful guidance to make sure I got the science correct. Any errors that remain are entirely my own, of course.

I would be remiss if I did not also thank the field crews I got to know. Tara Blackman, Kate (Kat) Culhane, Nina Ferrari, and Peter Satine made up Charlie's Crew and were always a source of good cheer. Mariah Vane also came to Mount St. Helens from time to time, and back in Seattle at the Burke Museum she showed me how to prepare a shrew skin for display. Pilita Carrera, Leif Castern, and Elsie Denton (and Tara again) were all very pleasant company when I visited Volcán Calbuco in Chile. Laurel Baum, Camilo Acosta, and Daviel O'Neill, three of Cynthia Chang's students, schlepped gear so I did not have to. Ken Burkart moved things around so I could fit in the boat with him and Jim Gawel.

Not everyone who was generous with their time and expertise ended up in the book, but the book would not be what it is without them. Carri

LeRoy and Shannon Cleason took me out to see their fascinating work on the new streams that are carving up the Pumice Plain. Rod Crawford showed me the spiders from Mount St. Helens in the basement of the Burke Museum at the University of Washington. Steven Gray, a biologist with the Washington Department of Fish and Wildlife, spent a day showing me steelhead redds on the South Fork Toutle River, and Chris Gleizes, also with the WDFW, was there for a couple of my fishless visits to the Fish Collection Facility. Tom Hinckley, a retired forestry professor from the University of Washington whom I have known for years, told me stories about his time in the forests near Mount St. Helens before the eruption.

At the University of Washington Press, I am grateful to Regan Huff for first suggesting and then commissioning this book, and to Andrew Berzanskis for helping see it through to its conclusion. Nicole Mitchell and Rebecca Brinbury kindly gave me an extra year to finish the manuscript when the research turned out to be much more involved than I anticipated. Neecole Bostick, Katrina Noble, Margaret Sullivan, and Julie Van Pelt deftly handled its design and production. I am thankful also to two anonymous reviewers for their useful comments and suggestions.

I was fortunate to receive an Ecological Society of America Travel Award, which helped me attend the society's annual meeting in Portland in 2017, where Charlie Crisafulli organized a symposium on volcano ecology. A Frank Allen Field Reporting Award from the Institute for Journalism and Natural Resources, a wonderful group, supported some of my research in 2016.

Eric Buhle climbed Mount St. Helens with me the year I was thinking about writing this book, and it was as we exited the Worm Flows route in the rain that I decided to give it a try. My friends Alex Hart and Carson Whitehead joined me for excursions of varying lengths and durations into different parts of the blast area, and Alex read and commented on part of the manuscript. I am also grateful to Sarah Gilman, then an editor at *High Country News*, for letting me test-run some Mount St. Helens thoughts in an essay for her. My writing group friends Kelly Brenner and Sarah DeWeerdt read several chapters and gave helpful comments and suggestions. And my parents Bill and Adele Wagner, to whom the book is dedicated, first took me and my sister Elise to Mount St. Helens in 1987, I believe—a visit that has stayed in my memory in a formative if gauzy way.

Lastly, and most importantly, all writers who have families ask a lot of them, I suspect. That is certainly true of me, and this book would not have been possible without my family's love and support. Among many other things, my mother-in-law, Jean Lee, watched my daughter during my ventures to the mountain, made smoothies for me while I later sat staring glumly at my computer—the list of all she did could go on, and probably should. Bay Wagner, the aforementioned daughter, bore my absences with relative aplomb, and I look forward to taking her all the way around the Loowit Trail (#216) when she is older. And my wife, Eleanor Lee, and I have climbed up and glissaded down Mount St. Helens every year for almost a decade now. Sometimes a crumb falls/From the tables of joy . . .

SELECTED READING

Andersen, David C. "Observations on *Thomomys talpoides* in the Region Affected by the Eruption of Mount St. Helens." *Journal of Mammalogy* 63 (1982): 6526–55.

Andersen, David C., and James A. MacMahon. "The Effects of Catastrophic Ecosystem Disturbance: The Residual Mammals at Mount St. Helens." *Journal of Mammalogy* 66 (1985): 5815–89.

———. "Plant Succession following the Mount St. Helens Volcanic Eruption: Facilitation by a Burrowing Rodent, *Thomomys talpoides*." *American Midland Naturalist* 114 (1985): 626–29.

Antos, Joseph, and Don Zobel. "Snowpack Modification of Volcanic Tephra Effects on Forest Understory Plants near Mount St. Helens." *Ecology* 63 (1982): 1969–72.

Bilderback, David, ed. *Mount St. Helens, 1980: Botanical Consequences of the Explosive Eruptions*. Berkeley: University of California Press, 1987.

Cairns, John, ed. *Rehabilitating Damaged Ecosystems*. 2nd ed. Boca Raton, LA: Lewis, 1995.

Carson, Robb. *Mount St. Helens: The Eruption and Recovery of a Volcano*. Seattle: Sasquatch Books, 2005.

Chang, Cynthia C., Charles B. Halpern, Joseph A. Antos, Meghan L. Avolio, Abir Biswas, James E. Cook, Roger del Moral, et al. "Testing Conceptual Models of Early Plant Succession across a Disturbance Gradient." *Journal of Ecology* 107 (2019): 517–30.

Chang, Cynthia C., and Janneke Hille Ris Lambers. "Integrating Succession and Community Assembly Perspectives." *F1000 Research* 5 (2016): 2294.

Colusardo, Christine. *Return to Spirit Lake: Journey through a Lost Landscape*. Seattle: Sasquatch Books, 1997.

Committee on Long-Term Management of the Spirit Lake/Toutle River System in Southwest Washington. *A Decision Framework for Managing the Spirit Lake and Toutle River System at Mount St. Helens*. Washington, DC: National Academies Press, 2018.

Crawford, Rod L., Patrick M. Sugg, and John S. Edwards. "Spider Arrival and Primary Establishment on Terrain Depopulated by Volcanic Eruption at Mount St. Helens, Washington." *American Midland Naturalist* 133 (1995): 60–75.

Crisafulli, Charles M. "A Habitat-Based Method for Monitoring Pond-Breeding Amphibians." In "Sampling Amphibians in Lentic Habitats," ed. D. H. Olson, W. P. Leonard, and R. B. Bury, special issue, *Northwest Fauna* 4 (1997): 83–111.

Crisafulli, Charles M., and Virginia H. Dale, eds. *Ecological Responses at Mount St. Helens: Revisited 35 years after the 1980 Eruption.* New York: Springer, 2018.

Crisafulli, Charles M., and Charles P. Hawkins. "Ecosystem Recovery following a Catastrophic Disturbance: Lessons learned from Mount St. Helens. In *Status and Trends of the Nation's Biological Resources,* ed. M. J. Mac, P. A. Opler, C. E. Puckett Haecker, and P. D. Doran, 23–26. Reston, VA: US Department of the Interior, US Geological Survey, 1998.

Crisafulli, Charles M., Frederick J. Swanson, Jonathan J. Halvorson, and Bruce D. Clarkson. "Volcano Ecology: Disturbance Characteristics and Assembly of Biological Communities." In *Encyclopedia of Volcanoes,* 2nd ed., ed. H. Sigurdsson, B. Houghton, S. McNutt, H. Rymer, and J. Stix, 1265–84. London: Elsevier, 2015.

Dale, Virginia H. "Wind Dispersed Seeds and Plant Recovery on the Mount St. Helens Debris Avalanche." *Canadian Journal of Botany* 67 (1989):1434–41.

Dale, Virginia H., Charles M. Crisafulli, and Frederick J. Swanson. "25 years of Ecological Change at Mount St. Helens." *Science* 308 (2005): 961–62.

Dale, Virginia H., Ariel E. Lugo, James A. MacMahon, and Steward T. A. Pickett. "Ecosystem Management in the Context of Large, Infrequent Disturbances." *Ecosystems* 1 (1998): 546–57.

Dale, Virginia H., Frederick J. Swanson, and Charles M. Crisafulli, eds. *Ecological Responses to the 1980 Eruption of Mount St. Helens.* New York: Springer, 2005.

del Moral, Roger. "Plant Succession on Pumice at Mount St. Helens." *American Midland Naturalist* 141 (1999): 101–14.

———. "Thirty Years of Permanent Vegetation Plots, Mount St. Helens, Washington." *Ecology* EO91 (2010): 152.

del Moral, Roger, and Lawrence C. Bliss. "Mechanism of Primary Succession: Insights Resulting from the Eruption of Mount St. Helens." *Advances in Ecological Research* 24 (1993): 1–66.

del Moral, Roger, and Cynthia C. Chang. "Multiple Assessments of Succession Rates on Mount St. Helens." *Plant Ecology* 216 (2015): 165–76.

del Moral, Roger, and Lawrence R. Walker. *Environmental Disasters, Natural Recovery and Human Response.* Cambridge: Cambridge University Press, 2007.

del Moral, Roger, and David M. Wood. "Early Primary Succession on a Barren Volcanic Plain at Mount St. Helens, Washington." *American Journal of Botany* 80 (1993): 981–91.

del Moral, Roger, and David M. Wood. "Early Primary Succession on the Volcano Mount St. Helens." *Journal of Vegetation Science* 4 (1993): 223–34.

———. "Vegetation Development on Permanently Established Grids, Mount St. Helens (1986–2010)." *Ecology* 93 (2012): 2185.

Edwards, John S., and Lawrence M. Schwartz. "Mount St. Helens Ash: A Natural Insecticide." *Canadian Journal of Zoology* 59 (1981): 714–15.

Edwards, John, and Patrick Sugg. "Arthropod Fallout as a Resource in the Recolonization of Mount St. Helens." *Ecology* 74 (1993): 954–58.

Fischer, Dylan G., Joseph A. Antos, Abir Biswas, and Donald A. Zobel. "Understorey Succession after Burial by Tephra from Mount St. Helens." *Journal of Ecology* 107 (2019): 531–44.

Fischer, Dylan G., Joseph A. Antos, William G. Grandy, and Donald A. Zobel. "A Little Disturbance Goes a Long Way: 33-Year Understory Successional Responses to a Thin Tephra Deposit." *Forest Ecology and Management* 382 (2016): 236–43.

Foster, David R., Dennis H. Knight, and Jerry F. Franklin. "Landscape Patterns and Legacies Resulting from Large Infrequent Forest Disturbances." *Ecosystems* 1 (1998): 497–510.

Franklin, Jerry F. "Organization and Conduct of Ecological Research Programs in the Vicinity of Mt. St. Helens." In *Mount St. Helens 1980: Botanical Consequences of the Explosive Eruptions*, ed. David E. Bilderback, 336–44. Berkeley: University of California Press, 1987.

———. "Biological Legacies: A Critical Management Concept from Mount St. Helens." *Transactions of the 55th North American Wildlife and Natural Resources Conference* (1990): 216–19.

Franklin, Jerry F., David Lindenmayer, James A. MacMahon, Arthur McKee, John Magnuson, David A. Perry, Robert Waide, and David Foster. "Threads of Continuity." *Conservation Biology in Practice* 1 (2000): 9–16.

Franklin, Jerry F., and James A. MacMahon. "Messages from a Mountain." *Science* 288 (2000): 1183–85.

Franklin, Jerry F., James A. MacMahon, Frederick J. Swanson, and James R. Sedell. "Ecosystem Responses to Catastrophic Disturbances: Lessons from Mount St. Helens." *National Geographic Research* 1 (1985): 198–216.

Frenzen, Peter F., and Charles M. Crisafulli. "Mount St. Helens Ten Years Later: Past Lessons and Future Promise." *Northwest Science* 64 (1990): 263–67.

Frenzen, Peter F., A. M. Delano, and Charles M. Crisafulli. *Mount St. Helens: Biological Responses Following the 1980 Eruptions; An Indexed Bibliography and Research Abstracts (1980–93)*. Gen. Tech. Rep. PNW-GTR-342. Portland, OR: US Department of Agriculture, Forest Service, Pacific Northwest Research Station, 1994.

Goodrich, Charles, Kathleen Dean Moore, and Frederick J. Swanson, eds. *In the Blast Zone: Catastrophe and Renewal on Mount St. Helens*. Corvallis: Oregon State University Press, 2008.

Halpern, Charles B., Peter Frenzen, and Jerry F. Franklin. "Plant Succession in Areas of Scorched and Blown-Down Forest at Mount St. Helens, Washington." *Journal of Vegetation Science* 1(1990): 181–94.

Keller, S. A. C., ed. *Mount St. Helens: One Year Later.* Cheney: Eastern Washington University Press, 1982.

———. *Mount St. Helens: Five Years Later.* Cheney: Eastern Washington University Press, 1986.

Larson, Douglas W. "The Recovery of Spirit Lake." *American Scientist* 81 (1993): 166–77.

———. "Science after the Volcano Blew." *American Scientist* 98 (2010): 324–34.

Larson, Douglas W., and Natalie S. Geiger. "Existence of Phytoplankton in Spirit Lake near Active Volcano Mount St. Helens, Washington, USA: Post-eruption findings." *Archiv für Hydrobiologie* 93 (1982): 375–80.

Lipman, Peter, and Donal R. Mullineaux. *The 1980 Eruptions of Mount St. Helens, Washington.* Geological Survey Professional Paper 1250. Reston, VA: US Dept. of the Interior, US Geological Survey, 1982.

Lucas, Robert, and Bruce A. Crawford. *Recovery of Game Fish Populations Impacted by the May 18, 1980, Eruption of Mount St. Helens.* Fishery Management Report 859–A-B. Olympia: Washington Department of Game, Fisheries Management Division, 1995.

MacMahon, James A. "Mount St. Helens Revisited." *Natural History* 91 (1992): 14–20.

MacMahon, James A., Robert R. Parmenter, Kurt A. Johnson, and Charles M. Crisafulli. "Small Mammal Recolonization on the Mount St. Helens Volcano, 1980–1987." *American Midland Naturalist* 122 (1989): 365–87.

Merrill, E. "Summer Foraging Ecology of Wapiti (*Cervus elaphus roosevelti*) in the Mount St. Helens Blast Zone." *Canadian Journal of Zoology* 72 (1994): 303–11.

Nash, Steve. "Making Sense of Mount St. Helens." *BioScience* 60 (2010): 571–75.

Olson, Steve. *Eruption: The Untold Story of Mount St. Helens.* New York: W. W. Norton, 2016.

Sedell, James R., Jerry F. Franklin, and Frederick J. Swanson. "Out of the Ash." *American Forests* 86 (1980): 26–30, 67, 68.

Snyder, Gary. *Danger on Peaks.* Berkeley, CA: Counterpoint Press, 2004.

Suzuki, Y., D. D. Roby, D. E. Lyons, K. N. Courtot, and K. Collis. "Developing Non-destructive Techniques for Managing Conflicts between Fisheries and Double-Crested Cormorant Colonies." *Wildlife Society Bulletin* 39, no. 4 (2015): 764–71.

Swanson, Frederick J., Charles Goodrich, and Kathleen Dean Moore. "Bridging Boundaries: Scientists, Creative Writers, and the Long View of the Forest." *Frontiers in Ecology and the Environment* 6 (2008): 499–504.

Tison, David L., John A. Baross, and Ramon J. Seidler. "*Legionella* in Aquatic Habitats in the Mount Saint Helens Blast Zone." *Current Microbiology* 9 (1983): 345–48.

Turner, Monica G., William L. Baker, Christopher J. Peterson, and Robert K. Peet. "Factors Influencing Succession: Lessons from Large, Infrequent Disturbances." *Ecosystems* 1 (1998): 511–23.

Turner, Monica G., and Virginia H. Dale. "Comparing Large, Infrequent Disturbances: What Have We Learned?" *Ecosystems* 1 (1998): 493–96.

Turner, Monica G., Virginia H. Dale, and Edwin H. Everham. "Fires, Hurricanes, and Volcanoes: Comparing Large Disturbances." *BioScience* (1997) 47: 758–68.

Walker, Lawrence R., and Roger del Moral. *Primary Succession and Ecosystem Rehabilitation*. Cambridge: Cambridge University Press, 2003.

Wissmar, Robert C., Allen H. Devol, Ahmad E. Nevissi, and James R. Sedell. "Chemical Changes of Lakes within the Mount St. Helens Blast Zone." *Science* 216 (1982): 175–78.

Wissmar, Robert C., Allen H. Devol, James T. Staley, and James R. Sedell. "Biological Responses of Lakes in the Mount St. Helens Blast Zone." *Science* 216 (1982): 178–80.

Wood, David M., and Roger del Moral. "Colonizing Plants on the Pumice Plains, Mount St. Helens, Washington." *American Journal of Botany* 75 (1988): 1228–37.

Zobel, Donald A., and Joseph A. Antos. "A Decade of Recovery of Understory Vegetation Buried by Volcanic Tephra from Mount St. Helens." *Ecological Monographs* 67 (1997): 317–44.

INDEX

salmon, coho, 146, 175–76, 178, 181, 186–87; salmon, Pacific, 146, 153, 178; steelhead, 146, 153, 175–90; Toutle River Fish Collection Facility (FCF), 175–76, 179–90; trout, brook, 145–46, 148; trout, cutthroat, 146, 148; trout, rainbow, 137, 145–59, 177
Fleming, Michael, 203
flood risk at Spirit Lake, 126–27
flycatcher, Hammond's, 34
Forest Service, US, 41–43, 76, 124, 129, 134, 155, 171
forest wars, 54, 123
Fowler, Hugh, 128
Franklin, Jerry, 35, 90, 102, 122, 170, 206; after eruption, 4–8, 39–45, 52–54; Andrews Forest and, 28–30; brook trout at Meta Lake, 144–46; del Moral and, 81–82; elk, 196–98; fireweed, 6–8; MacMahon and, 55; at Pacific Northwest Forest Summit, 124; snow cover and, 105; succession and, 45–51; Swanson and, 23–24
frogs, 138

G

Gawel, Jim, 135–43, 147, 151, 206
geology and ecology, connection between, 17
geology report (Paper 1250) (USGS), 17–23
Geostationary Operational Environmental Satellite-3 (GOES-3), 100–101
Gifford Pinchot National Forest, 52, 100, 172
Gleason, Henry, 85–87
goat, mountain, 194
Gonzalez, Mauro, 213–15, 218
gopher. See pocket gopher, northern
Gore, Al, 124
Green River, 173, 175, 182, 194
Grizzly Lake, 118–19, 207

grouse, sooty, 34
Guy, Harlan, 147

H

Harmon, Mark, 31–32
Harmony Falls trail, 114, 155
Harry's Ridge, 128, 133
hawkweed, white, 49
helenite jewelry, 109
hemlock, 44, 49
H. J. Andrews Experimental Forest, 24–26, 28–35, 117–18, 123–24
HOBOs (temperature loggers), 201–2
Hoffstadt Creek, 186, 188
huckleberry, 49, 61, 99–100, 105, 106
Hummocks Trail, 202
hunting, 204–5

I

insects, 71–72, 137, 141–42
International Biological Programme (IBP), 29–30, 33, 117–18
iron, 121

J

Jeffers, Robinson, 25
Johnston, David, 18
Johnston Ridge Observatory, 8
Jones, Julia, 27–28, 212, 216, 220–21

K

Kalama Falls Hatchery, 189
Keown, Keith, 176, 179–85, 188
Klebsiella pneumoniae, 128

L

lahars (mudflows), 3–4, 41, 94, 115, 166
Lakes Trail, 207
landslides, 3–4, 19
Lara, Antonio, 213
Larson, Doug, 129–34, 136–37, 139, 148–49, 156
layers Yb, Yd, and Yn, 115

ABOUT THE AUTHOR

Bill Wagner

Eric Wagner is a science writer in Seattle, where he lives with his family
and climbs nearby Mount St. Helens every year. He is author of *Penguins in
the Desert* and coauthor of *Once and Future River: Reclaiming the Duwamish.*
His essays and journalism have appeared in national magazines including
the *Atlantic, High Country News, Orion,* and *Smithsonian.* He earned a PhD
in biology from the University of Washington.